The Principles of Religious Ceremonial

BY THE RT. REV.
W. H. FRERE, D.D.
*Of the Community of the Resurrection
Bishop of Truro*

WIPF & STOCK · Eugene, Oregon

Wipf and Stock Publishers
199 W 8th Ave, Suite 3
Eugene, OR 97401

The Principles of Religious Ceremonial
By Frere, W. H.
Softcover ISBN-13: 978-1-6667-3423-2
Hardcover ISBN-13: 978-1-6667-2987-0
eBook ISBN-13: 978-1-6667-2988-7
Publication date 8/19/2021
Previously published by A. R. Mowbray, 1928

This edition is a scanned facsimile of the original edition published in 1928.

F. E. B.

OPUSCULUM NON SUUM SED IPSIUS

D.D.

W. H. F.

THE PREFACE OF 1906

IT will be evident from the title of this book that it does not aim at providing a handbook dealing systematically with the conduct of church services. There are already a number of such guides in existence, each speaking the language of the 'Crede Michi,' recommending its own way as the one way to be implicitly followed. There is no need to add one more to this motley multitude. To discuss the principles of ceremonial seems a more necessary task, for it is only by a recurrence to principles that the wide diversities of to-day can be brought to a better unity : and that is the aim which is here kept in view. There has been little, if anything, written hitherto on this subject in order to give in outline a historical conspectus of the growth of ceremonial, or to give an analytical examination of the principles upon which it rests. In entering thus upon untrodden ground, I must ask of the reader the indulgence which is due to those who in some sense are pioneers I have sufficiently stated in the book itself what general intention has been in my mind throughout ; but in order to avoid misconception, it may be well to add a further caution here. It must not be supposed, because I refer to ceremonies of various sorts, and to some of them in sympathetic language, that I therefore approve all of them, or wish necessarily the restoration of any of them which may not now be in use among ourselves ; still less that I recommend the adoption of any of them by individuals without ecclesiastical authority. On many of them I express no personal opinion, but merely cite them as instances. When I have, at intervals in the book, given vent to criticisms and passed judgements upon specific points, this has been done merely incidentally, just as it seemed to bear upon the matter in hand, and without any attempt to apportion approbation or disapprobation in a systematic way over the whole range of ceremonial observances. It has been throughout the principles rather than the details that I have sought to emphasize.

The notes have been kept within narrow bounds, and relegated to the end of the volume, in order that they may not hamper those who may be interested in the subject without having much technical knowledge of it. It would have been easy to multiply the bulk of them, and to add many references to ritualists both ancient and modern by whose labours I have profited, but to do this would to some extent have defeated the purpose in view. At the present time the subject of religious ceremonial is one of general interest. All churchgoers are expected to have some opinion upon it. It is too often discussed from a narrow and party point of view. So this volume is simply an attempt to provide materials from which to form a more tolerant and more independent judgement.

W. H. FRERE

S. Andrew's Day, 1905.

PREFACE OF THE NEW EDITION

IN preparing a new edition, the opportunity has been taken of making a considerable number of small changes both in the text and in the notes. There are also three changes on a larger scale which deserve to be recorded here.

(1) A new chapter (numbered chapter v) is introduced in order to describe the ceremonial of the Eastern Liturgies.

(2) The latter part of the original chapter on Authority for Ceremonial (now chapter xiii) has been omitted, as the argument in favour of the *jus liturgicum* is now superfluous.

(3) For the like reason the whole of the old chapter xiv on the interpretation of the Ornaments Rubric has not been reprinted.

✠ W. T.

S. George's Day, 1928.

CONTENTS

CHAP		PAGE
	Introductory	1
I.	Of Ceremonial in General	11
II.	Of Religious Ceremonial	16
III.	Congregation and Ministers	22
IV.	Stages in the Growth of Religious Ceremonial: I. Primitive	38
V.	Stages in the Growth of Religious Ceremonial: II. The Unchanging East	49
VI.	Stages in the Growth of Religious Ceremonial: III. Mediaeval West	59
VII.	Stages in the Growth of Religious Ceremonial: IV. The Later Middle Ages	75
VIII.	Utilitarian Ceremonial	92
IX.	Interpretative Ceremonial: I	104
X.	Interpretative Ceremonial: II	115
XI.	Symbolical Ceremonial	127
XII.	The Mystical Interpretation of Ceremonial	140
XIII.	Authority in Matters of Ceremonial	155
XIV.	The Rubrics of the Prayer-Book	168
XV.	The Application of Principles	195
	Notes	203
	Index	229

The Principles of Religious Ceremonial

INTRODUCTORY

THE subject of religious ceremonial is one which has a special faculty for stirring strong feeling. From time to time the outside world is surprised, and perhaps amused, at some sudden outburst of violent passions from this source. Bitter attacks followed by sarcastic recriminations are heard on the subject of the cut or colour of clerical vestments ; popular feeling runs high about the positions and movements of those who take part in a service. The excitement seems quite disproportionate to the cause ; it lasts longer than would have seemed possible ; for the attack is surprisingly vigorous, and the defence proves unaccountably stubborn. Moreover, these eruptions are as inexplicable as those of an earthquake, and as inevitable. If a chasuble causes them at one time, equally does a surplice at another,—at one time the eastward position of the celebrant at Holy Communion, at another the eastward turning of the congregation for the Creed at Morning or Evening Prayer.

In dealing, therefore, with so dangerous a subject it will be well to begin with some general considerations calculated to minimize the dangers of explosion, to disarm prejudice, and to bespeak caution, patience, and charity.

First, it is worth while to discover what there is in the subject itself, and in men's mental attitude towards it, that causes the explosive character of the topic. One chief cause will be found deep down in the constitution of human minds ; and thus an elementary inquiry into this phenomenon will be of use at this stage to prepare for a discussion of the subject.

The human mind is capable of great varieties of feeling, and these lead to great diversities of opinion ; but each man's mind is also furnished with a certain number of individual characteristics or even predilections and prejudices, which belong to his own personal nature and make him different in mental constitution from others. One of these differences concerns us here. Some minds are helped to grasp ideas by the aid of outward objects and symbols, others are hindered rather than helped by them. The more abstract-minded man likes to shut his eyes, or withdraw them, in order to be able to think the better ; but the simple mind finds it hard to think at all without something on which to fix his sight. Now the former type tends to undervalue, or even dislike, all ceremonial ; the latter to depend upon having it.

When the ceremonial in question is religious, the gulf between the two types of mind is often only the greater. To the former the externals seem especially distracting and derogatory, when they are associated with thoughts too high for mere mundane symbols ; and many a man who values the ceremonial of the Court, the Army, or the Freemasons' Lodge, dislikes ceremonial in church. To the latter class of mind the religious sphere, because it is the highest, is the one where symbolism is most needed ; and many a man who is indifferent to the ceremonial of ordinary life finds it very helpful, or even necessary, in prayer and worship.

Here are two widely contrasted types. The world might be classified according to them; for every one has his affinity either with the mind of the Quaker on the one side, or with the mind of the so-called Ritualist [*] on the

[*] The word is here loosely used in its popular and inaccurate sense. Strictly speaking, a rite is a form of service, while ceremony is the method of its performance. A ritualist is one learned about forms of service, liturgies, etc., and not necessarily either learned or interested in ceremonial. Henceforward the true distinction between ritual and ceremonial will be maintained in these pages.

other. And every one who handles the subject of religious ceremonial will do well to think beforehand what his own affinity of mind is, and to make allowance accordingly. It is only by recollecting continually his own personal bias that he will be able to be fair and considerate to others.

These two types of mind are not only widely separated ; they are also to a large extent inexplicable each to the other. When two men meet who have formed opposite opinions on a matter of fact or argument, there is always some hope that by discussion they may come to agree, or at least each to appreciate the other's view. But when the matter is one of taste and feeling, there is far less room for such hope : discussion can do but little to help matters. The one party still feels one way, and the other the opposite way. Each is confronted with something in the other of which he himself has no perception, which therefore he finds it hard to appraise or tolerate. Moreover, each is unable to explain or justify his own feeling or taste to the other ; and the irritation that he is liable to feel at not being able to grasp the other man's point of view is probably increased by his inability to express his own.

To this condition of things is due the well-authenticated experience, that there are no controversies so bitter as those of taste and feeling. Grievous are the animosities in the realms of art: and if the *odium theologicum* is thought to be stronger than the *odium artisticum*, it can only be because theology touches deeper currents of feeling even than art. How then shall questions of religious ceremonial, which are both theological and artistic, escape from the operation of this general law, and avoid acrimony and recrimination ? Again the warning note recurs, that only those can safely handle the subject of religious ceremonial whose minds have been trained to tolerate an alien, and even incomprehensible, point of view.

Besides these cautions suggested by mental considerations, there are others which spring from historical reflection. The broad general outlines of the history of ceremonial controversy have something to teach by way of caution and patience. Disturbances of this class seem to recur in cycles, and one phase of them follows upon another in a more or less regular sequence. The full cycle may be expressed by three divisions : first comes a period of experiment or innovation ; after this has continued for some time, as the controversy attendant upon it dies down, there follows a period of consolidation and settlement ; finally comes a period of quiet, tending to stagnation and formalism, before the cycle begins to recur. This general description is not uniformly accurate : a cycle may be interrupted or partial, or the periods may co-exist and overlap : but history gives continual instances of such an alternation in some such form and sequence.

The early ages of the Church show few signs of ceremonial controversy ; but even so, the first settlement of Christian ceremonial was not reached without something of the sort, as S. Paul's First Epistle to the Corinthians shows. There followed clearly the period of settlement as S. Paul set things in order ; and upon that a long period of quiet. A similar cycle is observable in Carolingian days, when the introduction of Roman ceremonial to the Frankish empire marked a period of experiment and innovation, with attendant controversy, which perhaps hardly ceased until the formation of particular local uses in the twelfth and thirteenth centuries marked the beginning of the second period. Thereupon ensued a long stretch of quiet, tending to stagnation and formalism, which lasted down to the Reformation.

Then began a fresh and a more familiar cycle. The sixteenth century in England exhibits in rapid succession the familiar trio, innovation in no small degree and with no little controversy, followed by partial settlement under Archbishop Parker in the early part of Elizabeth's reign, and a brief period of comparative quiet under Archbishop Whitgift at the end of the century and the reign. With the new century the cycle began afresh : the earlier part was full of experiment and innovation ; bitter controversy followed, until the crisis came of the Laudian era and the Great Rebellion ; settlement was not reached till the Restoration, and then followed the Hanoverian torpor.

When this sequence of events has once been grasped, it causes less surprise to find that a new period of restoration, innovation, and experiment should have begun with the revival of church life in the Victorian era, and that again controversy should wax hot. This is all according to analogy, and not in the least remarkable ; and the history should help churchmen to be tolerant towards uncongenial developments, and patient with rash but well-meaning experiment. Movement is of the very nature of the Church, as being a living body ; there is no real danger in this ; it is stagnation that is really dangerous. A living body must grow and must at least be susceptible of ' crisises.' The Church exhibits its life by experiencing them, and its divine character by surviving them, and emerging with added grace and beauty. So let the Muse of History sound a note not only of warning against rash judgement, but also of encouragement as to the results of conflict. These stirs are the birthpangs of some better order, more worthy of the beloved Church and of the worship of God Almighty.

But the services that history can render at this preliminary stage are not yet exhausted. It has further warnings to give. A warning against Erastianism, or at least against that form of civil aggression against the Church which is loosely called by that name. It is still possible that, in view of disturbances in the Church, the State, or even in these days the mixed assemblage of parliament, should hope to mend matters by intervening. But history warns us that such intervention has in past time marred rather than mended. The incursions of the government of Edward VI into the sphere of ceremonial were particularly unfortunate. The first parliament of Elizabeth's day could not but intervene ; but its intervention caused through the Ornaments Rubric the greater part of the troubles that followed in such matters : later ones were only restrained from ill-advised interference by the strong hand of the queen herself. When that was removed there came the disasters of the Commonwealth. More conspicuous because more familiar are the lamentable results of parliamentary intervention in the nineteenth century. Such precedents as these are discouraging.

Further, history reminds us that controversies of this sort are apt to evoke the cry of 'No popery,' and to become poisoned with a virus of anti-Roman prejudice. This cry is usually in England a political rather than a religious cry. It has little or no reference to the real points at issue between the English Church and Rome, which lie far deeper than ceremonial. A surplice worn in the pulpit, a choir installed in the chancel, a college cap, an organ, a litany desk—these and many other familiar features of English worship have in turn been branded as popish. History suggests that such outcries as these should be disregarded. The real matter to be considered, alike in ceremonial and doctrine, is not whether it is Roman, but whether it is legitimate and true. For, after all, not everything that is Roman is wrong.

Again, the conservative mind faced with novelty makes an appeal that is often fallacious to the principles of the Reformation against his antagonist. But history constantly warns us that the observances in whose favour the appeal is made are often mere survivals of Puritan lawlessness or Georgian slovenliness. After all, the main principle of the Reformers was fearless change from current abuses to the more ancient and uncorrupt ways.

The legal mind, it may be, makes a similar appeal to 'the law.' But again history warns us that this appeal is not so simple and conclusive as it seems. The law of the Church must be taken into account as well as civil law. That which is in the fullest sense binding, is that which is arrived at by joint action of Church and State. The action of the State is not ideally necessary for the settlement of ceremonial matters ; the civil power, unless forced by special circumstances, does not concern itself with them ; but the action of the Church is essential.

Chief of all, history utters warnings against the spirit of panic ; and this was a very disturbing element in nineteenth-century controversies about matters of ceremonial. When once panic spreads, argument fails. History is full of melancholy episodes of this character, and its warning in this instance comes as the climax of all. The Erastian tendency, the ' No popery ' cry, the hot appeals to misunderstood principles and more than dubious law, in these are the very elements out of which an ecclesiastical crisis is made. It cannot be denied that there are evils, abuses, and tendencies in the Church of to-day quite sufficient to cause misgivings to a devoted churchman—some of them, too, connected with worship. But these are not what are discerned in a panic, or are truly handled by panic orators, or healed by panic legislation.

History witnesses to the melancholy recurrence of such outbursts, and warns every sensible man against saying or doing anything that may help to evoke or forward them. It warns us also that it is not by such proceedings that God's work is carried on, nor the defects of the work remedied. There is more to be hoped for from patient investigation and sober deliberation ; more still from the quiet continuance of wise and patient episcopal government; most of all from the disappearance of wilfulness and contentiousness before a growing force of prayer, zeal, and penitence.

So much for the sedatives that may be found by reflection on the nature of the human mind in relation to externals, and on the lessons of history. There still remains a further consideration to be taken into account, which, like the others, is calculated to evoke patience, and that in a quarter where it often seems to be lacking.

The plain man has little interest in psychological or historical points ; his views depend chiefly on the judgements passed by an irrational and irreformable authority called his 'common-sense'; and he is apt to be more intolerant than the rest in matters of ceremonial controversy. The points at issue, he thinks, are so petty; they concern mere externals—mere 'man millinery.' He habitually mistrusts alike warmth and formality in devotion; this controversy brings him dangerously near to both of them; and his common-sense rebels in some alarm.

No doubt there is much truth in this view. The points directly at issue are petty in themselves and only concern externals: there always is a danger, whether ceremonial be much or little, that worship may degenerate into formalism. Ceremonial, it may be truly said, either safeguards piety or else degrades it; and any changes in traditional ways bring within the horizon the peril that some may value the changes, not as ancillary to devotion, but for some less worthy reason—for novelty's sake, for their artistic beauty, and so forth; and if so, degradation has set in.

But it is also to be remembered that there are, in reality, no such things as 'mere externals.' Every external implies and has reference to something internal, and must be estimated accordingly. Ceremonial is an external because it is an expression of an inner reality; this reality is often of such a sort as to baffle expression by any other means. Reverence, for example, is more eloquently signified by the Publican's bowed head, and blow on the breast, than in any other way. Irreverence too is equally plainly signified by an attitude or a gesture. No other method of expression could be so expressive. And in general it must be urged that externals are not 'mere externals,' but things pregnant with importance, because of that state of mind which they signify or express.

Ceremonial again is expressive of religious truths. Sometimes these are better defined by a gesture or a symbol than by theological definition. Many a poor sinner can express his trust in his Divine Saviour far better by kissing his crucifix than by attempting to expound his conception of the doctrine of the atonement. The like is true of eucharistic doctrine; and though there is, as there has been from the earliest times, an extensive scope for differences of opinion on these mysteries within the Church, and in fact English churchmen do differ extensively in their apprehension of them, yet that body of belief which is common to all the schools of interpretation which the Church can legitimately include, contains quite enough to justify, if not in some cases to require, a solemn and distinctive eucharistic ceremonial. Low churchmen as well as High churchmen express their views by externals over the larger area in which they are agreed as well as the smaller in which they differ; in fact it is impossible to do otherwise.

It is therefore a form of blindness, not common-sense, that prevents a man from recognizing that behind ceremonies there lie realities—principles, doctrines, and states or habits of mind. No one can hope to judge fairly of matters of ceremonial who does not see that the reason why they cause such heat of controversy is that they signify so much. The attack and the defence alike are worth all the force expended upon them, when under the guise of externals great realities are at stake.

No doubt there are externals which are not really significant of anything great, which are mere matters of custom or habit or taste, others even which are merely survivals. No doubt also there is a tendency to fight over these, as if they belonged to the class of significant externals and really stood for something of importance. Few things are so desirable in ceremonial controversy as the sorting out of the points at issue into these two classes, and the assigning to each point its own proper importance or unimportance accordingly. It is hoped that the discussion of principles which follows in this volume may help, at any rate in some small degree, towards this most desirable result. But if such a sorting is to be done by experts, or commended when done to the judgement of the larger world, including the plain man, it is essential that there should first be, not only among the experts, but also among the general public, a distinct recognition of the real importance of some externals because of that which they signify. When this is recognized there is better hope for the decline of controversy and the development of a fresh unity.

It is difficult to say how far unity of doctrine and feeling precedes unity of ceremonial, or how far it follows it. Ceremonial is at one moment the outcome of doctrine, and at another the inculcator of it, at another a perverter of it. The two are real allies, but really independent; for all might agree in ceremonial and yet differ to some extent in doctrine, and all might agree in doctrine and yet desire to express it externally in different ways. But this is no place to discuss the mutual relation of the two; it is enough for the present purpose to emphasize the intimate connexion subsisting between them, and to express the hope that along each line the Church may be led to a fuller expression of its own essential unity in Christ.

CHAPTER I

OF CEREMONIAL IN GENERAL

IN treating of religious ceremonial it is impossible to divorce the subject from ceremonial in general; for ceremonial is a general feature of human life, and appears in one or another form on all sides of it. Many misconceptions have arisen through treating religious ceremonial by other methods and canons than those applied to ceremonial in general; it will therefore be best to be clear upon this point from the beginning, and to look upon religious ceremonial simply as one province only of a larger territory.

We have called ceremonial a general feature of human life, because in point of fact it is found everywhere. Court life has its ceremonial, but so has family life. It forms no small part of the attraction of gatherings and societies of one sort or another: the lodge of Freemasons may be taken to represent this at one social level, and the Ancient Order of Foresters at another. It is one of the main safeguards of discussion wherever men meet to discuss, from the House of Commons to the ' Magpie and Stump.' It is called in to add solemnity to the administration of justice, and impressiveness to the Army and Navy. It is a masculine weakness, if weakness it be, rather than a feminine one; for it is the peacock, after all, who is most pleased with his appearance, and struts most bravely that all the world may know how pleased he is.

But if we inquire into the reason on which this general feature of human life rests, it is not a mere peacock's love of self-advertisement, but something much more inevitable. A task has to be done: then it must be done somehow. That 'somehow' may be good or bad; therefore prudence suggests that a method should be devised and laid down. Ceremonial has begun.

When this takes place in the case of an individual, and he pursues his method day after day, it begins to be habit, good or bad, or 'ways,' as we say colloquially, more or less desirable. So there grows up an individual code of ceremonial. Let a man run over in his mind such an everyday matter as the process of getting up in the morning. He has a regular course of ceremony—a ceremonial of washing or of dressing—extending to many minute regulations, carried out unquestioningly day after day : they prescribe which way he will use his sponge, which leg he will put first into his trousers, and so forth. Some of such things are *mere* habit—that is, they are matters of utter indifference in themselves ; but one way has been adopted, and it goes on. Others are the result of experiment, and are more or less deliberately arrived at. Others are the result of training, and have been more or less laboriously acquired. But they all owe their common origin to necessity. The things must be done somehow ; and in matters of habit this involves a ceremonial.

If this is the case with an individual, who has only himself and his own convenience to consider, much more is it the case with bodies of people where concerted action is necessary. The individual may, and if he takes enough trouble he can, avoid forming a ceremonial habit; he can vary his methods to the extreme limit of all known permutations and combinations. But a body of people must be corporately bound ; and a ceremonial rule of some degree of strictness or laxity must govern all joint action. This necessity is seen in its simplest form in drill—a rule prescribing uniformity of action to a number of individuals. A more complex form of evolution is exhibited by a ballet, where groups and individuals play into one another's hands by a system which is carefully prearranged and scrupulously carried out. A freer form still is seen in the ordinary dramatic art, where the actors are interdependent, and the performance goes along upon lines that are more or less fixed, and have been carefully rehearsed.

In such spheres as these no one doubts the wisdom of prearrangement, nor the need of rehearsal. The ceremonial must be carefully thought out and zealously practised beforehand; otherwise, instead of order and success there will be indecent confusion.

Still less does any one doubt the need of ceremonial in the ordinary social intercourse of daily life. The ceremonies are there called by another name, and figure as good or bad manners; and in consequence of the change of name many people do not realize that these are only ceremonial under another appellation. But, on reflection, what an elaborate code of ceremonial is seen to be represented by the terms 'manners' and 'customs'! It is found in all races and in all grades of the social order. When the savage rubs noses with his friend, he does it for the same reason as that which leads the European to shake hands, or to take off his hat to a lady, viz. because it is so prescribed in his code of social ceremonial. The etiquette of different classes varies even amongst ourselves as Englishmen; *e.g.* what is considered among one set of people a proper position in which one may leave the knife and fork on the plate, from which he has been eating, is considered improper among others. But the etiquette exists everywhere; and it is an elaborate and arbitrary system, which goes into great detail, and regulates with a relentless sway the veriest minutiae of life.

It does not follow from what has been said that all people are equally under the sway of such ceremonial laws as these which we have been considering. Plainly, it is not so: there is a good and a bad in each of these spheres—good and bad habits, good and bad ballets, good and bad drill, good and bad manners. But public opinion, if nothing else, supports the ceremonial code, and condemns those who infringe it with a severity which is often quite disproportionate to the crime. A fault in manners seems to many people more unpardonable than a fault in morals. The rules which are based on no intrinsic merit, but merely on convention or tradition, are often those that are most tyrannically enforced. People who are reasonable in other respects, are often quite unreasonable and unreasoning in petty punctiliousness. Obedience must be not only exact but unquestioning and implicit; for to hesitate is to be lost, and to criticize or question is in itself a crime.

Such in its best-developed form is social ceremonial; and it is well to recognize fully the character which this class of ceremonial has, and the sway which it exercises, before proceeding to consider the sphere of religious ceremonial; since in this sphere, for good probably, and for evil too, a different spirit is often manifested, and a different standpoint is adopted. Instead of conformity and obedience, it is found that questioning and criticism occupy a place which is often in inverse proportion to the critic's competence to criticize.

No doubt in all ceremonial, secular as well as religious, some allowance must be made for differences of temperament and training. The manners of a foreigner must often seem over-demonstrative to the phlegmatic Englishman, and the ceremoniousness of Court functions over-pompous to a blunt country squire. But this principle does not extend beyond the securing of a modification in details; and ceremonial remains still undethroned as a universal law governing human action in every sphere.

To recognize thus the necessity of a ceremonial does not necessarily mean that one is blind to its dangers or to its possible faults. It may readily be conceded at once that all ceremonial is exposed to dangers, and that the faults which mar it are many and various. Some of these faults and dangers, so far as they concern religious ceremonial, it will be our business to examine hereafter.

Of Ceremonial in General

But for the present it will be enough to meet one objection which confronts us at the outset.

It is constantly said that ceremonial must be 'natural'; and in many spheres and from many lips some protest is made against rules and codes of ceremonial on the ground of this contention. It is evidently true that in the right sense ceremonial must be ' natural ' ; but the question rises whether the ideal is that of nature untrained and unrefined, or of a refined and trained nature. For example, it is true with regard to social ceremonial that manners are not good unless they are natural. On the other hand, it is no less true that good manners do not come naturally, at any rate to people as a whole ; they are almost, if not quite, universally the result of careful and minute training in one form or another. Even in cases where a man seems to have them, as it were, instinctively, *i.e.* without special training *ad hoc*, it will generally be noticed that they are the outcome of a training and refinement of mind or of character ; in other words, they are not ' natural ' in the objector's sense of the word, but an artificial product all the same.

The truth no doubt lies in the old Latin maxim : *Summa ars celare artem*, ' Art is at its highest when it is not noticeable.'

The art of ceremonial proficiency, be it in good manners or in good habits or in good drill or in good religious ceremonial, is best exemplified when it is most concealed—when the best rules have been so well acquired and assimilated that they have become, as we say, ' a second nature.' Then the action so readily takes effect in the way which experience or propriety has laid down, that it is in this true sense of the word ' natural.' But this involves a full knowledge and a zealous practice of the rules of the ceremonial in question ; and if the objector thinks by his objection to obviate the necessity of ceremonial, whether religious or secular, he is thus seen to be entirely mistaken.

CHAPTER II

OF RELIGIOUS CEREMONIAL

MUCH of what has been said in the foregoing chapter as to the principles of ceremonial in general, applies also to religious ceremonial in particular; some applies even in a special degree, for religious ceremonial is action Godwards, and therefore demands the highest possible degree of excellence. Something analogous by way of climax is discernible in secular ceremonial; for while different degrees of pomp and circumstance surround such functions as those of Foresters and Freemasons, a higher degree surrounds municipal, parliamentary, and judicial functions, while the highest degree of all is reserved for the Sovereign and his Court. Heralds and high officers of state in gorgeously picturesque and quaintly antique costumes are those primarily responsible ; but all participate at least to the extent of an elaborate bow or courtesy, compared to which the ordinary bow and courtesy of social intercourse is slipshod and ineffective.

Further, Court ceremonial is also in a special degree centralized, for all has reference to the Sovereign himself, and is grouped round him. It is bound to present, so far as possible, a harmonious, symmetrical, and decorous appearance to the eye from any and every point of view ; but it is especially ordered with a view to the eye of the monarch and in relation to him.

In both these respects there is an analogy between the ceremonial of Court and the ceremonial of religion, and especially of the Holy Eucharist. There is no need to give proofs that the worship of God, viewed from its ceremonial side, must be the climax of ceremonial and must represent the very best that is possible ; and that no pains must be grudged to make it in every way worthy of the highest act of which man is capable, viz. the adoration of Almighty God. It is to be taken for granted that men must offer their very best to God in this respect, as well as in all other ways.

Here too the worship is highly centralized ; and in case any one should doubt that statement, it will be well to give some word of proof. It might be argued *a priori* that, because God is everywhere present, therefore any attempt at localization is of necessity a mistake. It might be contended that, since His presence is no less at the circumference than at the centre of a circle, all such centralization of worship is misleading and to be discouraged. But such a contention, which does in fact underlie some of the objections raised to religious ceremonial, is in direct contradiction to revelation. Wherever God has taught men in the Bible how to worship Him, it has been in a form of centralized worship. Under the Old Covenant this fact is most significant, since such worship was of necessity more akin to idolatry than a non-centralized and non-localized worship would have been. But in spite of that fact, the whole teaching of Tabernacle or Temple, and the whole practice of Levitical worship, rest upon the assumption that God's presence is for the purposes of worship to be considered as specially localized at one spot, towards which the worship is to be directed. Not only was this the case in actual Temple services, but from all parts of the world the Jew was accustomed, not without real Scriptural warrant, to direct his prayer towards the Temple. Thus Jewish worship was in the highest possible degree centralized ; and this centralized character of its ceremonial extended even to the private prayer of the Jew of the Dispersion.

Under the New Covenant no change was made in this respect : even our Lord's caution that ' God is Spirit ' was given in close connexion with the assertion that the Jews were justified in making Jerusalem and not

Gerizim the centre of their worship. Christian Churches have uniformly followed the precedent of the Jewish Temple in having a Holy place and a Holy of Holies—that is, in localizing for the special purposes of worship the presence of God, and, so far as ceremonial goes, in directing it to that centre. The visions of heavenly worship recorded by S. John in the Revelation entirely bear out this view, and have no doubt dispelled all scruples, if any ever existed in the mind of the Church, as to the rightness of this habit of centralizing. The throne of God and of the Lamb is in the highest degree the centre of the heavenly worship. Round it are grouped all the worshipping host of heaven, and towards it are directed all the ceremonial acts of the heavenly worship. The rainbow surrounds the throne; the four-and-twenty elders have their thrones grouped about it and prostrate themselves before it; the seven lamps of fire burn before the throne; the sea of glass is set before it; the four living creatures offer their ceaseless homage in the midst of the throne and round about the throne; while the myriads of angels are again round about the throne and the beasts and the elders, and fall prostrate before it; and all creation seems to represent yet a wider circle surrounding the same centre.

The significance of this is obvious : this revelation has been the model and ideal of Christian worship ; and in each church the altar has naturally stood for the throne of God and as the centre of all the ceremonial. Bible and Church alike prove that no objection can be raised to religious ceremonial for being highly centralized round the altar.

But besides taking count of these two points of resemblance between the ceremonial of Court and the ceremonial of Church, it is necessary to notice points of difference. Especially we must recognize that access to God is to a large extent a markedly individual act. The worshipper is throughout the service in an individual relationship to God, to which the analogy of the Court presents no close parallel. He makes his individual confession of sin, or gives his individual tribute of praise; and all, if we may so say reverently, for the private ear of God. To many English churchfolk this view of worship represents the whole, or nearly the whole, of the case. They have been trained in a theology which is highly individual; their view of religion is equally individual ; and even in public worship it is still this side of the question which fills their mind. Some may even say frankly that in their own view they can say their prayers as well at home as at church ; and that the purpose for which principally they go to church is to hear a sermon.

All this no doubt comes from the individualist view of religion, which is a very true side of it, and is moreover that which the last four hundred years of the history of the English Church have been especially occupied in enforcing. But it is only one side, be it remembered ; and those persons who set store by this side to the exclusion of the rest will not be very fair-minded judges of religious ceremonial. However, even the extreme individualist in worship cannot escape ceremonial. He has his private customs of reverence ; kneeling to pray, closing the eyes, covering the face—these, and suchlike common acts, are his ; and often he has also, besides the common customs, some very odd fads and habits of his own which he has devised ; and these, more even than the common ceremonial acts of reverence which he has adopted, show how impossible it is even for the most Quakerlike of individualists to escape from ceremonial. He may dislike other people's ceremonial, and even be intolerant of it, but he is bound to have a ceremonial of his own.

This is no less the case with clergy in their official capacity in the quire and the sanctuary than with the lay person in the pew ; and hence it is often to be observed that in churches where the puritan tradition is strong, and where pale horror would creep over the face of the minister if it was even suggested that he was a ' Ritualist,' there does exist a well-defined ceremonial. The vicar has his own ways of doing things, possibly the vicar's ways become by conscious or unconscious adoption the curate's ways also, and so it is fastened on the church. It is all highly individual ; it rests perhaps on nothing else but the vicar's own ways or oddities ; it has possibly no relation at all to the traditions of church worship; but it is ceremonial for all that ; and it differs from the ceremonial of the ' Ritualist ' only in being based on no authority, in being the result of individual caprice, and possibly further in being ill conceived, or even, it may be, grotesque in character.

It is necessary then to recognize fully the place of individualism in access to God even in public worship ; but that is no valid objection to the existence of ceremonial. So we may pursue our subject undeterred, and only less inclined than ever to leave religious ceremonial to be settled by the chance habits or ' ways ' of individuals, and more eager to seek out the true principles which must govern it and systematize it.

Public worship, besides being individual, is also essentially corporate : it is the approach to God not of a merely fortuitous conglomeration of individuals, but rather of an organized body. Just as the Court in its attendance on the Sovereign is a body performing a corporate action round his throne, so the worshipping Church is a body performing acts of corporate worship round the throne of God ; and it is this conception rather than the individualist view which underlies the major part of religious ceremonial.

Further, the Church, like the Court, is organized for this purpose in various grades, and consists of concentric circles, so to speak, in varying degrees of nearness to the throne. There is the broad distinction between the congregation and those who, in one or other capacity, perform different ministries in public worship. Further, there are great distinctions in the grades of ministry. There is a whole class or hierarchy of itself concerned with the singing; another whole class or hierarchy consisting of the clerk and others, who act as assistants to those who, in the narrower sense of the word, are ministers; again, the hierarchy of the clergy themselves in their different ministries. Here are three broad divisions, which correspond, roughly speaking, to the Quire, the Sanctuary, and the Altar.

The greater part of our discussion of religious ceremonial will necessarily concern these persons and their various ministries; but before closing this chapter something may be said about the ceremonial of the congregation.

It is in the congregation that most deference must be paid to the individualism of which mention was made above. Any one who is performing an official ministry in public worship can hardly count as an individual: his individuality must rightly be, to a very large extent, sunk in his office and ministry; and he must speak, move, and act as the servant of the whole body. But with the single worshipper in the congregation it is different. A rubric such as that which found a place in the Book of Common Prayer of 1549 is a very natural recognition of his individual rights, and applies even more strongly in his case than in the case of the clergy to whom the rubric seems primarily to be addressed.

'As touching kneeling, crossing, holding up of handes, knocking upon the brest, and other gestures: they may be used or left as euery mans devocion serueth without blame.'

But the congregation has its corporate acts and its corporate ceremonial: it is ordered as a body to stand, to kneel, to sit, to bow, to respond, and so forth; and all this, though naturally very much restricted in amount, is in a true sense its ceremonial. More elaborate action and fuller direction is reserved for those who are to execute special functions in connexion with the worship.

CHAPTER III

CONGREGATION AND MINISTERS

IT is but lately that we emerged from a state of affairs in which, so far as parish churches were concerned, the ordinary Sunday worship might be described as mainly consisting of a duet between the parson and the clerk. Of recent years great changes have come about, which have been mainly in the direction of causing not only large town churches, but even tiny village churches, to copy the methods of cathedrals. Whether this change has been altogether for the good, it is not our present purpose to inquire. It is a question that concerns music more than ceremonial, and we may leave the matter on one side. But we are concerned at this point to notice that the change has not necessarily introduced any better conception of corporate worship. The choral Mattins and Evensong of to-day may, in some places, no less than the services of the previous era, be described as a duet. The parson and choir take the place of the parson and clerk of old days—that is, in so far as the organist is willing to allow either of them to have a place—and the congregation has possibly, in proportion to its intelligence, a less part than it had under the old régime. The view of Divine Service* which conceives it to be a duet, is in reality the lowest term of a long history of degradation and decay ; and if our study of the principles of religious ceremonial is to be of any use, we must try to go back to earlier and better conceptions.

The history of the method of performing public

---

* The term is here used in its strict sense as the name for the system of Hour Services—Mattins, etc.—as distinct from the Eucharist and other rites.

worship is not uniform ; for, not to mention other services of less importance for our inquiry, the case stands differently with regard to Divine Service and with regard to the Holy Eucharist. As these two branches of our public worship have had a different origin, so in matters of ceremonial and in method of performance they exhibit a different history.

The performance of Divine Service did not necessarily at first involve the action of any ministers. Originally people came together of themselves for the most part, to say in common the devotions which they had been accustomed to say privately ; and Divine Service owes its beginnings in the main to the gregarious instincts of individual devotees, especially of the Religious, to use a more modern term for convenience, of both sexes.[1]

The same instinct which brought hermits together into community life, or joined in religious association those who so far had been living a life of special dedication in the privacy of their own homes, brought them together also in the fourth century for common worship of a voluntary sort, and additional to the eucharistic communion and worship which had long been the recognized duty of every Christian. So long as their common worship consisted almost, if not quite, exclusively of psalmody and religious reading, there was no need of any special minister. But when prayers and collects were added as an appendix to this, they seemed to call for the intervention of the clergy ; and when the main part was done the bishop was accustomed to come in at the end of the service to close it with the blessing.[2] But this intervention of the clergy long continued to be held unnecessary : the monks or nuns combined to conduct their own devotions. The clergy only slowly followed in the wake of the conventuals in developing worship of this sort ; it was not until public opinion demanded of them similar devotional exercises to those which the

[1] This and the subsequent numbers refer to notes at the end of the book.

conventuals had inaugurated and carried out for themselves, that there began to be anything clerical about the rapidly developing system of Hour Services. As the distinction between monks and clergy diminished, the clerical character of the system became more marked; when finally the recitation of the daily offices became a clerical obligation as well as a monastic one, this development was completed, and the Divine Service was clericalized. But, for all that, the system still was in its essence independent of any special ministerial function; and to this day the Latin services of the old system can be performed as well by a convent of laymen or a community of women as by a clerical body.

The ideal of services which had such a history and such a character was very different from our present practice. The ideal was that each person, so far as possible, should contribute something to the whole. Each lesson should have a fresh person assigned to read it, each respond a fresh person to sing it. Indeed the number of parts that could be allotted to an individual as his quota to be contributed to the whole was elaborately multiplied, in order that as many persons as possible should be employed. Even the precenting of the opening words of an antiphon, a psalm, or a hymn, might serve to give employment to a fresh worshipper, and so bring in fresh individuals to have each a part of his own allotted to him in a service. Thus an elaborate service like the Latin Mattins might come to provide a special task each for as many as forty or fifty different persons, all intrusted, either singly or in conjunction with one or two others, with the performance of some special part in the service:[3] and not only so, but others again might be utilized for purely ceremonial action, such as the carrying of a censer or a candle, and so bear their hand and take their share in the common worship. There was a great blending of the individual and the corporate.

It is clear that such a system as this has little or nothing in common with the idea of a duet which now prevails.

On the contrary, it may better be compared with an oratorio, where solos, duets, trios, and quartets alternate with choruses or are combined with them ; and where there is no hard distinction drawn between soloists and chorus-singers, but each member of the chorus in turn is intrusted with the more conspicuous and more responsible parts.

With regard to the Holy Eucharist the case stands differently ; for here, from the nature of the case, there has always been a distinction between the ministerial and the congregational parts of the service. This rite, however, was not in early days a duet, for the whole company of the faithful took its part in the Holy Mysteries in graduated order. The celebrant had necessarily his ministers to attend to him, some sharing with him in the recitation of the service, some ministering in the ceremonies accompanying the rite, some singing the music which alternated with the lessons and the prayers ; while the congregation itself, in the days of heathenism and under the system of church discipline, had its own gradations, and took a greater or a smaller part in the service accordingly.

In the Eastern liturgies the distinction between the ministers and the congregation is in some sense drawn more clearly than in the mediaeval Western rites. There the solid screen called the *Iconostasis* stands between the sanctuary and the body of the church, so that the action of the service is performed by the ministers to a considerable extent out of sight of the congregation, and independently of its co-operation. But, on the other hand, the deacon is deputed to be, as it were, a link between the two ; and, standing at the head of the congregation, he conducts the devotions of the congregation in the body of the church concurrently with the progress of the action of the Liturgy as it is conducted inside the sanctuary by the celebrant and his ministers.[4]

Here again, then, there is little or no sign of the idea of a duet with which we are familiar : all is co-operative. For example, in the due performance of the Latin rite, as seen before the great period of liturgical decadence had set in, the Liturgy was everywhere normally the work of the whole Christian community, worshipping God in its several grades. The celebrant had the solemn prayers to say—the variable collects and the fixed forms as well, including of course the actual consecration. The deacon had the Gospel to read and the subdeacon the Epistle ; while the former also was responsible for the leading of the people, though this duty soon shrank to very small dimensions in the West as compared with the East. These two sacred ministers, or two groups of sacred ministers, were also in attendance upon the celebrant ; they both waited upon him themselves, and also served as intermediaries between him and the lesser grades of ministers, such as thurifers, taperers, etc., so far as their ministry concerned the celebrant. Again, besides these ceremonial attendants must be reckoned the singers, or *Schola cantorum*, who were not concerned with ceremonial, but had their own part in the rite. They were responsible for the more elaborate and variable part of the music and such chants as employed soloists, especially the Introit and Communion with their psalms, the Gradual, *Alleluia*, and Offertory. Lastly, the congregation had its part both in the psalmody and in the prayers of the rite. At first the *Kyries* and *Sanctus*, and then later on the *Agnus Dei* and Creed, and lastly the *Gloria in excelsis*, represented the popular element or congregational parts of the singing, while the responses to the celebrant, and especially the solemn Amen after consecration, represented their share in the prayers.[5]

One can hardly fail to see, even in the dim obscurity which surrounds all early liturgical history, that the tendency to deprive the people of their part of the service, by making it so elaborate that it was of necessity confined to the choir, was one which showed itself at early stages. The simple psalmody which once went on between the lessons or during the ceremonies of the Offertory became ousted by the elaborate chants of the Graduals or of the Offertories. Next, the psalmody that still survived at the Introit and at the Communion was cut down, and became also uncongregational. Meanwhile the congregation was making its voice heard in new ways instead, and was singing the *Agnus Dei* at Communion, or on occasions the Creed. It managed for the time to retain its rights over these parts of the service and to acquire rights over the *Gloria in excelsis*, which at first was a purely sacerdotal element in the service ; but, on the other hand, to a considerable degree it lost the *Kyries*, as these ceased to be the simple responses to a litany and became the elaborated melodies of the later mediaeval period.

Yet, in spite of all such changes, the old ideal still remained, viz. that all should contribute their share to the corporate Christian worship ; and it is not too much to say that without any doubt this is the only true ideal of Christian worship.

It survived, however, down to the end of the mediaeval period only in a shrunken and a steadily shrinking form. A baneful process of decay was all the time in growing operation, which eventually reduced the oratorio to a mere duet, if not to a monologue, for the ordinary Latin Low Mass became little more than that. The congregation forfeited much of its share, partly through coldness and carelessness, but more still through the changes by which Latin ceased to be a tongue understood of the people. Simultaneously all the ministerial parts were also being cut down, and the co-operative principle was being lost. The Mass was said instead of being sung; so at one blow the whole of the functions of the *Schola cantorum* were gone, and the musical texts were transferred to the celebrant's part. Or it was said without attendant ministers except a 'server.' Thereupon the celebrant, with the server's help, took into his own hands so much of their functions as could be, or must be, managed, and the rest dropped out. So again by a gradual decline the co-operative principle was obscured and almost lost. Then the relics of the Liturgy which remained were conglomerated into the hands of the celebrant and formed the Missal, or compound sacerdotal book ; the participation of the faithful disappeared, and the resultant service was rightly called 'Low Mass.' For it represents the low-water mark of eucharistic service, and is a painful contrast to the true but almost lost dignity of the old celebration of the Holy Mysteries, carried out with the full and intelligent co-operation of all the faithful, each in their several spheres and grades taking their own proper part in the adoration of Almighty God.

It must not, however, be thought that all the causes which led to this lamentable decay were in themselves bad ; in many respects the contrary is the case. One cause was the multiplication of services. When the Eucharist was celebrated only on Sundays and High Festivals, the circumstances were all favourable for the preservation of the old ideal. But this weekly or rare habit of celebration was felt to be insufficient. In some parts of Christendom the practice of daily celebration began in very early days,[6] in other parts, even in the West, it came in only gradually and at a much later date. In the East the principle of daily celebration has never yet been adopted.[7] Now there is a very close connexion between the multiplication of Eucharists and the decay in the manner of celebration. It is only in special circumstances, as for example in monastic or collegiate or cathedral churches, that it has been possible to retain the old ideal together with a daily celebration. In ordinary circumstances a choice had to be made between the two things, the multiplication of celebrations and the retention of the old ideal. Here, roughly speaking, the East and West parted company ; for the East kept the ceremonial ideal and denied itself the advantage of daily celebrations, while the more utilitarian West sacrificed the ceremonial ideal to the practical advantage of frequent communion and daily Mass.

Other similar changes go alongside with this and influence the history similarly in the direction of decay. The spread of the Church into country places and the multiplication of village churches made it impossible to go on looking upon the bishop as the normal celebrant of the Eucharist, as was the case in the early days. When a priest took his place at the altar, the service was *ipso facto* less, not exactly because the priest was less in dignity than the bishop, but rather because the whole character of the assembly was altered. The faithful meeting for the Holy Mysteries in their several degrees round their bishop represented the Christian unit ; compared to this a body of Christians in a district church with a priest at their head was only a fraction, and their gathering merely sectional. The idea was thus different: the unity of the altar was gone ; and though it might be possible in a few places, as in Rome, to keep up for a time the idea of the unity by sending round from the pope's mass some of the consecrated host to each priest who was celebrating in the other churches, this clearly was only a despairing effort to retain what in fact was bound to disappear.[8] And if it soon proved impossible, even in the circumscribed area and among the conservative traditions of Rome, it could not be expected to be an expedient that would find favour in many places, or to be able to preserve the old ideal of liturgical unity. Thus the priest and not the bishop became the normal celebrant, and both the ideal and the practice were altered by the change.

For in practice, as the Church grew, and small churches and parishes belonging to special shrines or connected with landed estates took their place in the Christian economy side by side with the town churches,[9] the materials were not available for the old solemnity of the Liturgy. For choir and ministers the parish had to make the best shift it could with whatever materials were available ; and when it became necessary to define the lowest terms which should be considered possible for a celebration of the Eucharist, the minimum requirement was fixed at two persons, the priest and a clerk to serve him. And so we come to the duet. What wonder if the people soon came to regard the service as something done for them instead of something done by them?

This was a deplorable degradation of the ideal of corporate worship. It made little difference, so far as the present point is concerned, whether the priest was with or without any further congregation than his clerk to serve him, for the service in either case was reduced to a duet. Similarly, the question as to whether others communicated with him is unimportant from our present point of view, however important it may be from other and more significant points of view; the service was still a mere duet so far as the ceremonial presentation of it was concerned.

The multiplication of Low Masses of this sort had, no doubt, many advantages; especially as chantries and chaplains multiplied, the convenience of numerous classes of working people who wished to attend daily was met by two or three services daily at different hours. Whatever may rightly be said derogatory to the character of such daily worship at the Holy Eucharist in the pre-Reformation days, there is no doubt as to the extent of it; all classes of persons thronged the churches daily, especially in England, where an Italian visitor was astonished at the universality of daily attendance at mass.[10]

Such were some of the practical gains which must be set off against the loss or decay of the ideal of corporate worship. But we must be careful not to overestimate the extent to which that ideal had been lost before the Reformation. It was still maintained at its highest in monasteries, and in collegiate and cathedral churches. The decay of monastic life in the fifteenth century did not materially affect the case, since it was compensated for by the great development of collegiate churches. In such great centres as these the Hours of Divine Service were still the combined act of the whole body of clerks in choir, while the Eucharist was celebrated with at any rate so much of the co-operative action of ministers, choir, and congregation as is implied by the term High Mass. Even in smaller places and village churches something of this was kept up. There were two priests or more in many villages, especially in the latter part of the mediaeval period, for those who served the chantries were generally expected to help the parson on special occasions, besides often being responsible for keeping a school ; so that, at any rate on great days, Evensong and Mattins were solemnly sung and the Eucharist solemnly celebrated with sacred ministers, acolytes, and choir.[11] Moreover, the congregation had, in its old-fashioned way, some real appreciation of what the services were then held to imply. In the absence of books and of the power to read them, the people followed the gestures of the celebrant, and were guided by them through the course of the service.[12] So that, where all this was possible, the old ideal of corporate worship was not altogether lost, though the greater part of the everyday church-going consisted merely of hearing a Low Mass.

The character of pre-Reformation service-books in England was especially calculated to keep up a good deal of the old ideal. While continental mass-books very constantly contemplated nothing better than Low Mass, the English books always had High Mass in view. Indeed, this is so much the case that it is a matter of great difficulty to reconstruct what an English Low Mass was like before the Reformation, since the service-books make little or no provision for it.[13] Moreover, many of the service-books, both for the Eucharist and the Divine Service, incorporated as rubrics large sections of the ceremonial and ritual directions of the Cathedral Church of Salisbury. By this means there penetrated even to the village churches some echo of the dignified and corporate worship of that illustrious cathedral body ; and the smaller bodies were encouraged to do their best to maintain the same ideal, and to resist as far as possible the progress of liturgical degradation and decay.

The Reformation brought with it the opportunity for a great liturgical revision, but without enough knowledge of liturgical science and principles to make the best use of the opportunity. The new service-books were designed to carry out some much-needed reforms, principally to bring the services to correspond with the reformed doctrinal standpoint, and with the growing demand on the part of the congregation for their rights in the way of understanding and sharing in the services. The latter demand ought to have led to a restoration of the old ideal of corporate worship ; but unfortunately in fact it did not do so in any full measure. The reason of this was twofold. Partly it was because for the time the individual ideal of religion in general was overpowering the corporate ideal, and the reforms aimed more at securing for the individual his own unimpeded access to God than at securing him a fuller form of corporate worship. Partly also it was for practical reasons. The Great Pillage of 1547 had robbed every parish in England and stripped it bare alike of clergy, endowments, and ornaments, so that there were no longer either the persons or the things available in the ordinary parish churches for the richer ideal of worship.[14] Already most of the collegiate churches had similarly fallen victims to the right royal rapacity of the Crown and the Court, so that by 1549 and the issue of the First Prayer-Book the places were few and far between where anything more than a duet between parson and clerk, or congregation, was possible.

The new book contained only very scanty ceremonial directions by contrast with the old. The previous service-books had given a far greater fullness of rubric and prescribed the ceremonial to be used in Salisbury Cathedral, leaving smaller churches to do as much of it as was possible under their varying circumstances. The new book kept some traces of the participation of the clerks and the sacred ministers other than the celebrant. Succeeding service-books gave still scantier directions, and such, moreover, as contemplated Low Mass and the duet rather than the old co-operative form of service. A deadly blow was thus given to the old ideal of primitive and corporate worship; and it was left to be a matter of dispute for subsequent generations as to how the meagre outline was to be filled in.[15]

This failure to restore the ancient ideal of worship was probably not so much a matter of design as of accident. The reformers no doubt wished to reduce the elaborateness of ceremonial, to simplify the services and make them more congregational. They objected to the ceremonial partly because it seemed to men of that age, as the result of bad traditions, to be in itself an unspiritual thing, and partly also because it was intimately bound up in the popular mind with doctrinal views which they wished to eradicate. They did not see that, in abolishing the provision for it so much as they did, they were destroying good as well as evil, and were robbing a number of the people of the privilege of a share of their own in the worship. Nor did they perceive that, while attempting to abolish the sacerdotalism which they had seen so much abused, they were in fact, so far as service went, erecting a new barrier between clergy and laity, and a sharp line of demarcation between priest and people, such as had not existed previously in the days when priest, deacon, subdeacon, acolyte, clerk, incense-boy, and congregation still had each his appointed share, and ministered in his several degree.

The Prayer-Book of 1662 contemplates mainly but one officiant; though there are signs also of a less restricted view. While the Communion Service seems to imply that the celebrant will read both Epistle and Gospel, *i.e.* that there will be no sacred ministers, the Ordinal takes for granted that there will be both epistoller and gospeller at the Consecration of a Bishop; while even in the smaller scale of ceremonial contemplated for the Communion Office it is supposed that there will be a minister to begin the Confession. These small points are all that is expressed of the old ideal. The result of the change has been the extrusion of the laity from the sanctuary. Again, it was left free, so far as the book went, that the Litany might be sung by clerks; but no rule was laid down, and later custom has usually clericalized this part of the service.

While the meagre directions of the book preserved such few traces of the old ideal, tradition preserved more. In great churches where three clergy were available, in spite of royal rapacity and the diminution of clergy consequent on the doctrinal disputes, the epistoller and gospeller survived, and retained in more or less degree some of their old functions. The lessons at Mattins and Evensong have been assigned to different readers, generally, as in old time, in ascending order of dignity. In some cases even the Short Exhortation as well as the Confession has been assigned to one of the assistant ministers; and this plan is of especial interest, for it cannot be a mere survival. Those parts of the Prayer-Book rite are not features of the old High Mass at all; consequently the traditional use in regard to them must be the result of a general recognition of the principle that the assistant ministers should take their share in the service, and be responsible for the subordinate parts.

Traditions of this nature remained until recent years in many large churches and bore shrunken witness to the old ideal. Even in smaller churches the clerk retained his right to read the Epistle.[16] Many slight features survived even the Hanoverian decadence. That they were recently destroyed is due to a false High Church craze and to the unintelligent copying of Low Mass as seen in foreign churches. The epistoller and the gospeller, instead of being restored to their fuller functions, were banished, and a lay server substituted for them. The parish clerk was in many cases banished instead of being restored to a fuller execution of his duties. Even where epistoller and gospeller were retained they were made to cease from ' serving ' the celebrant, or otherwise robbed of their duties. The hand of the so-called ' restorer,' in fact, often dealt as cruelly with the ceremonial as with the fabric of the churches ; and the good that survived the old days of slackness and darkness often fell a victim to the new régime of strenuous enlightenment.

It is necessary, therefore, at the close of this chapter to protest against such false methods, and to urge a return to the old principles.

Liturgical worship must be co-operative and corporate. It is a false sacerdotalism that seeks to comprehend as much as possible in the one pair of hands of the priest or celebrant. It is always a gain that, with due regard to structure and liturgical principles, the services should employ many persons in divers functions. The clergy and other ministers, servers, clerks, and choir, all have their own part. The different parts of the ceremonial action must be harmonious ; but, so long as this is the case, it is no harm, but only good, that different people should simultaneously be doing different things. A good deal is needed to get rid of the false idea of the duet of parson and clerk, or parson and choir, or even parson and congregation. For example, it is far better that the psalms, when read, should be read as they are sung, from side to side ; that the lessons at Divine Service and at the Eucharist should be assigned to different persons ; that the first part of the Litany should be sung by clerks ; and that many other survivals of the old ideal be retained. And most of all it is desirable that the true ideal should be so clearly set before the congregation that it may become less of a cold critic of a ceremonial which it does not understand and perhaps dislikes, and more of an active and hearty participant in a great act of corporate and co-operative worship.

For this purpose it is necessary that the musical parts of the service which ought to be congregational, should be kept so simple that the congregation can, if it only will, take its part in them ; and of such moderate pitch that the men's voices can sing as well as the women's. All elaborate harmonized music is out of place for these parts of the service, except in those churches, which, though rare, do yet exist in England, where a large section of the congregation is able to take the various vocal parts, and is not confined merely to singing the melody.

The *Kyrie* and Creed at the Eucharist, and the psalms in Divine Service, are the special parts which both can be made, and ought to be kept, congregational ; and where psalms are congregational there is great gain in singing them for ' Introit ' and ' Communion,' as well as the best possible authority for doing so.

But when the congregation has its own part, it must not grudge others their part, nor expect to follow or share in all that others are doing. Such an expectation is a very common ground of complaint on the part of the laity, and it results from the misconception of the idea of corporate worship. No one expects or demands that on the stage only one actor should move at a time ; and if this is not expected on the stage, where all is done for the benefit of the audience, and adapted to the spectator's capacity for taking in the situation, far less is it to be demanded in religious ceremonial, which is done not for the benefit of the congregation, but for the honour of Almighty God ; and where, therefore, there is no need, as in the other case, that it should be adapted to the congregation at all, except so far as to be decorous and uplifting in its general effect.

Each person in his own sphere has taken his due part in the public worship if he has contributed his own quota, be it great or small, according to his responsibility and place, to the general sum ; and if at the same time he has followed generally the whole of the action. This is the ideal whether for the Eucharist or for Divine Service. These two differ widely in their general character, and therefore differ widely in the nature of their ceremonial. The Eucharist is one homogeneous and continuous action, and goes forward, if one may so say, like a drama ; it has its prelude, its working up, its climax, its epilogue. The Divine Service has no such unity ; it has a series of different actions which are not necessarily closely connected, and might almost equally well be placed in any other order as in their existing order. If the Eucharist may be called, in regard to the nature of the structure of the service, a dramatic action, the Divine Service may be called by contrast meditative or reflective. But, great as is this difference of nature between the two, they are alike in their ideal of corporate worship, and alike in requiring that the whole body of the faithful should as far as possible, and in very various degrees, co-operate. And in both cases this work of worship done by the Church on earth is a work in co-operation with the heavenly hierarchies in their celestial worship, whether it is the definite sacrificial climax of the Eucharist or the subsidiary work of preparation and thanksgiving, which, properly speaking, is the essence of the Divine Service.

CHAPTER IV

STAGES IN THE GROWTH OF RELIGIOUS CEREMONIAL

I. Primitive.

HITHERTO we have been occupied in recognizing the fundamental need for a religious ceremonial and in defining the persons who are concerned in it. We are therefore prepared to find that in some form or another religious ceremonial has existed from the very first beginnings of Christian services. There was no break in this respect between the Old and the New Covenant. Our Blessed Lord was pleased that from the first His earthly life should conform to the requirements of the Mosaic rites and their attendant ceremonial; and in accordance with this fact the Christian Church has thought well not merely to preserve the records of the Circumcision, the Purification, and the last Passover among the evidences of His conformity to Jewish ceremonial, but also to commemorate these in the ecclesiastical kalendar for the continual remembrance of Christian piety. The absence of break and the completeness of continuity is more especially brought out by the incidents of Maundy Thursday, when our Lord not only carried out the Jewish rite with its attendant ceremonial, but grafted on to it two new Christian ordinances—first, The New Commandment, with its attendant ceremony of the washing of the feet; and secondly, The New Covenant, sealed with the partaking of His Flesh and Blood, with the attendant ceremonies of blessing, breaking, outpouring, and administering.[1] These two new Christian rites, which, so far as the letter of the Gospels goes, seem equal and parallel, have in fact been shown by the interpretation and teaching of the Holy Spirit within the Church to be of very different calibre and importance. It is very significant that the one which is of primary importance as the abiding sacrament of the Christian's communion with the Lord and the Church's continual and corporate sacrifice and climax of worship, is the one which least of the two is an innovation, being grafted on to the Jewish ordinances both in its ritual nature, and in its ceremonial expression. The Maundy was never more than a significant parable ; it began thus and has continued to be no more than this ; but the Eucharist was to sum up and supersede the older rites and sacrifices ; and it has been from the first the central Christian sacrament, not significant only, but efficacious.

The nucleus of eucharistic ceremonial consists of those ceremonies which our Lord Himself used when He instituted the rite, and which, as having been annexed to it by Him, the Christian Church has perpetuated, at His express command. The blessing, the breaking, and the administering stand out clearly in the writings of the New Testament as features of the apostolic ceremonial.

Beyond these there is little to be found of any details of ceremonial, though there are evident signs of the beginnings of an order of service. The conduct of worship is a subject with which S. Paul deals. His Jewish mind, accustomed to the orderly ceremonial of temple and synagogue, was shocked by the want of order prevailing among the less decorous Corinthians. He did not think it below the dignity of the apostolic office to handle such matters ; but he wrote directions both as to the Eucharist and also as to the more informal meetings for prayer, preaching, and prophesying, and for the women's part in them, promising as well further directions to be given by word of mouth when he next visited the Church there.[2]

The pictures of heavenly worship recorded in the Apocalypse have already been cited as evidence of the divine character of ceremonial. It is more difficult to estimate their bearing upon the actual ceremonial worship of the primitive Church. It may be that they are an idealized picture of what S. John already well knew as being the continual presentation of the Eucharist in the Christian churches of the end of the first century. Or it may be that these visions served as a model, upon the lines of which subsequent eucharistic ceremonial was developed. Either view is possible, and it would be hard to decide whether the Apocalypse or the current practice of the Church has the priority. But in either case the connexion between the two is indisputable ; of the scanty facts that are known about the primitive ceremonial not a few fall in exactly with this outline.[3]

The form adopted for Christian churches was one which lent itself to such a *mise en scène*. Whether this was an adaptation of a dwelling-house, or an oratory established among the intricacies of the catacombs, or a large building planned on the model of a secular basilica, the essential form of it was a long rectangle ending in a niche or apse. At the entrance to the latter stood the altar, behind it was the bishop's throne, on either side of the apse were the seats of the presbyter-elders, while within the space surrounding the altar the ceremonial was performed and the Divine Mysteries were celebrated; on these were focussed the eyes and the worship of the congregation gathered in the body of the church.[4]

It is hardly to be supposed that in the early days there was any fixity as to the minutiae of eucharistic ceremonial; though most probably the general lines of it soon became customary and general. In this respect rite and ceremony were probably alike. It is clear, with regard to the rite, that no form of service or formulary of consecration was originally imposed upon the Church. The Church took some time to form its liturgical language and phraseology; and it was a further step beyond that when particular forms of prayer became stereotyped, and were repeated by various celebrants until they became a fixed rite. But while all this liberty was still current, and it was still left to the discretion of the celebrant to pray and consecrate in his own way, the general outline of the service was clearly laid down for him ; and it was only within certain well-defined limits that he was free to follow his own bent. Even when liturgical forms were stereotyped, their use was at first optional ; and even when they became binding on some celebrants, the old liberty was still reserved, *e.g.* to prophets and bishops and those of special dignity, of using other forms.5 The absolute fixity of rite was only the last stage of a long development.

It is probable that the growth of ceremonial proceeded along similar lines, from a mere outline, which, it may be, reached back to apostolic times, up to a clearly defined Order. The growth was slow in the case alike of rite and ceremony. Of the two it is probable that the former growth was the slower, because ceremonial involves the concurrence of various persons, and would therefore naturally have become more quickly settled than the rites or formulas of prayer, which concerned only the celebrant. In their case he could be left free in his prayer to go his own way, without disturbing others, as he would be bound to do if he went his own way in matters of ceremonial.

In the ante-Nicene period there is little evidence to show how far ceremonial had developed. There is nothing to cause surprise in this ; the literature of the primitive period is very scanty, and the Church was more occupied with carrying out its worship than in discussing, describing, or even formulating it. There can, however, be little doubt that the growth of eucharistic ceremonial was considerable, and that the services even in the straitened circumstances of the time were elaborate and as magnifical as they could be made. The early elaboration of worship had effects which are traceable in other parts of the Christian economy, particularly in the development of the Christian hierarchy.

From the beginning there was the closest connexion

between deacons and bishops. The seven deacons established at Jerusalem were the immediate helpers of the Apostles; and whether it be the case or not that the subsequent diaconate was the historical successor of the movement which created the Seven,[6] at any rate the connexion still continued between apostle and deacon. While the diaconate continued to exercise large administrative functions in conjunction with the bishop, it was also bound to him by liturgical duties.

The bishop, who was the normal celebrant of the Holy Mysteries in the early days, was ceremonially assisted not so much by the presbyters as by the deacons.[7] In Rome and in other large cities the number of deacons was maintained at seven in continuation of the original number; and on great days the seven deacons ministered to the bishop at the Eucharist.[8] This implied a developed ceremonial; and in fact the ceremonial was so far elaborated that deacons did not suffice to carry out all the parts of it, but gradually other orders grew up, chiefly in deference to the exigences of the worship. At Rome subdeacons came into existence at least as early as the first half of the third century, and a few years later the clergy of Rome comprised seven deacons, seven subdeacons, and forty-two acolytes, besides fifty-two inferior clergy. These formed the assistants of the pope for liturgical purposes, and they suggest an advanced stage of ceremonial development.[9] The part of the deacon was the custody of the chalice at the Eucharist; indeed, his part was so definite that he could even be said to 'consecrate' the chalice.[10] The subdeacon's duty was to attend on the deacons. The acolyte had amongst other duties in early times the carrying of the Eucharist from the altar to the faithful, or to the clergy of district churches in the form of the *fermentum* sent from the pope's mass to form a link between his offering at the central altar and theirs in their districts.[11] The exorcists developed as a special body to exercise the function of exorcising, and in particular connexion with baptismal ceremonial; the reader and doorkeeper had also a liturgical origin.[12]

When the beginning of the fourth century brought peace to the Church, and it emerged from twilight into daylight, at once much evidence becomes available to prove the elaboration of ceremonial that had taken place during the first three centuries. It is sufficient to look through the list of ecclesiastical ornaments given by Constantine and others to the great basilicas and stational churches of Rome, and recorded in the *Liber Pontificalis*, to see what standard of decorativeness had been obtained; and though it is probable that these gifts exceeded in magnificence what the Church had hitherto possessed, and in this respect began a new era, yet clearly the Church was already well accustomed to the use of such ornaments. The munificence of the emperor did not introduce innovation, but only further glorified a system which already existed.[13]

From this point forward there is a gradual increase both of direct and of indirect testimony as to the nature of Christian ceremonial. Indeed, the direct testimony in writings designed to be guides as to the conduct of services has its origin even in the earlier centuries. The great class of ecclesiastical handbooks which may be comprehended under the general heading of 'Church Orders' reached its main development in the fourth and fifth centuries. But this literature was based on earlier documents. The discoveries of recent years have brought two to light—the *Hippolytean Church Order*, which probably belongs to the first quarter of the third century, and the *Didache* or *Teaching of the Twelve Apostles*, which seems to be a Christian document of the end of the first century, and based indeed upon a Jewish work. The *Didache* has little by way of direction for services; there is much more of this in the *Hippolytean Church Order*; while the later stages of the development, especially the *Apostolic Constitutions* and the *Testament of the Lord*, represent richer and fuller reaches of the same stream of tradition.[14]

From the later Church Orders, and especially from the *Testament*, a fairly clear picture may be formed of the appearance of Christian services at the end of the fourth century.[15] The church is an oblong building with a court in front of it and turned to the east. It has two entrances at least, one for men and one for women, or perhaps three in honour of the Trinity, and two sacristies, or one at least on the right-hand side. Within, a light is kept burning day and night. At the further end on a daîs of three steps is the sanctuary, an apse containing the altar, but a veil hangs before it, just as a veil also hides the baptistery in the fore-court. Eastward of the altar is the throne of the bishop in the centre of the semi-circular seats of the presbytery. Within the sanctuary is also the place of the other clergy, who stand with the bishop at the consecration of the Eucharist in their degrees ; sometimes there are included with them those who have special *charismata*, or spiritual gifts, and even women, in the shape of the Order of Widows.

Outside the veil and northwards at the front of the congregation is the high place from which lessons are read, and perhaps also the deacon's litany is sung ; there also the oblations of the faithful are received at the Offertory. In the congregation the sexes are divided, either on opposite sides of the church, or with the men in front and the women behind. At the back are the various classes of penitents, and possibly also some heathen. The deacons and other officers move about, seeing that all are in the right place, keeping good order, and waking up those who go to sleep. A deacon keeps the men's door, and a subdeacon or a deaconess the women's. Late-comers are kept waiting outside until a suitable moment when they can enter without causing disturbance. The virgins and ascetics sit at the head of the congregation ; then the married ; the young of either sex sit or stand at the back.

The service begins with prayer and psalmody, during which the presbyter brings in the holy gifts, and the bishop censes the sanctuary and a presbyter censes the congregation. Then follow the lessons, one from the Old Testament, one from the Apostolic writings, and one from the Gospel. Between them psalms are sung according to what is known as the responsorial method; that is to say, each verse is chanted by a singer and a brief refrain is interpolated by the congregation after each verse. At the Gospel all stand, the chief deacon censes the Gospel-book during the reading, and then goes censing before it into the sanctuary. Then follows the homily. After it the catechumens are dismissed with the penitents and others who were not allowed to be present at the Mysteries. The deacon summons them, and after suffrages, a prayer, and a blessing from the bishop, each class goes out in turn. Then the Liturgy of the Faithful, the second part of the service, begins with further suffrages, a prayer, and the Kiss of peace, the bishop kissing the clergy, the laymen the men, and the women the women. After the Lavatory and the Offertory, the great Consecration-prayer begins with the 'Lift up your hearts.' The bishop, robed in white, stands at the altar, and crosses himself on the forehead as he begins. The presbyters stand round him, joining in the consecration; the rest stand in their order behind him, and further back outside the sanctuary all the people stand. At the Communion the clergy receive first, then widows, virgins, newly baptized, and children; then the bulk of the laity, the women with their heads covered. Meanwhile psalm xxxiii (xxxiv) is sung. Then follows the Thanksgiving, and after the bishop's prayer of dismissal of the people the deacon bids them depart.

All this evidence of highly developed ceremonial belongs most evidently to Eastern Christendom. One may look in vain for any information nearly so explicit with regard to Latin Christendom. In Rome itself the services were still Greek and allied to Oriental rites; the great transformation had not yet taken place by which Rome adopted Latin instead of Greek as its liturgical language, and by making a compromise between its old Oriental rites and the Western rites by which it was surrounded, produced the peculiar Roman type of eucharistic liturgy which has gradually permeated Western Christendom.[16]

In Africa a Latin liturgy had grown up which is only known from scattered references in African documents. With this must probably be classed the parallel evolution, which had as yet proceeded to a less extent, in Gaul and Spain, and a development even less clearly traceable in Italy apart from Rome ; thus in obscurity the ancient Western non-Roman liturgy and ceremonial had grown up. In the main outline its ways were those common to all Christian liturgies ; this much is clear from the relics that survive of the non-Roman rite of a later era. But evidence as to its details in the primitive period is very scanty. Of direct evidence there is practically none, and such indirect evidence as may be gleaned from the writers of these regions in the fourth and fifth centuries does little to fill in the outline or to make possible the reconstruction of a picture of Latin worship at that epoch.

The use of individual ceremonies, however, may be noted. Crossing had been in general use ever since the second century,[17] and had acquired such an official position that the sign of the cross seemed almost an essential part of sacramental actions such as the preparatory dealings with catechumens before baptism, the consecration of the font, the ritual anointings with oil, and the consecration of the Eucharist.[18] Similarly, the beating of the breast had become a stereotyped gesture of penitence at certain points of the service.[19] Holy Water was used in such ceremonies as the Consecration of a Church,[20] while at the Liturgy there stood out prominent the solemn offertory made by all the faithful, the kiss of peace, and the episcopal benediction.[21]

To some extent during the fourth century the liturgical and ceremonial uses were emerging from the stage of being regulated by custom, and were becoming the subjects of definite conciliar enactment. Thus, as early as the Council of Elvira (*c*. 305) there are canons dealing with the offertory and the services held in cemeteries; these were made, however, for disciplinary rather than for ceremonial or liturgical reasons.[22] Again, among the Canons of Nicaea (325) is the closing one which forbids kneeling on Sundays and in Eastertide. The canons of Laodicea which belong to the third quarter of the fourth century are richer in information of this sort. A number of canons prescribe the different rights and duties of the clergy in the services. There was evidently at this time a tendency among some persons to presume and take up the positions belonging to others. The priests, deacons, and to a greater degree still the subdeacons, need to be kept in their place. These last are not to touch the sacred vessels, nor wear stoles (which even readers and singers had presumed also to adopt), nor give communion, nor assist in the consecration of the chalice. Others are restrained from exorcising without authorization, or singing the responsorial solos unless they are recognized 'singers.' Further in this group of canons some liturgical details are also prescribed; the kiss of peace, the *agape*, the baptismal ceremonies are regulated. Here, then, are further signs of the stirring of liturgical and ceremonial questions in the East.[23]

No such evidence is forthcoming for the West until the group of African councils at the end of the fourth century, and then the ceremonial rules that are laid down, such as the prohibition of the custom of giving communion to the dead, or the regulation of the offerings that may be set upon the altar, spring rather from disciplinary than ceremonial reasons.[24]

Thus, in the primitive period, though there has been found a disappointing lack of information in detail as to ceremonial, there has been discovered plenty of evidence to show that the Church rapidly developed and elaborated a system of ceremonial. It carried on the Jewish traditions of gorgeous worship, developing them even under the penalizing restrictions of its early years ; and when these were removed, the development went on all the faster. There were, no doubt, some respects in which that spirit of puritan severity so characteristic of primitive Christianity operated in the direction of restraint or even prohibition. It seems likely that, for example, the non-use of incense in the earliest centuries, except at funerals, was due to prejudice against it, which could not fail to subsist as long as its idolatrous and pagan use was in vogue, and as long as it was the commonest medium of apostasy. But this spirit seems only to have touched certain details, while in general the Christian bodies inclined naturally and without restraint to make the outward presentation of their worship a glorious reflection of their inner joy and happiness.

The fourth century no doubt witnessed a very great development. It is only the want of materials in the first three centuries, and the continued dearth in the fourth, which prevents us from being able to state more fully the magnitude of the expansion that came with freedom of worship. Hitherto our view has been confined within these limits. The restriction is, no doubt, a somewhat arbitrary one, as no strict line marks off the fifth and succeeding centuries from the fourth. But by the end of the fourth century the first initial outburst of development consequent upon the liberation of the Church was over, and it therefore deserved separate treatment. Moreover, after it the first divergences in ritual matters began to make themselves conspicuous, the Western rites began to grow unlike the Eastern, and in the West the Roman and the non-Roman are seen to diverge. The first signs that such differences were causing surprise and difficulty are found in the letter of Innocent I to Decentius belonging to the year 416. Now ritual divergence implied ceremonial divergence too ; hence a new stage of self-consciousness as regards ceremonial also opened for the Church in the fifth century.

CHAPTER V

STAGES IN THE GROWTH OF RELIGIOUS CEREMONIAL

II. The Unchanging East.

THE Liturgy and its ceremonial seem to have developed much more rapidly at first in the East than in the West; and thereafter to have remained more stationary. Consequently it will do no harm to take first as representative a group of documents describing the Syriac liturgy towards the end of the fifth century; and to supplement it from a commentary belonging to the eighth or ninth.

Narsai, the founder of the great Syriac school of Nisibis, left behind him a number of homilies; and from a small group of these, and one especially of the group, the following description of the service may be taken. The rite described was not, it may be supposed, widely different from the Byzantine customs of the same date; it has remained substantially in use among the Nestorians.[1]

Narsai's account begins with the 'dismissals.' The introduction, and the lessons with their chants, and the offertory are done. The priest is 'in secret away from those that are without,' and ready to celebrate privately within the sanctuary. After the priest's blessing the three classes who are not allowed to remain longer are dismissed; and the 'hearers' are sent to guard the doors. The deacons bring in, and place the elements on the altar and veil them; the assisting priests come in procession to the sanctuary. Two deacons with fans stand, one on each side of the elements, while the rest are stationed before the altar. Then follows the Creed, recited by all.

The deacon bids prayer for the faithful; and also for the oblation that it may be accepted, consecrated by the brooding of the Holy Spirit, and profitable to the receivers. It is a bidding prayer rather than a diaconal *Ektenia* or litany.

The priest stands at the altar; makes three obeisances and kisses it; asks the prayers of the deacons and people, and makes his own *apologia*. The kiss of peace follows, at the direction of the deacon, both in the sanctuary and in the nave, and meanwhile are read the diptychs, the two lists of names of those living and departed who are commemorated.

When the deacon has exhorted the people, the priest unveils the oblations and proceeds to the great Consecration Prayer beginning with 'The Grace' and the usual versicles. At the beginning he makes the first of the crossings. The people are able to see the consecration, and distinguish ' the altar with the cross and Gospel-book laid upon it, the lamps shining, the censers smoking, and the deacons fanning'; and all keep silence. The priest genuflecting, says quietly the first section of the Prayer (or Preface), ending with the cue to the *Sanctus* said aloud, at which the people join in. Then, genuflecting again, the priest says the second part of the Prayer, which includes the recital of the Institution, ending with another cue or doxology, said aloud, at which the people join in with Amen, while he makes the second crossing over the oblations. Before the third section the deacon exhorts the people to pray; and the priest, as he begins, makes the third genuflexion or bow. This section consists first of the detailed Intercession, and then follows the Invocation of the Holy Spirit to dwell in the Bread and Wine and make them the Body and Blood of Christ. At the Invocation the priest stands upright with head and arms uplifted: he ends as before with a doxology said aloud, to which probably the people respond Amen. The deacon meanwhile utters a warning note and the priest make the third crossing, in order to show that the Mysteries are accomplished.

The fraction and commixture follow; then the blessing, and the breaking of the Body for distribution. The deacon summons the communicants; a prayer, said aloud by the priest, leads into the Lord's Prayer, which is said by all, and followed by two versicles and responses.

After the communion of the celebrant and clergy a great procession is formed of all the priests and deacons to escort the Sacrament to the communion of the people. Each receives communion in his right hand, resting crosswise upon his left hand; and kisses It before consumption. No account is given of the method of receiving from the chalice.

The deacon bids thanksgiving, the people respond; and the thanksgiving ends with the Lord's Prayer said a second time by all. Then the priest comes down to the door of the sanctuary and blesses the congregation with uplifted hands, signing them with his right.

It is clear from this summary that the ceremonial has developed considerably in the energetic Syrian Church of the end of the fifth century. Some of the things which become characteristic of the Eastern setting of the Liturgy are already noticeable. There is the threefold setting of the drama: the priest is saying the prayers in the sanctuary; the deacon is acting as his intermediary and as director of the people; the congregation is responding in the nave. As yet the sanctuary is not shut out from view by a solid screen: but the greater part of the solemn prayers are said in silence; only the conclusions are said aloud, to which there is made a response. As yet the deacon's part consists of directions, exhortation, and bidding of prayer or thanksgiving: the biddings have not yet developed into the form of a litany carried on by deacon and people while the priest's prayer is going on unheard in the sanctuary.

Further, in contrast to the West, it is noticeable that

the subdeacon has not been given any liturgical function. The bringing in of the oblations, at the Great Entrance, has already become a solemn procession. Of the earlier procession, the Little Entrance, we hear nothing, for Narsai's exposition begins at a later point.

In later days the closing up of the screen separates off the sanctuary. Doors and a veil shroud the Mysteries. Then the deacon when he has to lead the people, whether by exhortations or in developed litanies, comes out from the sanctuary to do so, and stands before the Royal Door that leads into the sanctuary.

Later on also took place the great development of the preparatory section of the Liturgy called the *Prothesis* : but this was performed out of sight, in the Chapel of the *Prothesis*, and does not concern the congregation, or the ceremonial as witnessed by the people. Apart from such developments as these the description of Narsai will serve as a general indication of Eastern Liturgy, though it belongs to Nisibis and to the latter part of the fifth century.

These homilies are valuable not only for giving the outline of the service, but also for providing a commentary and explaining the symbolism, which connected each part of the Liturgy with the story of Redemption. In Narsai we have an early stage of this. His purpose is, like that of S. Cyril of Jerusalem a century earlier, to enable those who were about to be admitted to the Liturgy of the Faithful to understand and follow the latter part of the service, from which all but the faithful were excluded. They are to see in the Great Entrance the funeral procession of the Lord, represented by the Bread and Wine carried in by the deacons and accompanied by the procession of priests. The altar is the tomb ; and the veil is the stone which seals it. The two deacons fanning on either side are like the angels stationed at the head and foot ; while the rest, standing round, represent attendant angels. The sanctuary is the Garden of Joseph. The commemoration of the incarnation of the Lord and of the acts of His earthly life, recited as it were over His tomb, leads up to the Invocation of the Spirit, Who 'causes the power of His Godhead to dwell in the bread and wine and completes the mystery of the Lord's resurrection from the dead.'

The movements made during the Prayer are all carefully described: but so far as symbolism is concerned the genuflexions or bows are not given any great importance, except that Narsai insists that all three should come before the descent of the Holy Spirit. In the later forms of Eastern Liturgies the bows also are not specially significant: the Prayer is made either bowed or erect; and change from one posture to the other is fairly frequent.

The crossings, however, are deeply significant. Narsai prescribes three—one at the beginning of the Great Prayer, one at the end of the second section, presumably following the recital of the Institution, the third after the Invocation. This systematic plan did not altogether hold the field. In some quarters it was obscured by the multiplication of crossings, as in the Liturgy of S. James: in others by the diminution of the number. The Byzantine liturgy has kept the signing of the Gifts only at the Invocation: the Liturgy of S. Mark shows it only when the Prayer is resumed after the *Sanctus*.

The symbolical interpretation increased as time went on. Since Narsai does not touch the earlier part of the Liturgy[2] it may be well to quote also some of the points set out in another commentary, that attributed either to Germanus, Patriarch of Constantinople († 733), or (more commonly in the MSS.) to S. Basil. It belongs in its earliest accessible form at latest to the ninth century.[3] The rite described is the Byzantine.

Two more or less consecutive schemes of symbolism may be distinguished and extracted from the rather tangled overgrowth, relating the service to the life of our Lord. The first is in the earlier part of the service: and there it is the Gospel-book which stands for the

Saviour. In the later part of the service it is the Holy Gifts of the Bread and the Wine which perform this function.

The entry of the Gospel, brought in with a great procession and preceded by lights, shows the coming of the Saviour into the world : the Book is regarded as representing the presence of the incarnate Lord. The *Trisagion* of the congregation corresponds with the *Gloria in excelsis* of the angels ; the *prokeimenon* or respond with the prophesies of the Old Testament ; the Epistle with the apostolic witness. The *alleluia* gives the attestation of David ; and the reading of the Gospel is the climax of the first cycle.

In the second the Lord is symbolized by the Gifts of Bread and Wine. The Holy Table is the sepulchre of Christ ; the corporal is the linen cloth enwrapping His body. The veil of the paten is the kerchief round His head. The larger veil or Aer, which covers both paten and chalice, is the stone with which S. Joseph closed His sepulchre. The Great Entrance is the Way of the Cross; the laying of paten and chalice on the altar is the burial. The consecration corresponds to the resurrection ; and this symbolism is worked out fully through the Anaphora. In later days there was a still further development of this symbolism.

But we must turn from the symbolism and go on to describe the chief ceremonial features of the Byzantine liturgy as now performed.

The two great ceremonial occasions of the early part of the service are the two Entrances. The doors in the *Ikonostasis* or screen, which have been shut since the public service was begun with three *Ekteniae*, or groups of suffrages, followed by three prayers and antiphons, are opened; and the deacon comes out, bearing the Gospel-book, accompanied by the priest, and preceded by lights. They come through the northern of the three doors in the *Ikonostasis*, and enter by the central Royal Door. This is the Little Entrance.

The lessons follow; and after the Gospel the doors are once more closed. They are not opened again until the next *Ektenia*, the Dismissal of Catechumens, and the two Prayers of the Faithful have been said. Then, while the Cherubic Hymn is sung, the sanctuary, icons, and people are censed by the priest or deacon. Next the priest places the paten on the head of the deacon, who holds the censer in his right hand. He himself follows with the chalice, while other priests, if there are such present, carry cross, lance, and other instruments of the Passion. They go out by the north door preceded by lights, and enter the sanctuary by the Royal Door. Thereupon the priest places the paten and chalice on the altar and censes them. This is the Great Entrance.

The doors are then shut and the curtain is then drawn over the Royal Door. According to modern usage the Door remains closed till the communion of the people; and so all the great ceremonial of the consecration, like the ceremonies of the two earlier times of closure, remains unseen to the congregation.

But there are here two degrees of closure. When the doors are shut after the Great Entrance, the curtain that hangs over the Royal Door is drawn, thus doubly blocking the view. This curtain is withdrawn at the beginning of the Creed, and so remains till the Elevation after consecration. Then it is drawn again; and the view is once more doubly closed, until the Door is opened at the communion of the people.

From this point to the end of the rite there extends a third period of ceremonial action visible to the people. The priest with the deacon comes through the Door to communicate the people. They come up in turn one after another with prostrations. Each one stands with hands folded over his breast to receive in both kinds together from the chalice by means of a spoon: he kisses the chalice and retires.

The priest takes back the chalice, and sets it on the

altar. The paten is given by him to the deacon, who carries it out into the *Prothesis*, or side-chapel near the altar in which the Gifts were originally prepared. The priest meanwhile takes up the chalice again, and goes with it to bless the people at the Royal Door: as he returns to the *Prothesis* he is met and censed by the deacon. After setting down the chalice there, he goes to the altar and folds up the corporal, whilst the deacon, standing before the Royal Door, says the last *Ektenia*. After this the priest lays the Gospel-book on the corporal, goes out of the sanctuary, and, standing behind the *Ambo*, reads the dismissal prayer which terminates the Liturgy. It is at this point in Russian churches that a sermon (if any) is preached. Finally the priest goes to the altar, takes from it the cross and holding it gives the final dismissal from the *Ambo*.

This brief description gives an idea of the rite as seen by the congregation. It remains to describe the very important part taken by the singers.

The choir is conspicuous throughout, as a mere mention of its duties will show. It will be best to classify them rather than to set them out in the order of the service.

(1) The choir is responsible for responding to the suffrages in the *Ekteniae*, or litanies, which the deacon conducts outside the sanctuary with the people, while the priest says the prayers within. Such suffrages occur at several places in the service—(*a*) at the opening, (*b*) after the Gospel, (*c*) after the Cherubic Hymn, (*d*) after the Consecration Prayer, (*e*) after the communion of the people.

(2) The choir also leads responses at other times. Some of these are familiar from Western use, *e.g.* at the Gospel, and at the beginning of the Anaphora or Consecration Prayer. Others are less familiar—at the Kiss of Peace, after the Creed, at the Elevation, after the Lord's Prayer, and so on. Some of these responses develop into chants of considerable size, especially at the Preface, after the

Sanctus, after the Lord's Prayer, and at the Invitation to communicate.

(3) As in the West, the Creed, *Sanctus*, and Lord's Prayer are, or may be, sung; and the first and third of these are points at which priest, deacon, and choir coalesce into one act.

(4) Two great hymns of the Eastern Church are almost of equal importance with the above-mentioned, viz. the *Trisagion*, sung before the lessons, and the Cherubic Hymn sung at the Great Entrance of the Holy Gifts.

Apart from a few special occasions these texts do not vary from time to time. But there are further several choral items to be considered, which are changed more often.

(1) After the opening litany there follow three Antiphons, originally whole psalms; they are sung by the choir, while the priest says corresponding prayers. These are to a certain extent varied: the third at any ordinary Sunday service is always the Beatitudes. This section of the service is not an early part of the Liturgy, but an addition modelled on a choir-office.

(2) At the Little Entrance of the Gospel-book which follows there is sung an Invitatory, usually the same but admitting a few variants: this is followed by *Troparia* proper to the day.

(3) The Graduals preceding the Epistle, and the Alleluias following it, are set according to the eight tones, and sung by the choir.

(4) Again at the later part of the service there are variables. At the mention of the Blessed Virgin in the Intercession a hymn in her honour is sung, chosen from a group of such hymns, suited to various occasions.

(5) At the communion of the clergy there is an anthem sung, which is proper to the occasion.

(6) Further, in the last part of the service several chants, provided for use before, during, and after the communion of the people, as well as the final dismissal given by the priest, vary on a few occasions.

Some of these singings, it will be noted, accompany an action which is taking place, while others are simultaneous with a prayer said by the priest.

This brief and analytical description gives little idea of the solemnity and majesty of the service, especially as performed in the Russian Church. It is dominated by the conception of the Eucharist as the Divine Mysteries. The great acts are performed within the veil, unseen, and to a large extent in silence, except in so far as the deacon, standing at the head of the people, leads them in prayer meanwhile. There is no chancel : the choir is heard rather than seen ; it belongs to the congregation. The eyes of the congregation are riveted by the processions, by the movements in and out of the screen, and by the mysteries performed within. The people as they worship, and communicate, are lifted up from earth to the heavenly places far more irresistibly than in any other rite.

CHAPTER VI

STAGES IN THE GROWTH OF RELIGIOUS CEREMONIAL

III. Mediaeval West.

NO clear survey of the ceremonial of the Western Church at the Eucharist, analogous to that which has been given for the Eastern Church in the fourth century, is possible until the seventh century. The three preceding centuries were times of great change, but only scattered fragments of evidence can be gathered here and there, insufficient to piece together into a picture, and somewhat tantalizing in their sparseness. The growing divergence of rite between Rome and the rest of Western Christendom revealed itself sharply, as has been noted, at the beginning of the fifth century in Innocent's letter to Decentius. The divergence probably had its origin in the fact that the city of Rome retained a Greek liturgy of the Oriental type, while Latin Christendom as a whole was developing a Latin type of liturgy more brief and more variable than the Eastern type. When Rome adopted Latin as its liturgical language, probably in the first half of the fourth century, it was disinclined to adopt the short and constantly varying formulas of the non-Roman liturgy. It formed for itself a single long fixed prayer by the combination of several short variable prayers of the type prevailing all around it ; and thus made a *Canon* or unchanging prayer, a sort of compromise between the ways of the East and those of the West.[1]

The natural effect of this change was to bring those parts of Italy which were in closest touch with Rome into line with Rome itself ; in other words, the Roman liturgy, and with it no doubt the Roman ceremonial, spread apace in the neighbouring districts. So it is that in 416 it is equally a source of surprise to Pope Innocent on the one side to find that at Eugubium (Gubbio), only some one hundred and twenty miles away, the Roman customs are not being followed, and on the other side to Bishop Decentius of that see to find that his divergences are regarded as being at all unusual. The correspondence,[2] be it noted, arises out of a wish on behalf of the provincial Church to conform to the ways of the Roman Church. It marks no doubt a general tendency that was growing and affecting the greater part of the peninsula. Among the points in question are the position of the kiss of peace and the intercession ; and of special interest is one answer of the pope, which does not insist upon uniformity. It was the custom in Rome, in order to secure a sort of unity among the various celebrations of the Eucharist on any given Sunday, for the pope to send round subdeacons or acolytes from his own Mass to take a part of the consecrated host called the *fermentum* or leaven to the priests preparing to celebrate at the district churches. This was their link with the central Eucharist. Innocent, however, does not advise that this custom should be adopted in a diocese with scattered parishes.[3]

Thenceforward the history of the liturgy in the West is the history of the gradual approximation of the two rites, the Roman ousting the non-Roman, but adopting many of its features in the process. This is not the place to trace out that evolution ; it belongs to the history of ritual rather than of ceremonial. Too little is known of the non-Roman rites, and less still of their ceremonies; but it was necessary to explain the matter so far, since the history of the ceremonial is only intelligible when at least the broad facts of the liturgical evolution are understood.

Other papal writings of a later date give evidence of the progress of this evolution, or of other ceremonial prescriptions. Pope Gelasius (492–496) had to deal [4] in regard to such matters with the bishops of Lucania in the south of Italy, and the papal influence spread southward through the peninsula. Northward it was less active because of the independence maintained by the great cities of Aquileia and Milan. In the next century the troubles that befell Africa ended the part which that flourishing province had taken in the evolution; but Spain and Gaul were brought more closely into it, and they, with eagerness or with reluctance, began to experience the influence of the Roman ritual and ceremonial. From the former country in 538 came a series of questions to Pope Vigilius as to the customs of his Church. The writer of the letter, Profuturus, Bishop of Braga, was in return provided with the text of the Roman Canon (with the Easter variants as a specimen of the changing parts of the rite) and with information as to the Consecration of churches, Baptismal Services, etc.[5] These were subsequently adopted by the province of which Profuturus was metropolitan; and thus we have another instance of the propagation of the Roman customs.

The incident also affords an example of the action taken by councils in this respect; for the adoption of these rites by the province was decided on at the Council of Braga (569). Further instances of the intervention of synods and councils in ceremonial matters become now more common, and especially the acts of the councils of the fifth and sixth centuries in Gaul and Spain reveal the growing influence of the Roman example.[6]

Liturgical books representing the papal rites of the fifth and sixth centuries are non-existent, and we have little or no information as to the ceremonies; on the other hand, the *Liber Pontificalis* in recording the biographies of the succeeding pontiffs continually gives small hints and pieces of evidence. A small record of their gifts of ornaments, or their church building and decoration, again and again throws welcome light into the dark places, and shows up some detail in the arrangement of the churches or the services.[7]

These scattered items lead up to a more complete survey of the papal ceremonial, which becomes possible with the appearance on the scene of the First *Ordo Romanus*. Gregory the Great had done much to organize and bring into system the liturgical and ceremonial customs of the papal court, besides making the larger liturgical changes, for which his name is renowned, in the Sacramentary and the music-books of the Roman Church. The *schola* or choir of the pope was reorganized by him, the sequence of churches in which the papal mass was celebrated on the great Sundays and festivals was revised, the domestic officers of the palace were increased, and also probably reorganized : in fact, it seems probable that within this whole sphere the Gregorian reforms introduced a new and lasting order where hitherto it had been lacking.[8]

The document known as the First *Ordo Romanus*[9] is more or less directly the outcome of these reforms, and the bulk of its contents goes back to the seventh century. The order of proceedings at the Solemn Mass there prescribed is so unlike what is now customary in the West that it seems desirable to give a full description of it and of the circumstances in which it took place.

The pope's service is held on solemn days at different churches in a rota ; in some cases it is preceded by a procession from another church. The place of the service or ' station ' is indicated in the old service-books and also the place of meeting for the procession. The selection depends upon the dignity of the feast and church, or else upon the connexion of the church with the festival, as dedicated to the same saint, and so forth.[10]

First, as regards the building, the basilica[11] where the liturgy is to be celebrated is a large oblong building divided into three or five long parallel sections by rows of columns, sometimes hung with curtains, forming a nave with two or four aisles. The basilica which the *Ordo* has in contemplation is S. Mary Major at Rome, where was held the chief mass of Eastertide, which is the one described.[12] At the east end (so-called)* is a semi-circular apse, and at the end of it the throne. In front of this, on the chord of the apse, is the altar ; or, if there is a transept between the apse and the nave (as is the case, for example, at S. Mary Major, but not at S. Lawrence), the altar is very likely in the transept or (as at S. Mary Major) under the triumphal arch at the centre of the western edge of the transept. Its position is determined by the *confessio* or place where the relics rest ; for the altar is set by preference over the actual grave or body of a saint, or over other relics set there, as it were, in a tomb. The grave is perhaps on the level of the nave ; and in that case the altar is raised well above that level, and there is very likely a grating underneath or on the western side of it communicating with the grave. In other cases the grave is below the level ; there is then less of grating to be seen from the nave, and perhaps there is a shaft from the grave ascending towards the church, and descending steps down towards the level of the grave. But in any case the level on which the altar stands is higher than the level of the nave. Steps go up to the higher level (called *bema* or *tribunal*) on the right and left sides of the altar, for the altar itself stands normally, having its western side flush with the *confessio* ; and there is no possibility of standing on the west side of it between the people and the altar.

The altar is a stone table ; that is, a stone *mensa* resting on a stone support or stone columns. Surmounting it is the *ciborium*, a solid canopy resting on four pillars at the four corners of the altar, richly decorated, and serving to focus all eyes on the altar itself. No ornaments stand out on it, for the candles used during the service are portable lights, and the custom has not yet come in of placing the head of a processional cross in a base on the altar when the procession has arrived there ; but a pyx in the shape of a dove hangs within

* For the purposes of this description it is assumed that the church is orientated.

the canopy and holds the reserved Sacrament, and there are probably hanging lamps as well. On the western side of the baldachin-canopy, and possibly also at the north and south ends of the altar, curtains are hung on rods fixed to the pillars; these are ready to be drawn at the most solemn parts of the liturgy so as to veil them from the gaze of the congregation.[13] In some churches there is also a *pergula* or screen in front of the altar, of open work with columns.

Westward of the altar, and on the level below the steps, is the enclosure now called the presbytery; the eastern part of the central nave is enclosed by low screens (*cancelli*) to form this enclosure. Here are the seats of the bishops on the north side, and the priests on the south side; for they have ceased to sit, as they formerly did, on the semicircular bench on either side of the pope's throne in the apse, perhaps because the developed ceremonial requires the whole space, and especially in churches like S. Peter's, where the altar stands on the chord of the apse itself.[14]

Within the enclosure is the platform or *tabula* where the choir assemble to sing,[15] and eastward of this, on the north side of the enclosure at least, and possibly on each side, there is an *ambo* or pulpit from which the lessons may be sung and the Gradual-psalm and other musical interludes chanted.

The easternmost part of the nave, or the transept, short of the presbytery is known as the *senatorium*, and is reserved for the high lay officials. In the rest of the nave and aisles the people sit, no doubt according to their degree, though the definiteness of distinction in position between faithful, penitents, catechumens, and heathen has almost if not entirely disappeared, and the curtains, which at one time divided the blocks in the different bays, have probably ceased to be drawn or have even disappeared. The sexes are divided, as has been the case from the first; the men are on the left and the women on the right.[16]

At the west end of the building is the vestry, called either *secretarium* or *sacrarium*, placed so that it is easily entered from the *atrium* or forecourt.[17]

Such is a general description of the type of the large Roman basilicas in which the solemn masses take place. As we turn now to consider those who take part in them, the first point for us to note is that the service demands the co-operation of a very large body of people. The clergy and lay officials who take part at any given church are partly those belonging to that church or district, and partly those who belong to the palace or to the general organization of the Roman Church. With the pope and next to him are the seven bishops of the suburban dioceses; those, that is, of the immediate neighbourhood. Apart from these dioceses the city itself is divided into seven ecclesiastical districts; each district has its own deacon, its subdeacon, and a body of six (or seven) acolytes, and is responsible in turn for the service. The deacon and subdeacon of each district is in attendance on the pope; and the acolytes belonging to the particular district which is responsible for the particular service act as taperers. On Easter day it is the district clergy of the third district whose turn it is to be in charge. The *schola cantorum* or choir belongs to no district, but is attached to the pope, and sings at all the solemn services. It consists of a *prior* or *primus* with three other officers under him, men singers (*paraphonistae*), some of whom at any rate are subdeacons, and the boys (*infantes*) of the choir school.

The lay officials partly belong to the palace and partly to the various districts. Among the former are the seneschal (*vice-dominus*) and majordomos under him, the treasurer (*sacellarius*), almoner (*subpulmentarius*), and remembrancer (*nomenclator*), besides chamberlains lay and clerical, grooms, etc. Each district has its two district councillors (*defensores*), who are grouped in a college under a president (*primicerius*), just as the notaries are under two officials, the *primicerius* and *secundicerius*.

These lay functionaries have also their part in the proceedings; especially they are prominent in the procession, at the offertory, and during the communion.[18]

The priests have a less prominent part than the other grades of clergy. The two attached to the church where the service is held are expected to be present to welcome the pope, and they with others who may be there help at the offertory, stand by with bowed heads at the consecration, and help, if necessary, in the breaking and distribution of the hosts at communion.

It is the acolytes who are there in largest numbers. Besides the seven of the district who carry the seven tapers, others are needed to carry the chrism (the *stationarius* and his fellow) in the procession, the lavatory bowl, the linen bags for the consecrated loaves, the chalice, and other bowls, to hold the paten and the linen receptacles for the offertory loaves or ' obleys,' and so on, while some apparently still keep to the traditional duty of minding the gates. In all, probably a score at least are in attendance. The seven deacons and the seven subdeacons are told off for special duties, a deacon to sing the Gospel and carry the Gospel-book, a subdeacon to sing the Epistle and carry the Epistle-book. Another subdeacon has a special part in the offertory (*oblationarius*), while a third is ' in waiting ' (*sequens*), and has also various special duties. Among the seven deacons, the archdeacon has a special pre-eminence and special duties.

As the hour for the service draws near the people assemble in the nave, and the clergy in the presbytery, with the exception of those whose duty it is to accompany the pope in his procession to the church. The porters bring some of the ornaments from the Lateran, and, with the almoner and cross-bearers, sit with the clergy in the presbytery. Presently the successive divisions of the cavalcade begin to appear—the seven acolytes of the district, who will act as taperers, others carrying the napkins, linen bags, ornaments, etc. The deacons, subdeacons, and district officials follow on horseback, immediately in front of the pope, while the *stationarius* acolyte, carrying the flask of holy chrism wrapped in a napkin, walks between them and the pope's horse. Grooms walk on either side, and immediately behind the pope walks the acolyte with the lavatory bowl. Then come the great officers of the household on horseback, bringing up the rear.

As the sound is heard of the approach of the pope to the church, a stir is observable in the presbytery, and a party goes out to welcome him. It consists of the clergy attached to the church, the majordomos of the Roman Church, with the acolytes and district councillors belonging to the district which is responsible for the services of the day. The clergy of the church and the sacristan carry incense to signify their respect, and bowing receive the pope's blessing. Escorted by them and supported by two deacons, he goes to the vestry, and there the final preparations for the service are made.

Presently one of the deacons-in-waiting is seen advancing up the nave, followed by an acolyte bearing the Gospel-book, and at once all stand. Coming into the presbytery in front of the altar he turns and takes the book from the acolyte, and, carrying it in his chasuble or 'planet,' to use the old Roman name, he takes it up to the altar and sets it thereupon. Next there comes out from the vestry one of the district subdeacons, who have been helping the pope to vest,[19] and after ascertaining from the precentor who are to chant the Gradual, he goes back and reports their names to the pope, together with the names of the epistoller and the gospeller. The precentor has followed him into the vestry, but he shortly returns, and after telling the taperers to light their candles and the subdeacons-in-waiting to kindle the incense, he passes up the church to the presbytery to warn the choir that all is ready. They thereupon form in a double line of men and boys on either side in front of the altar, and begin to chant the Introit.

Now follows the solemn entry of the pope. Supported

by two of the deacons, preceded by the incense and seven tapers (*Apoc.* i. 12, 13), and escorted by the rest of his attendants, he advances up the church. The deacons and he alike are in full vestments with planets over all ; but over his planet the pope wears his white pall. The deacons on entering the presbytery take off their planets, probably in order to have their arms free ; and these are given by a subdeacon to the acolytes in attendance on the deacons. As the pope himself enters the presbytery, a halt is made, and two acolytes bring him a box containing the Holy Sacrament. This was reserved from the previous Eucharist, and is now to be conjoined with the present consecration so as to emphasize the continuity of the consecrations. The pope or one of the deacons satisfies himself that the quantity is suitable, and bows in reverence to the Holy Sacrament. They then pass on through the double line of taperers and the rows of the choir to the top part of the presbytery below the altar, and there make their reverence. The first kiss of peace is now given by the pope to the senior bishop on his left and the senior priest on his right, as well as to all the deacons ; and his private prayers are said. The choir at his back begins the *Gloria Patri* of the Introit-psalm, and the deacons go up in pairs, the archdeacon last, to kiss the horn of the altar. They then return, and as the repeated verse of the Introit-psalm is sung, they conduct the pope to his throne. He passes up the steps on the right of the altar, kisses the Gospel-book, and so comes to his seat at the end of the apse, and stands before it, facing eastward. Behind him stand the seven deacons in two lines. The seven subdeacons meanwhile have made their reverence to the altar all together, and are now standing in two groups below the altar. Westward again of them are the seven taperers similarly grouped, and behind them in the presbytery the choir stands singing the *Kyries* ; below is the double rank of bishops on the left and priests on the right. This is the first tableau of the service.

The number of *Kyries* sung still depends upon the direction of the pope. When they are over, he turns to the people to intone the *Gloria in excelsis*, and then turns back again eastward. The Collect follows and is preceded by the Salutation, with a similar turn and return. For the Epistle and the chants following it the pope is seated facing the people; the bishops and priests likewise sit, the deacons stand near the pope, the subdeacons ascend the steps and stand on either side of the altar; while the seven taperers, perhaps to save space in the gangway, adopt a different formation, and stand in a single line east and west. All who are below the dignity of the priesthood stand throughout.

The subdeacon sings the Epistle from the epistle ambo (or if there is but one ambo, from the lower part of it), for the old first lesson from the Old Testament has already disappeared from most Masses; and the chant which once followed it, separating it from the Epistle, now follows the Epistle. The two chants—the Gradual and the *Alleluia* (or Tract)—are sung from the same place by the appointed soloists, while the choir, standing below the ambo, sings the choral parts.

Far more elaborate is the ceremonial that surrounds the reading of the Gospel. A deacon comes out from the group of deacons, kisses the pope's feet and receives his blessing. Coming from the throne to the altar, he kisses the Gospel-book and takes it from the altar; he then goes his way down to the gospel ambo, carrying the book on his right shoulder, preceded by two sub-deacons with incense and two acolytes with tapers. As he passes down the presbytery he receives a blessing first from the bishops on his right and then from the priests on his left. A halt is made while the subdeacon who is not carrying a censer helps the deacon to find the place in the book. They then pass between the taperers into the ambo; the subdeacons merely walk straight through it, leaving the deacon there, while they themselves turn back to wait for him at the steps of the ambo.

At the end of the Gospel the pope greets the deacon with 'Peace be to thee'; and, since the custom of singing the Creed has not yet been adopted at Rome, he goes on at once, unless he here preaches a sermon, to salute the people, and adds 'Let us pray.' No prayers, however, follow, for the intercessions which formerly were universally said at this point have disappeared out of the Roman liturgy. Meanwhile a subdeacon-in-waiting, preceded by the incense, is going round carrying the Gospel-book before him in his planet, so that all present may kiss it before it is returned to its case and put away.

As the deacon returns from the ambo, a subdeacon awaits him at the altar with the chalice and a corporal; the taperers set down their tapers before the altar; the deacon takes the corporal, and with the help of another deacon spreads it on the altar. He then goes up to the pope's throne, while the subdeacon follows with the chalice. The lay officials, headed by the chief notary and the chief councillor, also come up to the throne, and the two chiefs support the pope as he comes down to receive the oblations.

The Offertory begins at the *senatorium*, where the pope, attended by the archdeacon and other clergy, receives the obleys and wine offered by the nobles, gathering them respectively in a napkin and in large bowls. The offerings of the men and of the women of the congregation are received at the steps, on their respective sides of the church. As the pope passes from one side to the other, he receives the offerings of the chief officials at the altar in front of the confession, where also the clergy make their offerings, and finally those of the noble women. Bishops and priests help in the collection when the numbers are large. Meanwhile the Offertory-anthem with its verses is being sung. The lay officials escort the pope to his throne and retire to their places; the pope washes his hands there. The archdeacon does the same at the altar, and then the subdeacons hand up to him the offerings of the people to be set on the altar. He prepares the chalice from the wine offered by the pope, the deacons, and the lay officials, pouring in water in the form of a cross from a cruet offered by the choir, and brought up by the precentor.[20]

The pope now comes down to the altar from his throne, accompanied by the deacons. He receives in person the obleys of the clergy, and his own obley is handed to him by the deacon. When he has set this down, the archdeacon sets down on its right side the chalice, holding it by its handles, wrapped in a linen veil, which he then removes and places at the horn of the altar. At last the offertory is over; the sign can be given to the choir to cease singing, and the 'Secret' prayer can be said over the oblations.

Now begins the central action of the service; but it is probably at this point that the curtains are drawn, so that the people are unable to see what takes place at the altar. The greater part of the clergy are grouped on the far side of it; the pope stands in the middle, facing westwards, with the bishops in a line behind him, and the deacons similarly to right and left, the archdeacon being on the right. The acolytes stand by in attendance on their deacons. Westward of the altar stand the seven district subdeacons in a line facing the pope. The priests are still further west, in the presbytery, except on special days, when they join with the pope and concelebrate.[21] All stand with heads bowed, except when the subdeacons lift their heads to respond, *e.g.* at the Salutation and *Sursum corda*. After the sounds of the *Sanctus* have died away, the pope can be faintly heard in the church continuing the Canon, or great central prayer of the service.[22]

During the Canon an acolyte brings in the paten, wrapped in a cloth. It is handled with much reverence, and at the end of the great prayer it passes from him in quick succession into the hands of a subdeacon-in-waiting, a district subdeacon, and the archdeacon, who gives it finally to the second deacon, for him to receive on it the obleys which by then the pope has just consecrated. Meanwhile the archdeacon has been caring for the chalice, which is his special charge, and lifting it up (with the veil as before) to the pope at the closing doxology of the Canon for him to touch it on one side with the obleys. Both host and chalice are then raised from the altar and offered to God and replaced. Then as the newly consecrated obleys and chalice stand side by side on the altar, the pope takes the Sacrament reserved from the previous Eucharist, and with three crossings places it in the chalice. The consecration is completed, and the kiss of peace follows.

Next comes the Fraction, part of which is symbolical and part practical. The former part is performed by the pope, who breaks an obley and places one portion on the altar, to remain there throughout, while the rest is set (as already stated) on the paten. This done, the pope returns back to his throne ; for it is there that he will communicate, and make the commixture. Simultaneously the lay officials come up from the presbytery to the altar, and stand there in their order, right and left. A little later, immediately before the pope's communion, a strange custom is observed to take place. The pope's remembrancer and treasurer, with the seneschal's notary, make their way up to the throne, and ascertain whom the pope and seneschal wish to invite to dinner. They then go off at once to deliver the invitations.

The practical fraction of the hosts for the purpose of communion now goes forward. The greater part of the obleys that were set upon the altar are distributed by the archdeacon to the subdeacons-in-waiting and acolytes, who stand on either side of the altar, the acolytes presenting their linen bags and the subdeacons helping to hold them open to receive the loaves. The acolytes then carry them on to the bishops in the apse, and down to the priests in the presbytery, that they may break them ready for communion.

The portion that was set upon the paten is differently treated. The second deacon who was holding it gives it to the district-subdeacons, who carry it to the throne, while he follows with the rest of the deacons. Here the archdeacon joins them, and, at a sign from the pope, the deacons all join in the fraction ; at the archdeacon's bidding the *Agnus Dei* is sung meanwhile. While the junior deacon takes the paten to communicate the pope, the archdeacon returns to the right side of the altar to take the chalice from the district-subdeacon to whom he entrusted it before he began to distribute the loaves. On his return with it to the throne the pope makes the Commixture simultaneously with his own communion, placing in the chalice part of the same loaf from which he communicates himself. He then is communicated from the chalice by the archdeacon.

After this some of the contents of the chalice are poured into the great bowls to consecrate the wine in them, and the rest of the communicants receive from them, except the bishops, priests, and deacons. These receive their portion of the loaf or obley from the pope at his throne, but they go carrying it to the altar, and, resting each his hand upon it, communicate there ; they then receive the chalice from the senior bishop, standing at the end of the altar.

The Communion of the laity now begins. The pope is seen descending into the *senatorium* supported by the chief notary and the chief councillor. He communicates only the principal persons, and the archdeacon follows communicating them from the large bowls by means of a metal tube or reed. After this is done, the pope returns. The rest of the people are communicated by the bishops and priests, except the choir and junior clergy who receive after the pope's return. Meanwhile, the Communion-psalm with its antiphon is being sung by the choir. On returning to the tribune the pope and the archdeacon communicate there the councillors, the lay officials, and the lesser clergy. On solemn days the choir also has the privilege of communicating there rather than in the presbytery.

The Communion-psalm ends, as did its counterpart the Introit-psalm, when the pope gives the sign, and a district subdeacon hands it on to the head of the choir by crossing himself on the forehead. The singing is thus timed to end when the communion is over.

The close of the service is very brief. The pope comes from his seat to the altar, and there says the concluding Collect. He faces east, and does not now turn to the people for the Salutation, no doubt because the curtains are still drawn. A deacon at the pope's bidding goes and sings to the people the *Ite missa est*, and the service is finished. The pope returns to the vestry much as he came, preceded by the seven tapers and the incense. The congregation and officers receive his blessing as he passes into the vestry.

CHAPTER VII

STAGES IN THE GROWTH OF RELIGIOUS CEREMONIAL

IV. The Later Middle Ages.

THE effect of the papal ceremonial on the Western Church was very great. In the Carolvingian era not only the Roman rite, but the ceremonial with it, spread throughout the empire. When Amalarius [1] wrote his expositions of the new service for the benefit of the Franks, and from the midst of the literary school of Charlemagne's day, of which Alcuin was the chief organizer, he included among his treatises one explanatory of the ceremonial of the episcopal Mass; and this is altogether based upon a somewhat later recension of the same *Ordo Romanus* which was described in the last chapter. The full elaboration of the papal service was, naturally enough, not transplanted in its entirety over the Alps. In the service as set forth by Amalarius the clergy present are fewer, the offertory is far simpler, and the communion likewise. All this is the result of the smaller scale on which everything is done. But *mutatis mutandis* the ceremonial is the same. In some respects, however, there are signs of greater elaboration, if not in the ceremonial itself, at any rate in the record of it. And far fuller directions are given for the actions of the celebrant during the Canon, which were almost undescribed in the early form of the *Ordo*.

Another treatise of Amalarius deals more generally, and at far greater length, with the Liturgy, and from this it is clear that, while the ceremonial has been in the main transplanted, there have been changes. We begin, therefore, from this point to trace out some of the principal changes in the ceremonial. First comes to our notice a group of important and far-reaching changes which came about through the alteration in the position of the celebrant relatively to the people. There are four points in the service affected; the chief is the consecration. In the early Roman *Ordo*, as has been shown, the pope faced towards the people—*i.e.*, in an orientated church, westward—when he was standing at the altar to consecrate. All the early part of the service he said at the throne, turning eastward for the *Gloria in excelsis* and Collect, but westward only to salute the people. It was only from the offertory onward that he was at the altar, and then facing westwards. Hence no direction was required in the *Ordo* to tell him to turn to salute the people at the Salutation and *Sursum corda*. For, apart from the question as to whether or not there was a curtain between him and the people, rendering his attitude towards them immaterial, he was already facing them. Consequently no direction to turn at this point was placed in the *Ordo*.

Supposing, however, the position of the celebrant is changed, and he stands between the people and the altar, this want in the *Ordo* of any direction to turn will seem anomalous, and will probably evoke some explanation or comment. Such comment is actually found in Amalarius;[2] and it is clear therefore that he contemplated that the celebrant would be standing eastward at the altar, not westward. The existence, therefore, of the eastward position for the Canon as well as the westward, is proved as early as the time of Amalarius. Moreover he makes no allusion to any change having taken place, though he was familiar with the *Ordo* in some form, and had had the opportunity of seeing with his own eyes what was done in Rome; so it seems probable that the divergence of use between Rome and Gaul in this respect caused him no surprise. Probably, therefore, the westward position was a local Roman peculiarity which had not been adopted as a rule elsewhere, even in places where the Roman *Ordo* was the ruling authority.3

There are many other considerations which lead to the same conclusion. The westward position of the celebrant at Rome was intimately bound up with the existence on the western side of the altar of a 'confession,' or altar tomb, which in many cases precluded the possibility of standing on that side facing eastward.4 In Rome this connexion between the altar and the relics was the normal thing; but elsewhere martyrs were fewer, and such a connexion was unusual. Altars with confessions might be found in churches whose tradition reached back behind the peace of the Church, but not equally elsewhere. In Gaul or the later Frankish empire the altars had as a rule no confessions. The mediaeval custom of putting relics in the altar when it was consecrated, which was a natural survival in Rome and the older Churches, was unknown in the newer Churches till it was introduced from Rome as a result of the diffusion of the *Ordines Romani* in the ninth and tenth centuries.

A deeper reason still for this position of the celebrant at Rome may perhaps be found in examining the question of orientation. In discussing this, the terms east and west must be used in their strict sense according to the points of the compass, and not, as hitherto, in their ritual and conventional sense. The principal churches in Rome were turned not towards the east, but, as it happened, towards the west. The primitive instinct and the early rule in favour of orientation were not observed, probably merely because circumstances made it inconvenient or impossible. This being the case, it was necessary in them if the celebrant was to face towards the east that he should also look over the altar towards the people; and this is another reason that may account for the Roman custom. It clearly was not a wish to face the people, if the curtains veiled the altar and him from them, and them from him. But it is possible that the Roman position of the celebrant went back to a time when there was no such obstacle, and he could see them and be seen by them.

It may therefore be concluded that the westward position only prevailed in the great basilicas of the martyrs at Rome, and in some few other places where similar circumstances dictated it ; but that throughout the daughter Churches in general the eastward position was customary, and the borrowed Roman ceremonial was altered in that respect as early as the beginning of the ninth century.5

Closely connected with this is the question of the position of the celebrant at three other parts of the service. The pope, according to the *Ordo*, remains at his throne at the end of the apse till the close of the offertory, only leaving it in order to receive the first batch of the oblations that are offered ; he returns there to communicate ; he then descends to the altar for the closing Collect, but he says it on the easterly side of the altar, facing eastward and without turning to the people for the Salutation. As regards the first of these positions, it is to be noted that the same apsidal arrangement of the church which was usual at Rome was adopted elsewhere, and the bishop continued to follow the directions of the *Ordo* as to his position at the beginning of the service long after he had altered it for the Canon. The date at which the liturgical use of the east-end throne was given up cannot very clearly be established. It was, however, not later than the twelfth century, at any rate in England, for with the coming in of ' Early English ' (Gothic) architecture in place of Norman (Romanesque), the apsidal ending was given up, and a square end to the sanctuary was adopted in its place, which made no provision for the existence any longer of an easterly episcopal throne.* On the Continent the architectural change was less marked, for the apsidal ending went on after the Gothic style had superseded the Romanesque. But there is no reason to suppose that abroad the change in position

---

* The east-end throne survives still at Norwich Cathedral.

of the throne was deferred. It had probably been already made when the new style appeared—in fact earlier abroad than in England.

However, even when the site of the throne was altered, the liturgical position of the bishop did not at once follow suit. He went as before for the beginning of the service to his throne, even when it was moved, *e.g.*, to the north side of the altar. This custom commonly survived in the case of bishops, and in some places at any rate in France it was customary for priests also, to go for the opening part of the service not to the altar, but to their seat.[6] No sign of this survival has been noticed in the distinctively English ceremonial of the Middle Ages, in the case of either bishops or priests; but in this as in other respects the episcopal service generally preserved the old custom after it had been given up at the ordinary service.

A further alteration was effected as to the place where the celebrant communicated. This change no doubt followed upon the other. As long as the throne stood close at hand as a centre of attraction to command the presence of the bishop-celebrant, it was natural for him to move away there for his communion; but as this reason for a change of position ceased to be operative by the removal of the throne to a distance, it was more natural for him to stay at the altar to communicate, as, probably, priest-celebrants habitually did.

The alteration in position at the end of the service came sooner than the alteration in the position at the beginning. In fact, the same change which made the bishop say the Canon eastwards on the west side of the altar, *a fortiori* led him to say the Postcommunion there; for, unlike the Canon, the Postcommunion had always been said eastwards, and the change of custom was therefore less in this case than in that. Accordingly Amalarius again bears witness, and shows that the change has already been made, so far as his form of the *Ordo* is concerned. He records that the celebrant turns westward to bless and salute the people, and then eastward for the Postcommunion. This implies that he is standing between the people and the altar; and, contrary to the provisions of the early Roman form of the *Ordo*, he turns for the Salutation.[7]

This raises the question of another great transformation which was taking place. It has been already suggested that anciently the solemn part of the service was hidden from the people by drawn curtains; and, moreover, this circumstance was suggested above as the reason why the pope did not turn to the people for the Salutation before the post-communion. When, therefore, Amalarius speaks of the celebrant as turning at this point, the inference is suggested that he did not contemplate that there would be drawn curtains veiling him then from the congregation.[8] What, then, is the history of the change by which the action which had been hidden was subsequently done in the open? It seems natural to conjecture that this change went along with the change of the celebrant from the westward to the eastward position; but in point of fact the two cases are not parallel, since the veiling of the mysteries had become a general custom of the Christian Church, while there is no evidence to show that the westward position was anything but local and due to peculiar circumstances. The veiling came into use, and subsequently ceased to exist, apparently in the greater part of the West; and these changes were probably independent of any change of position in the celebrant. The history is very obscure, but it seems reasonable to suppose that the suppression of the western curtain was connected with a whole current of change in favour of laying open the mysteries to view, which was probably affected by the eucharistic controversies of the ninth and eleventh centuries, and reached its high-water mark, as will be seen later, in the institution of the Elevation.[9]

These are some of the earliest and most important modifications which the Roman papal ceremonial underwent as it spread through the West. The signs of its diffusion do not end with Amalarius and the ninth century, but they are found continuing, though in a decreasing degree, throughout the Middle Ages and down to the present time. While the effects were most marked in the Frankish empire, they were considerable also in England. The ceremonial of S. Gregory's missionaries was no doubt that of Rome, and the continuous tradition of conformity with Roman use is witnessed by such items of evidence as the Canon of Cloveshoo (747), which decreed that the liturgical services should 'be celebrated according to the written pattern received from the Roman Church.'[10] Whatever incorporation of distinctively Celtic customs there may have been, the system at this epoch was markedly that of Rome.

In the Frankish empire the blending of the local with the Roman was far more considerable. The Gallican ceremonies and rites had a firm hold; and it was only by incorporating a good many Gallican features that the Roman use made its way there. Thus it is probable that as England came increasingly under Frankish and Norman influences, it became less exclusively Roman in its use than formerly. It is mainly in the ninth and following centuries that there begins to be full and explicit evidence of the influence in England of the Roman *Ordines*; they are then the *Ordines* as modified by the Franks, and representing the mixed use. But earlier than this the purely Roman *Ordo* had probably come direct to England, if not with Augustine in the beginning of the seventh century, at any rate with Theodore and Benedict Biscop towards the end.[11] One of the few existing English MSS. of earlier date than the tenth century—the Pontifical of Egbert (Archbishop of York, 732–766)—may be taken as a proof of this. It follows the lines of the Roman *Ordines* and Service-books; and, moreover, in the case of the *Ordo* for the Consecration of churches, it is closely allied to the earlier and unmixed Roman form, while subsequent Pontificals of the tenth and eleventh centuries are allied to the more modified and later forms.[12]

There is no need to multiply further instances of the influence of Roman ceremonial in England and on the Continent ; nor is it desirable to attempt to give a close and detailed account of the changes which were introduced as years went on. It will be better simply to take a representative epoch of the late Middle Ages, and set the ceremonial of the mass at that stage alongside with the earlier picture which has been drawn already.

In the beginning of the thirteenth century a great project was carried out in the diocese of Salisbury which had far-reaching effects. The cathedral church of the diocese was transferred from the old town of Sarum, or Salisbury, to another site close by, where the new church then erected still stands, one of the least altered of all the old English cathedrals. In anticipation of this change, under the masterly guidance of the great Bishop Richard Poore, the opportunity was taken for the codifying and systematizing of the cathedral statutes and customs, and especially for the compiling of a complete directory of the services. This work survives in the *Consuetudinary*, and to that book we turn for a systematic description of a representative mass in the later Middle Ages.[13]

It will be well to be warned beforehand of certain marked changes that have already taken place. Some have been already alluded to, and their results will be now more manifest. The architecture brings one or two at once into prominence. The Romanesque basilica, with its apsidal end, has given way to a Gothic building which ends in a square sanctuary. The altar still stands away from the eastern wall, but the space eastward of it is no longer of any great ceremonial importance ; the whole action takes place on the west side. This is now open to view, and the curtains that once screened all four sides now only adorn the further three. Instead of the ' confession,' which rendered the altar inaccessible from the west, there are now two steps and a footpace ; the lower step belongs to the subdeacon, the higher to the deacon, and the footpace to the celebrant. A canopy or *umbraculum* over the altar, if it survives at all, is a mere survival. There are no longer lamps to be hung from it as of old, though candles stand on the altar and round about it ; but the hanging object over the altar is still a pyx containing the reserved Sacrament, which has a small canopy of its own and not belonging to the altar.

The whole quire is open, though in the conservative time of Lent a veil will be hung up to screen off the sanctuary ; the ambones have disappeared with the *cancelli* of the old type ; the quire is enclosed at the sides in the main by the choir stalls, while at the west end of it a solid stone loft called the *pulpitum* separates the quire from the nave. It has in a sense succeeded to the place of the ambones, for it is from there that the Epistle and Gospel, with the intervening chants, are to be sung on all great days, until the organs are set there, and, growing larger and larger, oust these ceremonies. A bay further west is the great rood.

As regards the ceremonial itself, in some respects it has been much curtailed.[14] The full magnificence of the papal retinue is of course wanting ; the ordinary *personnel* is a priest, with deacon and subdeacon attendant on him, and with the further co-operation of a small body of acolytes. For example, the taperers now number two only, and not seven as in the papal mass. But provision is made for some of the older magnificence when the bishop celebrates. He then has a number of deacons and subdeacons attendant on him, rising to the full number of seven on the great days, with three special acolytes. They do not now take up the old positions, but stand in a row on the step allotted to their order ; all, however, take part in the Gospel-procession ; and this gives to this section of the service a greater distinction than it had formerly.

Another reduction of elaborateness is due to the

shrinkage of the ceremony of the offertory. The custom of bringing up the offerings has long disappeared almost entirely, and only some small relics of it survive. This change has affected other parts of the service too ; for, in consequence, the elements are now prepared at an earlier point, after the Epistle ; and at the offertory it only remains for the priest to make an oblation of the already prepared chalice and paten. The ceremony of the *Sancta*, the mingling of the reserved Sacrament with the newly consecrated chalice, has now gone, and with it the symbolical link between one Eucharist and the next. A similar fate has also very naturally overtaken the *fermentum* ; and the service now stands unlinked by any special ceremonies with others alike in time and in space.

More serious still is the almost complete disappearance of communion, other than that of the celebrant. As masses have multiplied, the opportunities for celebrating priests to communicate have multiplied ; but for every one else the occasions of communion are infrequent, and no attempts by canon or exhortation to bring people to constant communion have had any lasting success. The congregation has ceased to communicate almost as entirely as it has ceased to offer. The Mass on most days has ceased to be a Communion ; and, while it is an opportunity of worship to the devout, to many it is little more than a pious spectacle. Moreover, even so, communion is now received only in one kind. Consequently the chalice is small, and one alone suffices. The paten rarely contains more than a single host. The hosts themselves are changed ; the old loaf is giving way to the round, flat wafer baked between two irons. The deacon's ancient privilege of having a special place in the consecration and administration of the chalice has dwindled to nothing. It is less regrettable that the linen bags for holding the hosts should have disappeared: but it is a distinct loss that the service has almost entirely ceased to be the 'Breaking of the Bread.'

Against these diminutions we must set some developments. The most prominent of these are seen first in regard to incense, and secondly in the introduction of the Elevation. The ceremonial of incense began to develop early. The processional use at the Introit and Gospel-procession is the only one in the purely Roman *Ordo* ; but the early Gallicanized forms show development, especially after the Gospel.[15] There the carrying of the Gospel-book round for the clergy and congregation to kiss has led them to draw to themselves in turn some of the smoke of the censer that precedes the Gospel-book ; this has led to the censing of each person in turn, and presently the thurifer is called away from this extended Gospel-procession for a censing of the oblations on the altar. When in the ninth century or thereabouts the singing of the Creed on certain days at this point becomes general, it comes in to divide the earlier part of the ceremony from the latter ; and thus in time the censing of the oblations comes to be regarded as a separate use of incense from that at the Gospel. Nor is this all. The censers are also carried round to the altars, probably for the censing of the relics there ; and out of this there has grown a censing of the altars and sanctuary, which, though still only outlined, is growing towards a more minute preciseness.

This and other similar developments are a natural growth ; but the case is otherwise with the elevation. This ceremony was adopted in the twelfth century as a definite result of the eucharistic controversies that went before, and as a definite protest against the minimizing views of Berengarius and his school. The showing of the Sacrament to the people was designed to stimulate eucharistic worship. It therefore differed in intention as well as in position from the older and less conspicuous elevation which, as we have seen, was made at the close of the Canon, and was the natural Godward action of offering. One of its results will be alluded to later ; viz. the postponement of the fraction from the centre of the Canon to a point subsequent to the elevation. A more serious one was the tendency to make a mystery, which had in old days been veiled, the central point of a spectacle, and to substitute ' gazing ' for devout offering and communion. There are no signs as yet in the Sarum Use of the early thirteenth century of this coming disturbance. The elevation, though it must have been in use, is not yet provided for in the document of that date, but figures first in the later form of it called the *Customary*.

One further cause of development deserves separate mention. In the early services great liberty was left as to all the opportunities for private prayer ; and it was only by degrees that there grew up sets of private devotions, belonging to the service, but of a personal sort. Thus at the entrance of the celebrant the early *Ordines* merely indicate the time and place of these private devotions, but the later books prescribe them. The same is the case at the offertory, at the celebrant's communion, and at the close of the service. Similarly, the ceremonies which at first were accompanied by no fixed form of prayer, tended to acquire them. In some cases this development took place early, *e.g.* in the case of the reading of the Gospel. Here the earliest form of the *Ordo* prescribes the formula by which the celebrant blesses the deacon who is about to sing ; but the later *Ordo* gives further directions as to the crossing and the giving out of the Gospel ; while later still come other ceremonial developments—the sign of the cross made by the people, and their response to the giving out.

Similarly, as the use of incense was elaborated, there began a blessing of incense, and then formulas of blessing were added. The lavatory acquires its formula. The ablutions become first prescribed, then elaborated and provided with accompanying formulas. In some cases the ceremony introduces a formula, and then the formula again leads to fresh details of ceremonial ; until the service of the celebrant, which once consisted of three or four collects and the Anaphora or Canon, comes to be overlaid with a multitude of secondary devotions; and *pari passu* the ceremonial grows also.

Other general alterations may be briefly noted before coming to the detailed description of the Sarum mass. The vestments are altered, for the deacon and subdeacon have almost entirely given up wearing their chasubles, and appear normally in dalmatic and tunicle; only in Lent their use of the chasuble survives, and the old ceremonies of removing it at certain parts of the service continue. The Gospel-book is still the centre of much honour, and it alone is brought in at the entrance of the celebrant and his ministers. The solemn entry of all the ornaments has been altered and is postponed; for the Gospel-book originally was brought in before the entry of the celebrant, while the sacred vessels, etc., which formerly came in with him, now are brought in subsequently.

In contrast with all these alterations are many survivals—ceremonies which lasted on after their original significance had diminished or perished. The first kiss of peace of the clergy at the Introit goes on, though the main ceremony of the *pax* follows the consecration. The paten is still treated in a peculiar way as being an innovation; it is banished from the altar during the greater part of the Canon, as of old, though the details vary. The old custom of touching the chalice with the host at the doxology before the Lord's Prayer survives now in a series of crossings made by the host over the chalice at this point; and a general direction, that the deacon is to come up to the celebrant and assist him by holding the corporal that covers the chalice, is all that is left of the control over it that the archdeacon formerly exercised.

It is high time now to turn to give a brief description of the service in general as exemplified in the old Salisbury Cathedral in the later Middle Ages.

The procession that leads up to the High Mass of the day goes round the church. At the head of it goes a verger, and a boy in a surplice carrying the Holy Water, followed by an acolyte bearing the cross, by two taperers, and a thurifer; then come subdeacon and deacon, and the priest in a cope. They are followed by the clergy in ascending order of dignity. They make a circuit of the whole church, going by the right either through the north door of the presbytery, or on great days through the west door of the quire. On the way the altars are sprinkled with Holy Water, except on great festivals. Passing by the font they come up to the rood at the western central pillars of the tower, where a station is made, and there follows the bidding of the bedes or notices of requests for intercession, like its modern survival the 'bidding prayer.' In this respect the cathedral differed from the parish churches; for there the bidding prayer came after the offertory. At the end of the prayers they enter the quire singing a respond; and with a Versicle and Collect at the quire step the procession ends.[16]

The priest and his ministers now disappear into the vestry on the south side of the sanctuary. When the Introit is begun by the choir they emerge again, preceded by two taperers and the thurifer. On ordinary days the subdeacon carries the Gospel-book, but if it is a greater festival the deacon and subdeacon each carry one upon a cushion. They halt at the lowest altar step, and, with the deacon on his right, and the subdeacon on his left, the celebrant says the preparatory prayers; at the end of them he kisses his two ministers and goes up bowing to the altar. There he kisses the altar, signs himself on the forehead, and then turns to bless the incense which the deacon meanwhile has been putting into the censer. Taking the censer from him, he censes the altar in the middle and at either end; next he is censed by the deacon, and is given by the subdeacon the Gospel-book to kiss. Meanwhile the choir, having finished the Introit, has begun the *Kyrie*; when that is done the celebrant comes from the south side, or from the sedilia, to the middle of the altar to precent the *Gloria in excelsis*. He then returns to the south side, and remains there while the *Gloria* is sung, with the deacon on his right and the subdeacon on his left. When he has signed himself on the forehead at its close, he turns to the people for the Salutation, and returns to say the Collect and subsidiary collects, if more than one is said. The deacon and subdeacon meanwhile stand immediately behind him, each on his proper step ; and this is their normal position, except at certain musical points in the service, when they stand on either side of him upon the footpace. The deacon turns westward when the priest does so, being in some sense his intermediary throughout, and not only on special occasions when he has to proclaim the end of Mass with the *Ite missa est*, or announce in Lent the time to kneel or stand at the solemn Collects.

During all this time there has been much movement in the quire ; not among the singers and congregation, for they remain in their places, the canons in their stalls, the vicars and other clergy in the seats below them, and the boys again below them ; all face choir to choir, except at a few points in the service, such as the intonation and certain subsequent clauses of the *Gloria in excelsis* and Creed, or at the *Gloria tibi* of the Gospel, when they turn for the moment eastwards. But the taperers have been busy. When they had set down their candles at the altar during the Introit, they came out to fetch the cruets and the lavatory bowl ; and having brought these in, they take up their candles and come down the presbytery. Meeting there an acolyte in alb and tunicle, who is bringing in the chalice, wrapped in a silken veil, they escort him while he sets the chalice ready and lays the corporals on the altar.

Now begins the series of journeys to the *pulpitum* : first goes the subdeacon to read the Epistle, then the singers for the Gradual and other chants, while a taperer goes also with a boy to get ready the desk for the Gospel there. Up in the sanctuary the deacon and subdeacon prepare the chalice and spread the corporal, while the celebrant sits in his seat. Then all is ready for the climax of the preliminary part of the rite—the Gospel-procession. The deacon censes the middle of the altar where the Gospel-book lies, takes it up, bows to receive the celebrant's blessing, gives the book to the subdeacon to carry, and follows him, the taperers, the thurifer, and on high days a crucifer, to the *pulpitum*. There in a group they stand, the subdeacon facing the deacon and holding the book, the taperers flanking him, and the thurifer behind the deacon. He faces north, though that is not now the direction where the men are to be found, and, in fact, the whole congregation that is in quire would have now to turn westward to face him after the *Gloria tibi* has been said eastward. Such is the force of conservatism.

The procession returns, and the kissing of the Gospel-book with censing begins, while the Creed or the Offertory is being sung. As soon as the celebrant has done his part, the shrunken ceremonies of the offering take place; they now consist of no more than the bringing up by the deacon of the paten and chalice, and their being set upon the altar with a ceremony and prayer of offering by the priest. Thereupon follows the censing of the oblations, which, as has been already explained, is now a separate and highly developed ceremony. For the censing at the Introit and Gospel there are no very precise directions, but here it is otherwise.[17] The *Consuetudinary* prescribes three crossings with the censer, three circles and a swing on either side of the chalice. The *Customary* adds a censing of the altar, and places here the kissing of the Gospel-book and censing of the priest, which the older rules of the *Consuetudinary* prescribe immediately after the Gospel.

While the deacon censes the south end of the altar and the relics set around it, the subdeacon ministers the lavatory to the priest; and when this is done, other private prayers, crossing, and kissing of the altar follow, forming the more immediate preparation of the priest for the central part of the service. Then this preliminary section of it is closed by the ' Secret ' collect.

From this point forward the ceremonial, as usual, is less ; the preparations have been solemnly made, but the action itself is done in stillness and quiet. Except for the removal of the paten at the *Sursum corda*, and its restoration at the Lord's Prayer, the celebrant is left to himself. His own actions are now more minutely prescribed : they form to a considerable extent a guide to the congregation which watches. The introduction of the elevation has established a new point for them to look for, but there is no censing during that ceremony.[18] At the *Agnus Dei*, as previously at the *Sanctus*, the ministers come up to the footpace on either side of the celebrant. After the Commixture the deacon receives the kiss of peace and hands it on to the subdeacon ; so it comes to the rulers of the two sides of the choir and goes the round of the whole body in descending order of dignity.[19]

After the priest's communion and his prescribed private devotions, the Ablutions follow at the south end of the altar. They are also minutely prescribed and furnished with accompanying prayers. They are concluded in the middle of the altar ; the priest then washes his hands at the south side, while the subdeacon transfers the book there, and the deacon folds up the corporals, and gives them, with the vessels, to an acolyte to carry out at the end of the Postcommunion collect. This is said at the south side, preceded and followed by the Salutation ; and then the deacon sings the *Ite missa est* or its equivalent. With a closing private prayer of the celebrant, said in the middle of the altar, the service ends. The clergy bow, and leave the sanctuary in the same order in which they came, the priest repeating the Gospel, *In principio* (*S. John* i. 1 and ff.).

CHAPTER VIII

UTILITARIAN CEREMONIAL

THE preceding descriptions have served to give an outline of the history of ceremonial development and of the contents of the eucharistic ceremonial at different stages. It will be evident from them that the whole body of ceremonial observances, which are or have been in use in the Christian Church, is a collection of very varying history, character, and aim. It is difficult to classify such a miscellaneous collection ; but the attempt is necessary if the underlying principles are to be brought to view. For the purposes of discussion it will be best to attempt three main divisions, arranging the various actions according to the motive which may be taken to underlie them, or to have been the cause of their introduction.

A large part of ceremonial began and still goes on upon purely utilitarian grounds ; another section may be called interpretative, because the ceremonial is meant to explain or comment on the circumstances to which it is annexed ; while the third division will contain all such ceremonial as is purely symbolical. The class of ceremonial which we have called utilitarian is necessarily first and chief. If a thing has to be done, it must be done somehow ; and it is the duty of ceremonial to explain or prescribe the best way of doing it. A considerable number of the rubrics of the Prayer-Book are simply of this nature. Such, for example, are those which direct the changes of posture in the clergy or people, the transition from kneeling for prayer to standing for praise, or the turning of the officiant to the people in order to address them ; while the postures themselves, and, to some extent it may be, the changes (such as the turning back of the priest when he resumes the work of prayer after addressing the people at the *Sursum corda*), may by anticipation be noted here as interpretative, since they emphasize either a state, or a change, of mental attitude, and explain what the people or the priest is doing.

Again, the directions for the ordering of the bread and wine, for the communion of the people, for the taking of the child into the priest's arms to be baptized (there is no direction to give it back), and those for the actual baptism, are utilitarian. In some cases the directions are in a special sense utilitarian, since they are dictated by cautious prudence. For example, the sick person is to be communicated last at the Communion of the Sick for fear of infection ; and for the like reason provision is made for holding, when it seems desirable, the whole of the Burial Service in the churchyard.

But besides the few ceremonial directions of this sort that are given in the rubrics, a large number of other ceremonial customs are continually growing up, merely from the necessity of settling some way of doing a thing that has to be done. Thus, customs, which are very often of a considerable degree of elaborateness, grow up round the entry of the clergy and choir into church. In some churches which would blush to be called 'ritualistic,' these have attained the proportions of a piece of pompous ceremonial. In other places a custom has grown up of magnifying the process of going into church at Mattins or Evensong by the singing of a processional hymn. This custom exists in defiance of all liturgical propriety, and stultifies both the penitential prelude to the service and the petition, *O Lord, open Thou our lips*, which introduces the service proper. In some cases, as though to emphasize the anomaly as much as possible, this versicle and response are previously said as a vestry-prayer, and the liturgical use of them is made a still more meaningless absurdity. Similarly, it is found to be impossible even to leave church when service is done without further pomp and ceremony; and a 'recessional hymn' has been invented to magnify the exit of the choir and clergy. Such ceremonies as these, even in their exaggerations and absurdities, can only be classed as utilitarian.

Again, the collection of alms by churchwardens and sidesmen necessitates a certain amount of ceremonial. In this ceremony, and others like it, customs are constantly growing and decaying as ways and fashions change; and curiously enough it is not at all an uncommon thing to find such ceremonial as this, which is entirely independent of rubric or church authority, being far more carefully carried out than the ceremonial which has better authority, or is really bound up with the due performance of the liturgical service. Most Englishmen have a deep-seated love of ceremonial if it is of their own invention.

The ceremonial directions of the Prayer-Book thus require to be supplemented by a body of extraneous customs, which are in a continual state of flux, and constantly change in varying circumstances and with varying fashions. This is a somewhat precarious position; but freedom is valuable, and except in a certain few points, the Prayer-Book has not attempted to secure ceremonial uniformity. The book has brought in a uniformity of rite which was unknown in pre-Reformation days, but the places are few in which it gives ceremonial directions and even aims at ceremonial uniformity. Ever since the beginning of the new series of English Service-books in 1549, the performance of service has been partly regulated by church tradition, partly by ecclesiastical authority, and partly left to the discretion of individuals. While the latter method is, as already has been remarked, precarious, the two former are safer and wiser, and, moreover, they have had far the greater share of responsibility, at any rate until recent times, in prescribing the supplementary non-rubrical ceremonial which is necessary for the performance of the services of the Prayer-Book. A large part of this traditional ceremonial belongs to the utilitarian class. Many of the most familiar features of Anglican worship rest upon no other basis than this. The large numbers of churchmen who are not very familiar with their Prayer-Book would no doubt be surprised in many cases, if they looked it up, to find that customs associated with their old and deepest memories of churchgoing were additional ceremonies not prescribed by the rubric at all. Such at any rate is the case ; and they rest for the most part on church tradition, and are to be justified partly by that fact and partly by mere utilitarian considerations.

Why, for example, should a celebrant bring in with him the chalice and paten at his entry ? There is no mention of either of them till the Prayer of Consecration, no use for them at all at any rate until the Offertory ; but he follows the old custom of Low Mass if he brings them in then, as distinct from the ceremonial of High Mass, which is quite different ; and he does so because it is practically convenient.

Again, why should the reader of the Epistle, be he the celebrant or be he the epistoller, turn to the west, as is the custom in many churches, when there was no direction for him to do so ? It is simply a matter of convenience. He turns to the people to read to them, as the reader of the lessons at Mattins or Evensong is directed to do ; and the New Prayer-Book now directs him to do so.

In some churches a contrary custom has been recently imported, by which the celebrant reads the Epistle facing eastwards. In doing so he has followed the example of the priest at a Latin Low Mass, who does not turn to read to the people because they cannot understand what he reads ; and because, that being so, it is not worth the trouble to turn to them—especially if the altar-book, from which he has to read, is cumbrous or heavy. This custom was thus also in its origin utilitarian ; but it can hardly claim to be so, as adopted by a priest reading to a congregation what it wants to hear. It may well disappear.

The case is the same with regard to a large part of the ceremonial of earlier English use, which has in many places been restored and recovered and utilized to regulate the many points in the performance of the services of the Prayer-Book which the rubrics still, after all the revisions, leave undecided. Thus, when the epistoller and the gospeller follow the old ceremonial of the Church, and carry out their part in its fullness instead of being content merely to intervene for the Epistle and Gospel, a large part of their movements is dictated by purely utilitarian considerations. If the epistoller carries in the Gospel-book with him at his entry, it is part of the general series of actions by which the ornaments requisite for the service are gradually brought in.[1] If a cross is carried at the same time at the head of the sacred ministers, this represents a survival from the time when there was no distinction between the processional cross and the altar cross, but the one which was brought in procession, was placed upon the altar.[2]

Again, the candles of the taperers were meant for subsequent use in the service, and were sometimes identical with the altar candles. These same taperers then, having brought in cross and candles, were next responsible for bringing in first the bread and the cruets of wine and water for the oblations, and then the water-bowl and towel to be used for the lavatory; and then they attended the acolyte who solemnly brought in the chalice with its veil and the two corporals, one to lie under the chalice, the other to cover it.[3] Thus by the time of the reading of the Epistle the necessary ornaments are all ready for the epistoller and gospeller, who, when the reading is done, begin to prepare them for the use of the celebrant. The only exception is the paten, the use of which is a later importation; there is, therefore, no provision made on the old lines for it to be solemnly brought into church.[4] All this is extremely practical and utilitarian, though to many it is unfamiliar. The exigences of Low Mass, and the absence of ministers to wait upon the celebrant, have introduced less solemn ways ; so it has become the common habit for the priest to bring in all the ornaments that he can carry, and to find the rest placed ready for use before the service begins. But one custom is no more rubrical than the other.

The actual 'serving' done by the epistoller and gospeller—the spreading of one corporal on the altar, the preparation and presentation of the elements, the assistance at the blessing of incense or at the lavatory, and suchlike actions—are so obviously utilitarian that there is no need to go into them in detail. But even some, which might seem to be of little practical use, were in fact, in their origin at least, dictated by mere motives of convenience. For example, in the early days chasubles were full and cumbrous, fell in great folds, and were bunched up on the wearer's arms. It was then distinctly a convenience that when the celebrant turned to the people, and the deacon, as being (properly speaking) his mouthpiece to the people and the director of their actions and devotions, turned with him, the subdeacon should occupy himself with the celebrant's chasuble so as to facilitate his turning.5

Perhaps it was also originally motives of convenience which arranged that the subdeacon should remove the paten and veil from the altar at the beginning of the Anaphora (*i.e.* the central section of the Communion Service) and give it to the acolyte to hold until the Canon was finished and the Lord's Prayer begun, returning it then to the deacon, who gave it to the celebrant at the end of the Lord's Prayer. The use of the paten, as has been already noted, was an innovation. The deacon placed the host upon it when he prepared the elements before the Gospel, and gave it so prepared to the celebrant at the offertory ; but the celebrant seems not to have taken to the innovation, for he still continued the older custom of using only the corporal upon which to lay the host and consecrate it. For a time the paten rested under the corporals on the right-hand side ; but it would seem to have been felt to be in the way when the time came near for the consecration, and to have been removed in the manner described, so as not to hamper the Manual Acts.[6] Similarly, the deacon's customary action at the consecration of the chalice, of standing at the right of the celebrant and lifting the second corporal, with which the chalice was covered, was probably in part a matter of convenience, though it has its roots far back in the old rules which gave the deacon special rights over the chalice, as has been already shown.[7]

The same utilitarian motive is clearly discernible in much of the ancient ceremonial of the celebrant. The old rule, that after breaking the host he should keep his finger and thumb closed, is one of practical utility, since it diminishes the danger of scattering any minute particles of the Holy Sacrament which may be adhering to his finger or thumb. The danger no doubt is diminished by the use of good wafers ; but where ordinary bread is used, the old rule is still of the highest practical value. In giving communion the like considerations of practical utility dictate that the same thumb and finger should be used for handling the Sacrament. For the administration they have of course to be separated : this is natural, and forms a good utilitarian exception to the general utilitarian rule ; but beyond this the only exception that was recognized by the old rules is in the acts of blessing or crossing made during the Canon.[8] Corresponding with this was the direction for rubbing the thumb and finger together over the chalice to detach any particles that might be adhering to them.[9]

This instance leads naturally on to another which shows the same practical common-sense and is closely connected, viz. the method of cleansing the vessels after the communion, called the Ablutions. The same reverence which dictates the care in the use of thumb and finger dictates also a careful method of cleansing to secure after the communion the entire consumption of what remains unneeded of each species. The Prayer-Book contains only a general direction which will be easily recognized to be of a utilitarian character. The older directions were more elaborate and their utility is perhaps not so easily recognized. The first ablution provided for the cleansing of the celebrant's fingers and thumbs in the chalice with wine and water; and so brought to a natural end the precautions which we were just now considering; and this is as clearly utilitarian as they were seen to be. There followed a second ablution of the chalice with water. In many churches, a previous ablution was made by pouring wine alone into the chalice to be received as a *purificatio oris*: but at Sarum this is not prescribed.[10]

Here again it will be noticed that the paten was not taken into account; it had in fact hardly been used, as has been mentioned, and the only part that it had in the old rules for the ablutions was in forming, as it were, a saucer upon which the chalice was set inverted after the second ablution, which received any liquid that there might be still remaining after it had been drained by the celebrant.[11] When all this is considered in view of the circumstances it is seen to be eminently practical.

In modern days it has become usual to have an ablution of the paten as well as of the chalice, and commonly this, the third ablution, is one of water only, and takes the place of the water poured into the chalice. In view of the modern way in which the paten is used—unless a ciborium for convenience sake takes its place at a large communion—and the need of cleansing which results from it, this additional ablution seems on utilitarian grounds to be a very suitable addition to the old ceremonial.[12]

There is no need to multiply further examples to show what is meant by utilitarian ceremonial. No objection will be raised, in theory at least, to such ceremonies by the plain man; but yet in practice even ceremonial which is purely utilitarian meets with its objectors, not only among the laity, but also among the clergy. There are not a few persons who dislike and rebel against any rules, even these practical ones, whose only *raison d'être* is, that the thing that is to be done, should be done in the best way. Men very often prefer their own way, not because it is really better, but because it is their own. Or they will not take the trouble to find out, or even consider, what is the best way; they act in the way that comes natural to them. Unfortunately, as has been already noted, this habit is not a safe guide.

It is distinctly utilitarian and a gain, that actions and postures and groupings should be seemly and symmetrical; but, to secure this, reflection and training and rules are necessary. The way that comes natural to many of us is a clumsy or an ungainly or an inefficient way; and clumsiness or inefficiency is not to be excused on such a ground. This is recognized in the technical training of other professions in which men figure before the public eye. An actor has to learn not only how to speak, but even how to walk suitably for public appearance; and it is not many men, and especially few Englishmen, who by nature can do either of these things presentably. A priest has much to learn from an actor's training and method; and though he should be the first person to shun whatever could be rightly blamed as theatrical, he ought to be the last person to shirk whatever trouble is required to fit him for the conspicuous place that he occupies in public worship. The layman has every right to protest warmly against the bad mannerisms of the clergy in divine worship; they are simply the result of their doing things in their own way, instead of taking pains to learn to do them habitually and naturally in the best way.

One instance may be given to exemplify this point, which will be all the more telling because in itself it is small. When the celebrant at the altar turns northwards to read the Gospel, according to the old custom, there are two ways in which he may do it. If he, facing east, turns by his left, he has about a quarter of a circle to turn; while if he turns by his right he has about three-quarters of a circle to turn. One way is good and the other is bad. Ceremonial lays down that he should turn to the left, and this is only common-sense. But there are some people who go through all the fuss of turning by the right through three-quarters of a circle; and there are many more who would be irritated if they were told to turn to the left, merely because they dislike rules. Nevertheless, the rule justifies itself, and it is a pity if people turn the worse way, whether out of ignorance or out of obstinacy.

Again, if the celebrant has to use one hand in a marked manner, symmetry demands that he should suitably dispose the other. If he is holding out his hands extended in prayer and has, *e.g.*, to turn over in the book with one hand, he should fold the other on his breast or set it at rest on the altar. The direction may sound fussy; but he is, in the nature of the case, a very conspicuous figure, his appearance from behind matters; the law of symmetry comes in therefore and demands that attention should be paid to such minutiae till they form good habits.

Minute directions of this sort are more important still when not one person merely but several are concerned. When the celebrant, epistoller, and gospeller come down from the altar at the close of the service, and turn to bow at the sanctuary step, it may be either a decorous or an indecorous movement. It is decorous if the two sacred ministers, being on the outside of the celebrant, each turn inwards, *i.e.* one by the left and the other by the right; it is much less so if they both turn outwards; and it is positively ugly if one turns outwards and the other inwards. This point, again, is of course a very small and unimportant one, but that is no reason why the movement should not be made in the right way instead of the wrong way. Again even in such *minutiae* it is a gain to have utilitarian rules.

These need little justification so long as their utility remains and is recognizable. But it does not follow, because a practice began on good utilitarian grounds, that it therefore will remain as a useful practice for ever after. Indeed, it is very possible that it may survive as a practice long after its utility is gone; for ecclesiastics are, next to lawyers, the most tenacious class of society. What justification is there for such cases? It is over such survivals as these that the antiquarian and the practical mind come into conflict. Now it is possible that the ceremony, having lost its original utility, may be found to have an interpretative value, and so be retained under that head. The eucharistic vestments, for example, were at first utilitarian, for they were the ordinary dress of the day; but they acquired a representative value on wider grounds, and may be well justified on those grounds.[13] For other points, on the contrary, there may be no obvious justification remaining, when once their utility is gone. The man of practical and progressive views will then very probably wish to get rid of them, while the man of antiquarian or conservative mind will wish to retain them. 'Why retain the use of a corporal,' says the first, ' now that the custom of consecrating upon it is given up and the paten takes its place for this purpose?' The other replies, 'Why not keep it? It has always been used.' Further, perhaps, he adds some mystical interpretation of it; *e.g.* that it represents, as its very name implies, the winding-sheet of our Lord; and this argument only has the effect of widening the divergence of view between him and his opponent.

Here we touch one cause of constant disputes, arising out of some point of ceremonial, which confessedly is in itself unimportant. It is hard for any one to try and mediate between the two views. There is a real religious value up to a certain point in this reverent conservatism, though it has its great drawbacks; and there is real value also in the sensible spirit, which has a zeal for simple efficiency unhampered by traditions, though this too has its drawbacks. Perhaps the most that the mediator can hope to do, is to bring both parties to realize the unimportance of the matter. If he does this, he has done a great deal ; he has secured a truce for the moment, together with some prospect of further agreement to come later. In time perhaps the point will seem to both parties unnecessary and superfluous ; or perhaps the practical man will come to feel, *e.g.*, that there is the same sort of propriety in spreading a special cloth under the chalice for the consecration as there is in having a fair linen cloth with which to cover the elements when consecrated.

CHAPTER IX

INTERPRETATIVE CEREMONIAL

I

A LARGE part of the duty of ceremonial is to interpret. There are many things, in all services, of which the eye can take no account, because there is nothing visible in the things themselves which can appeal to the faculty of sight. Now the larger part of mankind is incredibly dependent upon the eye, and has little power of grasping things unless by the help of sight. This is particularly the case with poorly educated people, who have not been trained to assimilate by unaided thought ; but it is the case also with many others, and to a greater extent than is commonly realized. Good and attractive sermons again and again fail to get attention, because they are delivered without action ; while, on the other hand, a speech or address of very inferior quality wins the attention of the hearers, because it is given with gesture that rivets their eyes.

In the same way a great amount of ceremonial action has for its object the securing of attention for the service as it proceeds, and the bringing home to people of its significance through the medium of their eyes. Sometimes such ceremonial may take place in silence, and be meant to interpret a mental state ; more often it accompanies actual words said, and acts as their interpreter.

It has already been mentioned that the ordinary postures of devotion are of this class, since they are an outward and visible expression of what in itself is invisible. Some of these postures express the reverence due to God. When we kneel to pray the attitude is expressive of the mind, and also illustrates the actual words of prayer that are said ; when we stand for praise the like is the case ; and even sitting at the lessons expresses the attitude of attention and teachableness.

Attitudes such as these are partly prescribed by rubrical directions. Thus the congregation is told to kneel from the Confession to the end of the second Versicle and Response at the beginning of Divine Service, and then to stand for the *Gloria* and the remaining Versicle and Response. Again, when the Creed is reached there is the direction to stand, followed by the counter-order to kneel when it is finished, and to remain kneeling till the end of the third Collect. Again, in the Eucharist the people are directed to kneel for the first part of the service, and again at the Confession, and again at the reception of communion. But these directions are manifestly incomplete, and much is settled by tradition or custom, which has not always been uniform, nor is so now.

Thus the position of the congregation during the singing of the psalms is not only not defined, but it has varied, and to a certain extent still varies. In the early post-Reformation days standing was by no means usual ; indeed the Puritan regarded it as a grievance when the bishops tried to make the people stand for psalms and hymns, and face eastward at the *Gloria*. This habit had probably survived from the pre-Reformation times till then, and was not therefore an innovation ; but, nevertheless, the Puritans resisted it and wished to sit covered during the psalmody.[1] At the present day it is so usual to stand throughout the psalms that churches where the contrary custom prevails seem eccentric, and no man now wears his hat in church. On the other hand, the retention of the old custom of turning to the east for the *Gloria* is comparatively rare. There is thus no uniformity of use in these two points.[2] Similarly, there is no uniformity of use in parts of the Communion Service ; at the *Gloria in excelsis* sometimes two different customs prevail in the same church on different occasions ; nor is there any uniformity at the Offertory-sentences. At the Prayer for the Church Militant, though there is still no direction given, it is customary to kneel ; but at the Short Exhortation which follows, in some churches it is customary to kneel and in others to stand. The former habit is, in many cases at least, a recent innovation, and probably is connected with the disuse of the Long Exhortation. Again, when the penitential preparation, Confession, etc., for which kneeling is prescribed, is finished, it is becoming customary in some churches to follow old custom and stand from the *Sursum corda* to the end of the *Sanctus*,[3] and there is much practical convenience to recommend the custom, especially at a choral Eucharist. No position is prescribed for the Lord's Prayer and the prayer following, nor even at the Blessing. There is a general uniformity at these points which is the result of tradition ; and it shows that, in spite of such differences of posture as have been quoted, there is still good reason for saying that the postures are interpretative, and are meant to explain and express what is going on.

All such expression is merely conventional. To us at the present day kneeling is the natural expression of prayer ; but this identification is comparatively modern and Western. The early Church stood to pray, and even forbade kneeling throughout the whole of Eastertide. In the East standing is still the normal attitude of prayer. The mediaeval Church kept some part at least of the rule which prohibited kneeling in Eastertide, and reserved the attitude of kneeling in Divine Service for special times and forms of prayer. Thus we have gone to unparalleled lengths in our great identification of prayer with kneeling ; and therefore we shall realize more readily than others the interpretative character of the attitude of kneeling.

It is partly the strength of this feeling and partly the effect of post-Reformation tradition which has caused the present almost universal custom of kneeling for the Litany. There is no direction given for the posture to be adopted either at its ordinary use or at the Ordination Services. The bulk of the influence of early history and pre-Reformation usage is in favour of its being said in procession ; but soon after its first appearance in English form this was given up in favour of kneeling, ostensibly because of certain inconveniences and disorders which at the time had become attached to the processional use.4

In Queen Elizabeth's time the processional use was occasionally resumed,5 but until recent years there was almost unbroken tradition since that date in favour of kneeling ; and it seems to have attained to such uniformity mainly through a feeling that this attitude was the most appropriate, at any rate for our form of the Litany ; in other words, our custom of kneeling is interpretative.

There are other things which are best expressed by this attitude of standing. While sitting, though not prescribed, is the attitude that seems to be expected during the reading of Holy Scripture, the rubric orders standing for the Gospel, both in the Communion Service and the Baptismal Service, as a posture of greater respect expressive of the special attitude of mind with which the Gospel is to be heard.6 Of recent years the significance of this direction has been much obscured through a habit adopted in some churches of kneeling through the Epistle. This is subversive of the purpose of the rubric; for instead of marking the Gospel with special reverence, it assigns to it a less reverential posture than to the Epistle. There have been probably two chief motives at work in bringing about this innovation ; namely, first, a feeling that it is reverent to avoid sitting during the Eucharist, and second, a desire to follow the custom of Roman Catholics. The first is a mistaken feeling and to be resisted on practical grounds as well as on those grounds already urged ; because the change of posture and the rest of sitting is very desirable, and the strain of continuous kneeling unnecessarily trying, especially at an early service where the habit is chiefly in vogue.

It may be natural enough that a Roman Catholic worshipper should make no change from kneeling, for he very likely does not hear the Epistle read at all, nor know when it is begun or ended ; nor could he understand if he did hear. But all this has no bearing at all on the case as it affects English church-people.

The real interpretative value of these ordinary postures of devotion is clearly revealed by the controversies as to the posture to be adopted in receiving communion. No direction was given on the subject in the First Prayer-Book, for it was taken for granted here, as in so many other cases, that the existing custom would continue unless a contrary direction was given. But this was not to pass unchallenged. An agitation was being conducted in favour of sitting. This was done in the interest of the crude bibliolatry which was fast becoming the main tenet of the extreme party of reform, and it was also due to the low sacramental views which found favour there. The controversy was not a mere matter of external posture ; the question really at issue was the interpretation of the act of communion. Some wished to sit, in order to show that they regarded it as a partaking in a mere memorial supper. On the other hand, the order to kneel was (for the first time) inserted in the Second Prayer-Book, in order to emphasize the truth that it is an eating of the Flesh of Christ and a drinking of His Blood ; and the Black Rubric, as it stood for a few months in that book, was a well-meaning but clumsy attempt to interpret the act of kneeling on the negative side, and to say what it did not mean. Thus both sides of the controversy were equally convinced of the interpretative value of the posture of reception.[7]

The same may be said of the act of genuflexion in reverence to the Blessed Sacrament, which is, as it were, an extension and development of the act of kneeling for communion. The custom does not seem to be traceable further back than the later Middle Ages,[8] and in England (so far as is known) it was never adopted as part of the ceremonial of the sacred ministers at the altar down to the Reformation, except at Exeter where much English ceremonial was deliberately given up in favour of Roman ceremonial in the middle of the fourteenth century.[9] The due reverence was paid, but in the form of profound bows. Thus, whichever custom was adopted, the purpose was the same, viz. to interpret by outward gesture the veiled mystery of the sacramental presence. And to the present day most people, other than trained theologians, can better express their belief as to the Blessed Sacrament by their deep bow or their genuflexion than they could by any words, definitions, or arguments.

Posture, again, in some cases expresses not so much the reverence due to God as respect due to man. It is from this, no doubt, that the custom has grown up of late years that the congregation should stand at the entry of the choir and clergy. It is one of the many pieces of ceremonial custom which have come in with the increased feeling for decorum which has made the modern Anglican service so ceremonious and even pompous a thing as it is in many churches. But it is very natural, and it has many parallels in other circumstances, as, for example, when people stand in the presence of royalty, or rise at the entry of a judge into his court because he is the representative of the Crown.

More often than this a posture is the expression of a third idea, viz. of ministerial authority. The rubrics of the Prayer-Book are often explicit on this point, and prescribe the position of the minister while they pass over in silence the position of the congregation. Standing is prescribed for the priest alone as the right attitude for saying the Absolution at the beginning of Divine Service; the same is the normal position of the celebrant, apart from one or perhaps two exceptions, as expressive of his ministerial authority. The same is his attitude again throughout the Baptismal Service, at any rate until the actual baptism is done ; and for the same reason. Absolving and blessing are so obviously ministerial acts, that it is only natural that the minister should stand for them. In a less degree the same is true about saying solemn collects. The Collect for the day is said as the climax of Divine Service ; the whole history of this custom shows that it is in a very real sense a special ministerial act. In the Latin service the priest said it with much solemnity standing ; and when there were preceding Suffrages, which were said kneeling, as was the case at some times of the year, he was expressly directed to rise for the closing Suffrages, the Collect, and the Memorials which followed it. There can be no real doubt that this custom is meant to be continued in the Prayer-Book service, and that the priest should stand for the Collect of the day and the two or more Collects which follow.[10]

In the case of a bishop, sitting as well as standing is a position of ministerial authority. It is not only prescribed in the Ordination Services at the preliminary presentation and at the examination, but it is also the attitude in which the bishop continues for the laying on of hands in the case of deacons, and which he resumes in the case of priests, though there is no rubric in the book to direct it. In this case the position is the more significant, because, while the bishop sits, the priests who join with him in the laying on of hands emphasize the difference of their order by standing. As the person to be ordained meanwhile is kneeling, there is at this point a simultaneous exemplification of the meaning of each of these three postures.

No direction is given as to the position of the bishop during the act of Confirmation, nor is there any uniform tradition on the matter. The analogy of Ordination suggests that he should be seated for the imposition of hands if the candidates are brought to him. If however he goes round to them the case is naturally different.

We have thus far considered the interpretative significance solely of the ordinary postures of devotion ;

but the services abound also in special actions and pieces of ceremonial which have the like expository value, and it will be well to consider some of these. We will take first those which concern the congregation, as distinct from those that concern the ministers. They are not very many, but some are of considerable interest. There are various bowings, some of which are made in silence, and are therefore interpretative of a state of mind and not of words spoken. Such, for example, is the bowing towards the altar at entering and leaving church, which was commended by the seventh canon of 1640, and therefore has whatever authority attaches to that code of canons.[11] This is a continuation of old usage, but in a somewhat simplified form as compared with the custom formerly prescribed in cathedral, collegiate, and monastic churches. There a double bow was prescribed on entering and leaving, called *ante et retro* ('before and behind'), and comprising first the bow to the altar and then a bow to the bishop, dean, abbot, prior, or person of dignity present.[12] Naturally there was no scope for this double bow in parish churches, but the bow towards the altar survived the Reformation, was a frequent ground of puritan attack, was encouraged by the canon, and survived in a few places throughout the gloom and decadence of the eighteenth century, till it was taken up again in the beginning of the catholic revival.

Another bow made in silence by the members of the congregation is that made to the thurifer who censes them ; but its motive is somewhat different, since it is an act rather of human courtesy than of reverence ; and it is analogous to similar acts which will come up again for consideration as part of the ceremonial of the ministers. Others are sometimes made by devout persons, as, for example, to the cross carried at the head of the procession or to the celebrant as he passes by in procession ; but these are private exercises of piety rather than church ceremonial.

Other bows are made as the accompaniment of words,

such as the bow ordered in the Elizabethan Injunctions and in the eighteenth canon of 1604, at the Holy Name of Jesus. This has a much more authoritative position in post-Reformation usage than the bow towards the altar; but it does not seem to have had as good an authorization in Anglican ceremonial before that date, and there is no mention of it in the Sarum customs. It was, however, probably a well-established custom. Perhaps it was introduced from abroad,[13] but possibly its popularity was also connected with that special reverence for the Holy Name which was a marked feature of English piety in the later mediaeval period. This custom, too, formed a great point of puritan attack, but it weathered it more successfully and completely than the custom of bowing to the altar. It had one stronghold from which it was never dislodged; and though the bow might be little or rarely made in other places, yet in the Creeds the custom universally survived down to the days of ceremonial revival.[14]

The meaning of the crossings made by the congregation is more difficult to discern. To judge by the analogy of the crossings made by the ministers (hereafter to be discussed), these too should be interpretative; but it is a little difficult to see in what sense they are so. According to the Sarum customs the members of the congregation were directed to cross themselves publicly at three points during the mass, viz. at the end the *Gloria in excelsis*, at the response *Gloria tibi Domine* made to the giving out of the Gospel, and at the *Benedictus qui venit*, which came at the beginning of the second part of the *Sanctus*.[15] The first may perhaps have been due to the commemoration of the three Persons of the Blessed Trinity which is made at the end of the *Gloria in excelsis*, and the crossing may have been meant to emphasize this. At the second point the signing was no doubt copied from the deacon's action in giving out the Gospel. He was directed to make a cross on the book first, and then on his forehead, and lastly on his breast with his thumb. In his case the reason of the cross is fairly clear, since it is parallel to many other cases in which it was used by the minister to define and localize and indicate visibly that which he was doing.[16] The cross on the book defined the Gospel text, and the crosses on his forehead and breast brought his head and heart into connexion with it. But this purpose did not exist in the case of the congregation, nor were the people directed to make the three crosses, or even the two, but merely in general terms to sign themselves with the sign of the cross. After the Gospel it was customary to do what was often done in other cases for private devotion, viz. to make the sign of the cross on the desk or the floor or in some convenient place, and then kiss it.[17] The simplest explanation of the first crossing on the part of the congregation at this point seems to be one already suggested, viz. that, as is the case in other points, it was done by the people in imitation of what they saw the minister do. The Roman ceremonial which prescribes three crosses was probably influenced by the benediction said over the gospeller, which spoke of his mouth as well as his heart; and this mention seems to have led to the making a cross upon the lips. If this is so, the triple crossing is far less appropriate for the congregation, whose place it is not to read the Gospel, but to listen to it.

The third crossing which is prescribed at *Benedictus qui venit in nomine Domini* is more difficult to explain with certainty. It is probably due simply to the word *benedicere*, which from its use in blessings became naturally associated with crossing and suggested it.[18]

It will be observed that no mention is made of crossing at the end of the Creed. In fact this was not done in England at the Latin services, only a bow was made towards the altar at the end of the Nicene Creed.[19] This was similar to the triple bow made towards the altar in the middle of the Creed at *incarnatus*, at *homo factus*, and at *crucifixus*, which was not superseded in general in

England by the Roman custom of kneeling during the first two clauses and somewhat illogically rising at the third.[20] The signing of the cross at the end of the Apostles' Creed has come in of late, probably through false analogy in imitation of the Roman custom of crossing at the end of the Nicene Creed.[21]

Another interesting gesture on the part of the congregation is the beating on the breast as a sign of sorrow. It is a natural expression of inward feeling. The Jews used it, and it passed into Christian usage, as S. Augustine bears early witness.[22] Equally expressive was the holding up of hands in prayer. From the early pictures in the catacombs showing an 'Orante,' down to pictures of the Eucharist in the fifteenth century,[23] the posture is graphically shown; directions also are found ordering this during the service and at the Consecration. Lovers of Dean Colet will not forget the tender charge that he gave to his boys at S. Paul's School to hold up their little white hands in prayer for him.[24]

The discussion of interpretative ceremonial as it concerns the minister had better be reserved for another chapter.

CHAPTER X

INTERPRETATIVE CEREMONIAL

II

A LARGE part of the ceremonial of the clergy and others who minister in church may be defined as honorific in character ; it arises from religious politeness or is designed to show respect. It thus forms part of interpretative ceremonial. For reasons such as these the verger with his verge goes before the choir or clergy ; or vergers in ascending degrees of dignity precede the various dignitaries, as in a cathedral or collegiate church. This form of ceremony is not peculiar to religious observances, but is universal. The heralds at a court pageant or the outriders at a royal progress are doing exactly the same thing, and for the same reason. When the verger conducts the preacher to the pulpit in the Communion Service it is no doubt an additional ceremony not prescribed by the rubrics of the Prayer-Book ; but it is one to which, so far, apparently no aggrieved parishioner has taken exception, and on the legality of which no lawyers have as yet been called in to pronounce. In similar cases even greater pomp has been usual. It was customary to honour the Roman emperor[1] with torches or lights and incense, and when he was not in person present, but was represented by his picture, the lights and incense accompanied in procession the symbol of his authority.[2] By a natural transference into the ecclesiastical sphere the lights and incense were in early days carried before the Gospel-book in the procession to the ambo for the reading of the Gospel at the Eucharist, and in some cases similar ceremonies surrounded sacred pictures or 'eikons.' The lights and incense similarly preceded the Gospel-book as it was carried back after the reading of the Gospel, and they went before it first to the celebrant, and then to the rest of the clergy and dignitaries, as it was offered to each of them in turn to kiss.3 From this arose the custom of censing the clergy and others after the Gospel, or, when the Creed had been imported into this position in the service, after the singing of the Creed.4 By this change the censing passed from being an act of respect paid to the Holy Gospels into being an act of respect done to the clergy and people. It remained honorific in character, but with a different object of honour.5

Another class of ceremonial acts which may be called honorific has grown up out of the mutual relations of the various ministers who are associated together in the performance of service. At constant intervals in the services one person waits upon another, brings him what he requires, or in some other way ministers to him. In ordinary circumstances the obligation would be acknowledged by a 'thank you,' or at least by a smile or a bow. In the course of the service the last of these three is obviously the only one suitable, and a bow makes a very suitable acknowledgement. In some mediaeval rites there was more ceremony than this, for according to the First *Ordo Romanus* the deacon kissed the pope's feet as he went to read the Gospel, and in the Sarum rite the minister kissed the shoulder or hand of the celebrant as he ministered to him.6 But the rationale of the act was the same; it was honorific and interpretative, it expressed in action what could not well be said in word.

In this connexion it is natural to refer to a far older piece of ceremonial custom. The kiss of peace goes back to the earliest days of Christendom; it was in apostolic times the sign of Christian fellowship and love. S. Paul in his First Epistle to the Thessalonians directs that it should be given, and the direction was no doubt carried out on the occasion of the public reading of the letter ; that is, in the Christian assembly. It cannot be stated that this was a liturgical assembly ; but, even if it was not, the importation of the kiss of peace into the liturgical assembly was natural and obvious. Its use as a formal part of eucharistical ceremonial is attested by some of the earliest records of Christian worship, *e.g.* Justin Martyr's account of the Eucharist.[7] Its method has varied considerably from time to time. Originally it was given in all simplicity, and with no further regulation than that the men kissed the men and the women the women. But later, probably in the thirteenth century, it was found more suitable to pass round some article for each to kiss in turn, either some object of devotion, such as the paten, or else a specially made *osculatorium* or pax-brede.[8] But under whatever circumstances the ceremony was carried out, the character of it was the same. It was an action interpretative of the inner love with which the Christian assembly met before the throne of God.

Special significance attaches to the actions of the celebrant or the principal officiant at divine worship. In his case, more than in any other, actions are significant and interpretative. Sometimes they alone interpret what is being done, as when in silence he ' presents ' the alms. But more often the actions take place while words are being said ; and they serve to bring out their meaning more clearly, or else to indicate some point in connexion with the words that needs to be brought out.

The most primitive and universal of the gestures of the Consecration-prayer are those which are a following of our Lord's own action. The Manual Acts prescribed in the Prayer-Book of 1661, and practised previously, though not prescribed from 1552 onwards, are the continuance of primitive tradition in imitating the institution.

The mediaeval rubrics directed similar action, though with some differences. It was customary to consecrate upon the corporal, not upon the paten ; therefore the first direction was an innovation. The custom of making a fraction at this point had been given up in the later Middle Ages; for as the novel custom of the elevation of the host at the consecration became general from the twelfth century onward, there grew a sense of inconvenience in making the fraction before the elevation; thus the second direction of the Prayer-Book was a restoration, and a characteristic restoration, of what was a natural custom based on scriptural precedent. The documents of the Sarum Use had no direction for the taking up the bread, but where the earlier books ordered a fraction (*frangat hostiam*) the later ones ordered a touch (*tangat hostiam*).[9] There were no directions for the celebrant to lay on his hand, but there was ordered a similar action interpreting the words, viz. the signing with the sign of the cross at *benedixit*, both in the case of the host and the chalice. This action is one of the highest antiquity, for S. Augustine speaks of it as indispensable to the due performance of such sacred rites as the hallowing of the font, the admission of catechumens to the privileges of the Church, the consecration of Holy Oil or of the Eucharist;[10] and this dictum of his became a generally received principle in the Church. The maintenance of this custom seems therefore the best way of carrying out the existing rubric.

As regards the chalice, the Sarum rubric ordered that, like the host, it should be lifted a little at this point, and thus falls in with the directions of the Lambeth Judgement of 1890 in ordering that the manual acts should be conspicuously made. Thus these manual acts of the Prayer-Book are in a very obvious way interpretative. Similarly, though with a different object, the later mediaeval rubrics ordered an elevation of both host and chalice after each had been consecrated.[11] The ancient elevation at the end of the Canon had been a natural act of uplifting to God. The new elevation was meant to exhibit the Sacrament to the congregation. Though so widely different, each was in its way interpretative.

Other directions for gestures in the old services may

be cited as further instances of interpretative ceremonial. There were from early days further crossings made in the Canon. In the eighth century the Pope Zacharias sent a roll to S. Boniface at his request to indicate the points at which this should take place. The MSS. of that date show much variation in most of the groups of crossings which ultimately became universal, and know nothing of one of them—that in the section *Supplices te rogamus*;[12] but a century later the place and number of them were settled, except that the additional group was subsequently inserted, and in the sixth and last group three additional crossings were added. The interpretative nature of these crossings is evident. The first group, for example, comprised three crosses at the words *haec dona, haec munera, haec sancta sacrificia illibata* ('these gifts, these boons, these holy, spotless sacrifices'). Similarly in the second, fourth, and fifth groups crossings are prescribed at the words *corpus* and *sanguis* ('body' and 'blood'). They thus simply indicate what is being mentioned.

In the second, the fifth, and the sixth groups, as in the third (the consecration already discussed), the cross is made at the word *benedicere* (to bless) or the like ; these crossings are therefore linked with those at the consecration, and share in the general convention by which the action of blessing is outwardly expressed by the sign of our redemption.

Crossings are not the only expressive gestures of this solemn prayer. The celebrant is to bow at the words which speak of supplication and at the consecration ; he is to look intently at the host as he draws near to the handling of it, and to look up, as our Lord is said to have looked up to the Father, at the recital of the institution. More significant still, as he comes after the institution to speak of the passion, he is to stand with his arms outstretched in the form of a cross. This attitude, a familiar one in old days,[13] and constantly adopted in private prayer, has a special significance here. It was prescribed, here at any rate, not as merely an act of private personal devotion on the part of the priest, but as a gesture full of meaning to the congregation. *The Lay Folks' Mass Book* directs the congregation when they see this to pray for the dead.[14] Langford is more natural, and directs them to bear in mind the passion at this point.[15]

The congregation was similarly guided in its devotions by the gestures of the celebrant. In *The Lay Folks' Mass Book* a series of prayers is provided for the unlearned laity, being, like the directions themselves, in verse. The faithful are instructed to take their cue from what they see going on. When they notice the second group of crossings, for example, they can tell that the consecration is close at hand, and they are to say the Lord's Prayer in preparation for it. The sacring bell was a still more marked provision for the guidance of the people in their worship at the elevation, as well as of the absent.

The series of prayers in this directory follows fairly closely the action that is going forward. Other directories, with a less clear kind of interpretation, bade the congregation see in each part of the service some representation and symbol of a part of our Lord's passion ; this thought was to be before them all through, and not only at the time when the priest stands with outstretched arms as though crucified, or carries out the fraction at the end of the Canon. Again in this case, it was the gestures of the celebrant that were to be their interpreters, and guide them through the course of their meditations.[16]

Most obvious of all is the lifting of the hands at the *Sursum corda* ('Lift up your hearts'). The words carry us back at least to the time of S. Cyprian in the middle of the third century, or even some decades earlier, it seems, to the *Hippolytean Church Order* ; and it can hardly be doubted that so expressive a gesture is coeval with the words.[17]

We turn now from the special ceremonial of the Holy Eucharist, first to some pieces of general interpretative ceremonial, and then to some further instances from other services. At intervals it is customary that the officiant, instead of maintaining the ordinary still position of prayer, should disjoin, extend, and then rejoin his hands. This was commonly done as an act of salutation at *Dominus vobiscum* (' The Lord be with you '), though the Sarum rubric only orders the joining of hands, which was taken to be significant of a suppliant attitude. The same action is repeated at *Oremus* ('Let us pray'), but in a different sense. In this connexion, it would seem, the waving of the hands invites co-operation. This is also the case elsewhere, as for example in precenting, where this gesture is employed to call upon the congregation to join in. The celebrant uses it at the Creed and the *Gloria in excelsis*, because these are meant to be congregational. There is no such action at the *Kyrie*, because this is not precented, nor at the *Agnus Dei* for the same reason. The reason why there is no precenting by the celebrant here, is because these were not matters in which he was concerned. The *Kyrie* was originally the response of the processional litany introductory to the liturgy ; the clergy and people sang it as they accompanied the celebrant to the church and up to the altar, but it was no part of his duty. The *Agnus Dei* arose in like manner, independently of the celebrant, as a popular devotion during the communion. There is equally no precenting to the *Sanctus*, and no waving of hands, but for a different reason. The Salutation, *Sursum corda*, and Preface have already formed the introduction to the *Sanctus*, and given to the people the invitation to join in at the proper moment.

There is a third reason which explains the absence of precenting or waving at other chants of the liturgy, such as the Introit, Gradual, etc. These are choir chants and not congregational chants ; the duty of singing them belongs to the choir, and the celebrant is therefore not responsible for starting them. All this variety of use in varying circumstances makes the more clear the purport of the celebrant's waving of hands at precenting, and also at the invitation ' Let us pray.'

Turning now to other services, we are constantly confronted with the practice of the imposition of hands, used under varying conditions and with different intents. The references to the practice in Holy Scripture are numerous and various. Our Lord used it for healing and for blessing, but not in giving His chief authoritative commission to His apostles. On that occasion He breathed on them,[18] thus indicating by an even more expressive ceremony their endowment with the ministerial gift of the Holy Spirit. These uses were continued by the apostles after His ascension; and they further used the imposition of hands in imparting to others the gift of the Holy Spirit that they had themselves received. S. Paul is recorded to have received such an imposition twice; first when Ananias came in to him immediately after his conversion, and again when with S. Barnabas he was separated for the missionary work.[19] The former of these was similar to the use established later of using the imposition of hands in giving absolution; the latter was more akin to the employment of the same gesture in ordination.

It is difficult to say how far the laying on of hands, either in S. Paul's case or in the case of the Seven,[20] can be placed in line with the universal use thenceforward of the imposition of hands in ordination. The references to the practice in the Pastoral Epistles [21] are more definite, but are not wholly conclusive. Two of them are references to the imposition of hands upon Timothy by S. Paul and the presbytery, and certainly refer to his being set apart for his office. The third, 'Lay hands suddenly on no man,' has been interpreted by some to refer to ordination, by others to the reconciliation of penitents.

The laying on of hands for this purpose, even if it is not the one here in question, is at any rate of extreme antiquity. It is found for example in general use in the West at the time of the controversy about those who had lapsed in the Decian persecution in the middle of the third century. Though S. Cyprian and the Roman authorities differed as to the method in which the lapsed were to be treated, they agreed in speaking of the imposition of the hand as a ceremony accompanying absolution.[22]

Besides these four uses another may also be cited, viz. the employment of this gesture in exorcizing. There is no mention of it when our Lord or His apostles cast out demons. This silence is no proof that there was no laying on of hands; it only suggests that, if so, it was no special feature of the course taken in exorcizing. Later, however, both the purport and method of exorcism was extended. The exorcism itself was applied not only to persons possessed with a demon or demons in a special degree, but to those also who, being heathen and outside the covenant of Christian sanctifying grace, were, to say the least, at the mercy of evil spirits. This conception of the position of the heathen may appear strange and repugnant to modern European Christians; and they may easily make the mistake of thinking it an unworthy relic of superstition. Those, however, who live and work among the heathen know that the primitive view is a true view; for they have plenty of evidence continually before them of the power of evil spirits in heathen surroundings, and even over those who are turning from them to the sphere of the grace of Christ.[23]

Thus exorcism was a preliminary procedure to baptism. The exorcist in time became a regular officer of the Church, whose main duty, apart from special cases, was to deal with the catechumens, and exorcize them repeatedly as part of their preparation for the font. As early as the beginning of the third century we hear from Tertullian of the ceremonial laying on of his hands.[24]

In all these cases the action may be said to be in one or other form interpretative.

Clearer still and more familiar are such actions as the joining of the hands of bride and bridegroom at marriage, or the casting of earth at burial. The officiant in each case interprets his words by his action, so that even a bystander, ignorant of the language which he spoke, could understand what was being said and done. The action in each case is, properly speaking, the action of the priest, though the present Prayer-Book has in the latter case transferred the responsibility to 'some standing by.'[25]

In a special sense the ancient use of Holy Water is interpretative. Like the use of oil, it has a quasi-sacramental character,[26] since it is the outward sign of an inward effect. The hallowed oil or water accompanies blessings or other operative words, and emphasizes in a visible way their meaning. And when there are no words, as in the most usual sprinkling of Holy Water, yet the idea is plainly conveyed. The water is the sign of hallowing, and the use of it has the nature of an acted prayer, or exorcism, or blessing.

Many other picturesque ceremonies have the same purpose, such as the receiving of ashes, the bearing of palms, the creeping to the cross, among the primitive devotions laid by at the Reformation.[27] The same or similar objects have been aimed at in recent days by such novel ceremonies as the penitents' form, the Way of the Cross, the Flower Service, and others. They appeal to the simpler instincts of devotion, and provide for them intelligible methods of expression.

It may easily happen in course of time that interpretative ceremonial may cease to interpret, just as utilitarian ceremonial may cease to have any utility ; and a question arises as to its retention in the altered circumstances, similar to that already discussed in the analogous case in the eighth chapter.[28] The ceremony will perhaps on losing its original interpretative value acquire a fresh one. The use of incense, for example, which was in one way honorific, became, as it was adapted to fresh circumstances, expressive of fresh ideas. It associated itself especially with the idea of prayer ; and just as the incense in Revelation viii. 4 expressed in visible form the ascent of the prayers of the saints to the throne of

God, so the censing of the sanctuary at the beginning of Holy Communion created as it were an atmosphere of prayer. Still more obvious was this connexion when the incense was offered at the versicle of Evensong, ' Let my prayer be set forth in Thy sight as the incense,' and during the *Magnificat* that followed. Towards the end of the Middle Ages this use of incense became more closely connected with the altar, till it passed into being a censing of the altar. The idea, however, which it expressed remained the same, and even in this shape the incense is expressive of prayer, and the object is to create a visible atmosphere of devotion.[29]

Interpretative ceremonial may therefore acquire a new and valuable significance in addition to, or in place of, its original significance. But it may also lose its significance altogether, and so become what is called in the preface to the Prayer-Book a dark and dumb ceremony. In such cases even the most conservative mind must be content to forgo it. But an old ceremony must be well tested, and perhaps given a chance to recover its meaning and value, before it is condemned as dumb or dark ; and due disregard must be paid to those who only think it dumb and dark because they are constitutionally deaf to the appeal of such things and blind to their beauties.

Lastly, it is interesting to note that in some cases the ceremonial instead of interpreting already existing words has created formulas to express in speech what so far had been only represented by act. Thus, at such points as vesting, the approach to the altar, the lavatory, the mixing of the chalice, the censing, the offertory, communion, etc., there grew up in later mediaeval days, and much subsequent to the ceremonies, various sets of prayers and devotions introduced in order to give utterance to the thoughts expressed in the ceremonial action. These devotions were at first of a purely private character. As they became at all general, they began to win their way into the Service-books ; but there was no uniformity.

In fact, the main diversity of rite in the later Middle Ages, so far as the Ordinary of the Mass was concerned, lay in these new and secondary devotions created by the ceremonial. This process represents an inversion of the more ancient and natural procedure by which the ceremonial came into being, in order to express what was already in the words. In the study either of ritual or of ceremonial the distinction is one to be remembered.

CHAPTER XI

SYMBOLICAL CEREMONIAL

IT is a little difficult to define precisely what should be included under the above heading and what not. The essence of symbolical ceremonial is that it involves the importation of some fresh ceremony not otherwise demanded on other grounds, which serves at the same time as a symbol to introduce a fresh idea not hitherto present. It differs therefore, on the one hand, from interpretative ceremonial, for that is only the use of ceremony to interpret an already inherent idea. It differs, on the other hand, from the mystical explanation of ceremonial, for that is only the attaching of new meanings to ceremonies which already exist on other grounds. In other words, the characteristic feature is, that in symbolical ceremonial both the symbol and the thing symbolized are imported simultaneously.

If the difficulty of making a clear theoretical division is considerable, the difficulty of distinguishing in practice what is symbolical from other classes of ceremonial is greater still. It requires not only a keen analysis, but sometimes also a thorough knowledge of the history of the ceremonies in question, to be able to determine to which class they should be assigned. For example, when S. Patrick, according to the legend, picked the shamrock and based upon it an exposition of the doctrine of the Trinity, he was giving to the trefoil a mystical interpretation, because he was attaching a new meaning to something which existed independently of it. When, however, in subsequent ages an artist paints a shamrock as part of a scheme of church decoration as an emblem of the Trinity, he is using it symbolically, not mystically, for he is introducing the symbol and the idea simultaneously where neither of them was before.

Historically speaking, therefore, the symbolical and the mystical may be said to generate one another. For by first acquiring a new mystical meaning an object may come to be regarded as a symbol ; and then, having been introduced as a symbol with the new meaning attached to it, it may attach to itself other additional meanings, which will be rightly described as mystical.

But to make the point clearer it is perhaps better to pursue the subject back a little further.

It is a universal custom of mankind to express an idea by a symbol. In fact there is no other way than this of giving a graphic expression to an idea. Thus the alphabet is nothing else but a series of symbols ; and though many of the letters have ceased to express an idea singly, they do so in combination ; and it seems that the letters are all descended from primitive symbols, which in their origin each singly represented an idea, just as a hieroglyphic does or a Chinese character. The same fact is even more clearly seen in the case of numerical figures. The Arabic figures are each of them symbols conveying a certain idea. Indeed, in cases as familiar as these the idea of symbolism almost entirely dies out ; the connexion between the symbol and the idea conveyed by it becomes so close that we consider them practically identical. Thus we no longer say of 4 that it symbolizes or represents ' four,' but that it *is* ' four.' It has acquired a primary meaning devoid of the suggestion of symbolism; and we thenceforward only say ' 4 symbolizes so and so,' or ' four is the symbol of so and so ' when we have begun to attach further and secondary meanings to the symbol and the idea of ' four.'

Symbolism in this secondary and more usual sense is not at all peculiar to the sphere of religious ideas, though it is there that it finds its fullest development. Numbers have their symbolism apart from religious influence, and have had at least since the days of Pythagoras. The symbolism which they bear in the religious sphere is only part of a general symbolism which has belonged to them probably since primitive times.

Personal names, again, may also be taken as examples of a symbolism which is wider than the specially religious sphere. They may even be used as a further instance to show the difference between what is interpretative and what is symbolical. When Isaac's first-born received the name of Esau—the Red—it was in regard to his already existing characteristics ; but when Jacob's youngest son was called by his mother Ben-oni—the son of my sorrow—and by his father Benjamin—the son of my right hand—the name was in each case symbolical, for it brought with it a fresh connotation and fastened a new idea upon the child.[1]

It is not surprising that the religious sphere should be one in which symbolism specially germinates, for it is a sphere fruitful in freshness of thought. Symbolism thus comes to have a natural place in the development of Christian ceremonial ; and in divine worship the instances are frequent where a rite is enriched by the acquisition of symbolical actions and a group of ideas introduced along with them.

It is best to cite first of all instances that are clear, where there is no ambiguity, either on the score of history or analysis, concerning the class to which the ceremony belongs.

Among the ceremonies which from early times have been attached to the rite of Holy Baptism, one of the most poetical is the giving of honey and milk to the new Christians as they came fresh from the font and fresh from their first communion. The ceremony is of great antiquity, since even by the beginning of the third century two varying explanations were current as to the meaning of the symbolism. Tertullian mentions it twice ; and one of the passages seems to suggest the exposition found elsewhere, viz. that the newly baptized are like infants fed on children's food.[2] Later on Jerome in citing Tertullian's other passage gives it this sense ; [3] and this is also the explanation which finds most favour in the *Hippolytean Church Order*.[4] On the other hand, Clement of Alexandria connects the symbolism with the entry to the land of promise, the land that flows with milk and honey.[5] This seems also to be alluded to in the *Hippolytean Church Order*, and is the explanation which was given in the Latin prayer used in the Canon of the Mass for the benediction of the water, milk, and honey down to the time when the custom disappeared, probably at the end of the sixth century.[6] But whichever of these explanations be taken, it remains equally true that the ceremony is essentially symbolical in its origin. It would have no place in the rite except as introducing a new and suitable thought which was not there already, but was imported with the ceremony in a form that could be readily understood.

Baptism was rich in such ceremonial ; for indeed it is natural that sacraments, being of themselves so closely akin to symbolism, should attract to themselves symbolical ceremonial. Moreover, the immersion was itself, from the first, symbolical of the death to sin. The renunciation of the devil and the confession of the Christian faith are primitive features of the rite, and, like the ceremony just discussed, are found in Tertullian's account of baptism.[7] The African Father merely alludes to them in the course of a rapid summary, and describes none of the ceremonial belonging to them. But in the contemporary *Hippolytean Church Order* it is directed that the candidates should face west for the renunciation, and then turn eastwards to make their confession of faith.[8] This action is best explained as a piece of symbolical ceremonial. The points of the compass acquire very early in the thought of man a mystical meaning. The east is the quarter of the rising sun, and therefore the quarter from which good comes ; while the west, on the contrary, is the quarter of the setting sun, the quarter of failure and lost causes. From this mystical interpretation the east and the west became familiar symbols of spiritual success and failure, and so forth. A turning to the west is therefore naturally introduced with a renunciation of evil, and a turning to the east with an acceptance of good.

If this action stood alone in Christian ceremonial, it might be questionable whether it should not be classed as interpretative; for to any one who is familiar with the recognized symbolism of the points of the compass, the movement expounds the words that are being said. But the eastward attitude reappears in many parts of Christian ceremonial. Just as the devout Jew turned for his prayer towards the Temple,[9] and the Mohammedan follows the line of the Kiblah in his mosque that indicates the direction of Mecca, so the Christian instinct led worshippers to turn eastward for their prayer; and they adopted the custom though it brought upon them considerable suspicion of being sun-worshippers. It was well established as a personal custom in the third century;[10] and a century later at any rate the orientation of churches began.[11] With this is connected the eastward position of the celebrant at the Eucharist. When it was customary for him to face the people there was a tendency to place the altar at the west end of the church, so as to secure that he faced eastwards. When his position was otherwise, and he stood at the head of the people facing in the same direction as they, then the altar was set at the east end of the church. When a further change was made at the Reformation, this symbolism ceased, and the new position at the north side of a table set tablewise was substituted in order to symbolize other ideas. With the change in the placing of the Holy Table, which brought it back again to the altarwise position with which we are familiar, the north side became an impossible position, and the eastward position with its symbolism returned. And it is valuable now, not merely for its original symbolism, but also because it is one of the bits of ceremonial universal in the Catholic Church, and therefore testifies to the unity of the eucharistic service throughout Catholic Christendom.[12]

When this widespread use of the symbolism of the east is taken into account, it is natural also to classify the ceremony of turning west and east in baptism as symbolical rather than interpretative. After these two baptismal ceremonies, one of which may be taken to be an undoubted case of symbolical ceremonial, while the other illustrates the difficulty of classifying by hard and fast lines, two further ceremonies may be cited from the same service. The use of the chrysom or white dress was adopted in order to show the baptismal purity. This is the explanation that S. Cyril of Jerusalem gives to his catechumens (348), and it is an obvious one.[13] Colours, like the other things already cited, have mystical meanings attached to them ; they then become the symbols of those ideas, and are introduced, as in this case, in order to bring in the ideas. White has naturally the meaning of purity, and therefore the clothing in a white garment, or 'chrysom' as it was called later, was a natural piece of symbolical ceremonial. Its omission from the Prayer-Book rite of 1552, after it had been retained in the book rite of 1549, is a loss that may well be deplored.

This symbolism is paralleled by other uses of white, which, though less of the nature of ceremonial actions, are too closely connected with ceremonial to be passed over in silence here. Clement of Alexandria recommends white clothing to Christians in general as suitable to the uniformity and simplicity of the truth,[14] quoting the white robe of the Ancient of Days in Daniel vii and the white robe of the Apocalypse (*Rev.* vi. 9, 11). The white dress of a bride was a natural extension of this, and seemed to find a sanction in the 'fine linen, clean and white' in which the bride is arrayed in Revelation xix. 8.

The earliest specialization of dress on the part of the officiating clergy lies also in the assignment of a white dress as becoming his office.[15] This precedes any special

cut of ecclesiastical vestments, for it was only as the
ordinary Roman dress adopted in the early days went
out of common use that it acquired, by surviving among
the clergy, any specially clerical or ministerial connotation ;[16] but the colour is special, and sometimes it is
also contemplated that special clothes will be reserved
for use in celebrating.

At a later date the other colours brought their symbolism into connexion with Christian worship, and these
evolved in the later Middle Ages the liturgical colour
sequences based upon an elaborate symbolism of colours.[17]

The further baptismal ceremony that remains to be
cited is the giving of a lighted taper to the newly baptized.
This is alluded to by S. Ambrose and S. Gregory Nazianzen in the fourth century, and became a very usual
ceremony in the East and in the West. Already the
connexion had established itself between illumination
and baptism. The beginnings of this connexion may be
seen as far back as the two passages in the Epistle to the
Hebrews, where the Christians are appealed to as men
who 'after being illuminated' had 'endured a great
fight of afflictions,' and where being 'enlightened' is
enumerated among the stages of Christian life, after
which it is said to be impossible to renew again the fallen
unto repentance.[18] It soon became natural to use this
as technical phraseology : 'those who are being enlightened' was a phrase descriptive of the catechumens,
and 'those who have been enlightened' of the baptized.
The connexion between symbol and idea was thus clearly
established ; the ceremony of the candle was a natural
one to introduce, and no one could mistake the meaning
that it brought with it.

This ceremony formed one of the points of conflict
between two great French exponents of ceremonial at
the beginning of the eighteenth century. Dom Claude
de Vert, the Cluniac monk, wrote his *Explication simple
litterale et historique des Cérémonies de l'Église* in a state of
reaction against the mystical tendencies of many of his

predecessors in that sphere of labour, who vied with one another in giving fantastical reasons to explain the simplest and most natural ceremonial. He therefore tended to ascribe everything as far as possible to merely utilitarian considerations, and to deny in a great degree the symbolical. His account of these candles is, that they were given unlighted originally, and only lighted when they were required to enable the newly baptized to go through the darkness of the night of Easter Even from the font to the altar. This contention he based upon the practice of the ninth century, when it is clear the candles were given unlighted in some places, and only lighted at the *Agnus Dei* of the Mass. This argument proved too much ; for if this was the case, the very time at which the light of the candles was required was long past before the lighting took place. And De Vert's opponent Le Brun, the Oratorian, was not slow to show the absurd extreme to which in this instance De Vert's zeal for historical truth had pushed him, by asking why, if light was needed in going from the font, it was not needed in going to it ; and if needed by the newly baptized, why not equally by the clergy, godparents, and faithful. In this instance at any rate the worthy monk's zeal outran his discretion, though he may easily be pardoned for his wish to recall the criticism of ceremonial from the fantastic sphere into which it had strayed, and even more for his success in recovering it.[19]

Hitherto it has been the Baptismal Service that has been mainly in question ; but it is clear that symbolical ceremonial has gathered no less round the Eucharist, and especially at its central point. The action of our Lord Himself in the ceremony of the fraction was in some degree symbolical, for it brought with it a new idea, and connected the whole action with His crucifixion. In reproducing our Lord's example in this respect, the Church seems (as has been noted) to have been influenced more by a wish to follow our Lord's example, than by the wish to make a symbolical fraction. The former seems to have been the dominant consideration, though of course it by no means excludes the other. The fraction therefore has been dealt with under the heading of interpretative ceremonial ; so it is enough to call attention to it under this heading also.

The case stands otherwise with the chalice. Here too, in using a mixture of wine and water and not simple wine, the Church is probably following our Lord's example. But in this case imitation is a motive of only secondary importance. In retaining the mixed chalice the chief motive has been a symbolical one, at any rate from very early times. Though imitation of our Lord, and perhaps, too, practical convenience, may have had something to do with the custom in its origin, its universal retention and diffusion are due to the symbolism. It is therefore more proper to classify it under this heading than to treat it as a utilitarian or interpretative ceremony, to which subsequently, after it had been adopted on one of those grounds, a secondary and mystical meaning was attached. In other words, it is a case where the meaning attached to the ceremony is its *raison d'être* and not an afterthought.

It is true that the earliest evidence of the custom has with it no such meaning expressed. Justin Martyr merely says ' there is brought in to him who presides over the brethren bread and a cup of water and wine.' The two other passages of the same writer where it is mentioned are equally simple ; but the description was written for the heathen, and no explanation would be rightly expected in such a context. Justin confines himself to explaining the relation of the Blessed Sacrament to the Body and Blood of Christ. Equally simple is the reference to the mixed chalice by Irenaeus, who is concerned with the same great point and pays no attention to the smaller one.[20]

S. Cyprian in one of his letters deals at great length with the mixed chalice, and insists upon it, not in order to secure the presence of the water, but in order to secure the presence of the wine, and to stop a most reprehensible custom which was found in some places, probably as a relic of heretical rites, of consecrating and administering water only. He therefore insists that our Lord's example must be followed; and that, if there is no wine this is not the case, for our Lord took wine. Such an argument as this cannot fairly be taken to prove that S. Cyprian, if asked to explain the presence of the water, would merely have said that it was a following of Christ's example.

On the contrary, when he does explain the mixture, his explanation is different. He says that our Lord *in His passion* fulfilled what had been said before (*Prov.* ix. 1) of Him : ' Wisdom hath builded her house . . . she hath mingled her wine.' He alludes in fact to the view that the mixed chalice represented the blood and water that flowed from our Lord's side. This view is so natural and so widespread that it may well be thought to have been responsible for the ceremony of the mixed chalice as a practically universal custom. No doubt it is true that other meanings were attached to the mixture. S. Cyprian himself in the same letter has another to give. The water represents the people, and the wine the blood of Christ. The mixture represents the indissoluble union of Christ with His people, of the believers with Him in Whom they believe.[21] But the accumulation of secondary meanings in this way is a very familiar feature of Christian thought, and is in no way of necessity derogatory to the primary meaning. S. Cyprian adds a new mystical interpretation to a piece of symbolical ceremonial ; this proceeding is of constant occurrence, as will be shown in the next chapter. And it is noticeable here that the original symbolism is so well known that S. Cyprian need only allude to it, while his mystical interpretation requires a full exposition. The original symbolism is found constantly recurring in later writers in a more or less explicit form,[22] and in a closely allied form, explained as a reference to the Eucharist and Baptism, in the *Testament of the Lord*.[23] It is again found combined with the reference to the union of Christ with His people in S. German of Paris (*c.* 576). But Cyprian's example was a strong lead, and was followed by Isidore of Seville and others after him, down to the English *Rationale* of 1541.[24]

Another group of symbolical actions at the very centre of the Eucharist comprises the various ways of dealing with the sacrament between consecration and communion. The most general ceremony to be noticed is the commixture—that is, the uniting of the two sacred species by placing part of a host into the chalice. This usage is common to both Eastern and Western rites,[25] and is to be carefully distinguished from three other usages which are outwardly identical, and were even in early days constantly confused, but had a different history and purport. These are (1) the placing of some of the consecrated bread into unconsecrated wine for the purpose of effecting its consecration;[26] (2) the placing into the newly consecrated chalice the *sancta*, or portion reserved from a previous occasion, and now brought thus into the consecration in order to emphasize the unity of the sacrifice which is in progress with the previous Eucharist; (3) the sending of the *fermentum* to the local churches from the central Eucharist of the bishop or pope.[27] The symbolism of the commixture proper was the reunion of our Lord's body and soul in the resurrection. The separate consecration of the host and chalice had so far emphasized the separation of the Flesh and Blood and the thought of our Lord's death. The ceremony of the commixture owes its existence to the wish to redress the balance by a ceremony which should symbolize our Lord's risen life.[28]

The second and third of the other forms of inserting the host into the chalice may equally be taken as an example of symbolical ceremonial. The *sancta* was reserved from one Mass to another, or the *fermentum* was distributed from the pope's altar to others, purely as a symbol of unity. But these customs were much less widespread, and therefore are less conspicuous instances.

Moreover, they have disappeared, while the commixture proper has survived.

More elaborate still is the symbolism which dictated several curious methods of handling and arranging the fragments of the host after the fraction. According to the Liturgy of S. Chrysostom the four fragments are simply arranged in a cross;[29] but in the Mozarabic rite the nine fragments into which the host is subdivided are each named after one of the 'nine mysteries' of the Creed, which has just been recited over the consecrated elements, and they are then elaborately arranged in this order on the paten so as to form a rough cross.

```
         C 1
      M 6 N 2 R 7
         C 3 G 8
         A 4
         P 5
```

The ninth,* which rests temporarily under the one marked G, is used for the commixture.[30] These methods are survivals from an early time when many and strange arrangements of the fragments were common. The cruciform arrangement was ordered by the Council of Tours in 567, no doubt in order to put an end to varieties and probably superstitious patterns.[31] But in far-off Ireland the old ways went on; the number of fragments varied from five on ordinary days to sixty-five on the three chief festivals of Easter, Whitsun Day, and Christmas, and the complexity of the patterns varied accordingly.[32]

It must be remembered in this connexion, that at the time when these ceremonies were introduced the questionable custom had not come in of substituting a number of small wafers for the eucharistic loaf; still less had an unfortunate distinction been created between the celebrant's wafer and that of the communicant. The celebrant selected from among the loaves offered one to be consecrated; this was the 'one loaf' of which S. Paul

* The names in full are—1 Corporatio, 2 Nativitas, 3 Circumcisio, 4 Apparitio, 5 Passio, 6 Mors, 7 Resurrectio, 8 Gloria, 9 Regnum.

SYMBOLICAL CEREMONIAL 139

speaks, from which all (so far as possible) communicated. Besides the fractions for ceremonial purposes, there were also the fractions for the practical purpose of subdividing the host among the communicants. But all shared the one. Here was a genuine piece of symbolism which it is a great pity to surrender. This feeling for the unity of the sacramental loaf can be traced back step by step to S. Paul's time. It is no real compensation by way of symbolism to be told that the individual round wafer now symbolizes the coin which the communicant in fact offers instead of his obley loaf. The First Edwardine Prayer-Book took a step in the right direction when it said that each wafer should be subdivided. It is easily possible to go beyond this, and to use for the consecration either wafer or bread which is ready to be subdivided into a number of small pieces. Unless the number of communicants is large, it ought still to be possible to have actually the 'one loaf' to be consecrated in one whole and then broken into its parts for distribution. This is not a case in which the Church as a whole has altered its custom, for in every Eastern rite the host is, according to the old plan and symbolism, subdivided for communion. The changes made at the Reformation form a safe guide as to the direction in which it is desirable to move; and conformity to the Eastern and primitive use is far better than conformity to the late mediaeval and Western.

Many further instances might be cited of symbolical ceremonial, some quite clear, others more doubtful. For in fact many of them are capable of being variously classified. The use of lights is a good case of a doubtful point. Jerome, for example, in one place repudiates all but a utilitarian use of lights, while immediately afterwards he speaks of the lights burnt everywhere in the East at the reading of the Gospel as being, not utilitarian, but symbolical of the joy of the Gospel.[33] These instances, however, must suffice, and it is time now to make still more clear the distinction between the symbolical and the mystical by treating more fully of the latter.

CHAPTER XII

THE MYSTICAL INTERPRETATION OF CEREMONIAL

MYSTICAL interpretation is an attempt to give not the primary meaning of things, but their hidden and recondite meanings. It is addressed not to the plain man, but to the man who is initiated, who has a certain insight into what lies below the surface, and an interest in the hidden principles and obscure workings of things. Such a habit of mind lies somewhat remote from the average Englishman, who is practical, not thoughtful, who hates to reflect, but loves to act. But it is not by any means a rare or a despicable part of human character. Consequently mystical interpretation has from the earliest times been applied to all the objects of thought, and has won in different times and places a strangely varying meed of respect.

As applied to religious thought, this method has the highest sanctions. The literature of the Old Testament is full of it ; and the Jewish exegetes, in applying this method of interpretation to the sacred Scriptures themselves, were only following the example set forth in the very literature which they were interpreting.

The use of this method has further sanction in the New Testament. Our Lord's interpretation of ' an eye for an eye and a tooth for a tooth ' was certainly not the literary or primary one. In the writings of S. Paul there are many uses of Scripture which more obviously still rest on mystical interpretation. Some are as bold, or, the scoffer might say, as wild, as any mediaeval fancies. The two sons of Abraham are interpreted to represent the Law and the Gospel in Galatians iv—to say nothing of the more mysterious identification of Hagar with Mount Sinai. The children of Israel drank in the wilderness of a ' spiritual rock that followed them ; and that Rock was Christ.' Here is mystical interpretation in unmistakable form.[1]

Later, and especially under Alexandrine influence, this became a recognized method of interpretation of Scripture. The Bible, like man, is composed of three elements, and needs to be interpreted literally and historically (this corresponds to the body), morally (to the soul), and spiritually (to the spirit). Such a view as this, which was formulated by Origen,[2] opens the way wide to mystical interpretation ; and it was a way which was long popular in the biblical sphere before it became so popular in the liturgical. There can, however, be little doubt that as soon as there were any settled Christian ceremonies at all, they began to acquire mystical meanings side by side with their primary intentions and objects. Already attention has been drawn to the close connexion, in one relation or another, which subsists between the visions of the Apocalypse and Christian worship. Now the record of these visions is full of mystical interpretation, and especially in the parts which have affinity to the worship.

The seven lamps are the seven Spirits of God (iv. 5) ; the golden bowls full of incense are the prayers of the saints (v. 8) ; the fine linen is the righteousness of saints (xix. 8), and so forth. Thenceforward there is a continuous tradition of the mystical interpretation of ceremonies, welcomed and elaborated in congenial circles, looked upon with wonder and some amusement in uncongenial circles, but always and inevitably there, and to be reckoned with. When it has been adversely criticized, this has generally been the result of a misunderstanding of its position. The mystical interpretation, let it be said again, is always a secondary and additional meaning ; and it does not claim to be anything else but that. The ceremony has a primary meaning or origin, which may be, according to our previous classification, either utilitarian, interpretative, or symbolical. This does not preclude its having mystical meanings; on the contrary, it is the necessary preliminary to a mystical interpretation. When the primary and the secondary are thus kept distinct, there is no confusion, and each is found to have a very proper sphere of its own. Mistakes are made and mutual misunderstandings begin only when the two are confused—when the prosaic man is so full of the prosaic meaning that he is contemptuous of any other, or when the obscurantist is so much in love with the secondary meaning that he ignores the primary.

After this attempt to reconcile the two opposite tempers to toleration of one another, it will now be easier to give some account of what has actually been the case with the mystical interpretation of religious ceremonial.

In the early days of the Christian Church ceremonial was only slowly acquiring fixity; rite and ceremony were alike left to be settled partly by tradition and partly by individual judgement. Even when some fixity was reached, the worship of the Church on both its ritual and its ceremonial side was not a subject of comment or discussion. The early Christians did not talk about worship; they simply worshipped. The explanation of the familiar ceremonies was not a point of interest to them; they were clear enough for practical purposes, and no theory or comment was needed. Thus even Origen in Alexandria itself could be content not to inquire as to their meaning.[3]

'Among ecclesiastical observances,' he says, 'there are many of this sort which every one of necessity carries out, though all by no means see the reason. I suppose, for example, that it would not be easy for every one to give the reason why we kneel to pray, or why we choose the east out of the various possible directions in which alone to say our prayers. Who again would find it easy to explain the meaning of the reception of the

Eucharist, or of the ceremonies involved in it, or again of the performance of Baptism, the words, the acts, the series of questions and answers?'

If this was the attitude of mind towards the ceremonial of worship that was found in Origen—a man above all others inclined to inquiry and interpretation of all sorts— it is not surprising that the early Church was as a whole, with reference to its services, like a child that has not yet become self-conscious. It did the things in obedience to tradition or instinct, and did not ask the reason why.

There are, however, even in the first three centuries some sparse signs to be noted that the habit of mystical interpretation was by no means in abeyance, though it was not to the fore. The instance of the mixed chalice, which has been already cited, shows this. S. Cyprian puts a new interpretation upon the custom by taking it to represent the union of Christ with His people. This interpretation recurs again later, and side by side with the original symbolism of the blood and water, in an anonymous writing of the fifth or sixth century.[4] But even so the limit of the possibilities of mystical interpretation is not reached. There is no need to be restricted ; if one such interpretation is admissible, equally so are others. This is of the essence of the conception. Consequently mystical interpretations multiply almost indefinitely.

When the fourth century is reached the material is far more copious, and there is much more evidence of the prevalence of mystical interpretation. But still there is nothing systematic. The Church is not in general interested in such exposition ; and though the several ceremonies have acquired certain mystical meanings, yet when the services are to be explained, as for example in the courses of instruction to catechumens, it is the plain literal meaning for the most part that has to be set out. Thus S. Cyril of Jerusalem [5] explains to his catechumens the symbolism which led to the introduction of the lavatory before the priest begins the central part of the Liturgy and of the kiss of peace. He then passes to a very literal and straightforward exposition of the *Sursum corda* and the rest of the 'Anaphora' or central section of the service, *i.e.* of the rite, not of ceremonies. Yet a little bit of mystical interpretation comes out, where he tells them in communicating ' to make the left hand a throne for the right which is to receive the King, and so to receive the Body of Christ in the hollow of the hand.' The exposition of S. Ambrose in his *De Mysteriis* is even more matter of fact, and the book of instructions for neophytes based on this work of S. Ambrose a century later, the Pseudo-Ambrosian *De Sacramentis* has practically nothing further in the way of mystical interpretation, though it expounds some of the points which we have cited as symbolical.

In the Church Orders [6] belonging to this century the tendency is more marked. Thus in the *Apostolic Constitutions* the deacon's ministry to the bishop at the altar is compared to the relation of the Son to the Father, and more strangely still, the work of the deaconess to the work of the Holy Spirit.[7] A similar instinct dictates in the *Testament of the Lord* that the church is to have three entrances as a type of the Trinity, while the baptistery is to be twenty-one cubits in length and twelve in breadth to match in number the prophets and the apostles.[8]

While such sporadic evidences of the tendency belong to the first four centuries, it is necessary to descend as far as the end of the fifth century or the beginning of the sixth before there can be found any systematic application of the principle of mystical interpretation to the ceremonial of the Church. An earlier chapter (v) has already given some account of this as it figures in Narsai. It is then found in the writings which pass under the name of Dionysius the Areopagite,[9] a collection of four anonymous treatises expounding a view of Christian thought which has much in common with neoplatonist views, and may be called the first systematic exposition of Christian mysticism. It is natural to expect to find in such

MYSTICAL INTERPRETATION OF CEREMONIAL 145

a writer some mystical interpretation of services and ceremonial if he touches them at all ; and he does so in his *De Ecclesiastica Hierarchia*. The treatment is methodical. He takes as his topics Baptism, the Eucharist, Unction, Ordination, the Monastic Profession, and the Funeral Services. In each case he deals with the topic in a threefold manner, first expounding its general utility, then describing the rite, and finally giving a mystical interpretation of it. The greater part is concerned more with ritual than ceremonial ; for example, in the chapter devoted to the Eucharist the bulk of the exposition has to do with the rationale of the service in its broad outlines[10]—the psalmody, the lessons, the dismissals, the offertory, the diptychs, the consecration, communion, thanksgiving. But ceremonial is to a certain extent included ; for example, the natural explanation is given of the lavatory and the kiss of peace. The method of interpretation may be called mystical, more because of the general habit of mind and style of the writer, than because there is much of mystical interpretation in the strict sense. There are, however, the beginnings of this, as the following passage shows.[11] It is a commentary on the opening ceremony, in which 'the priest having accomplished his pious prayer at the holy altar, starts from thence censing, and making a complete circuit of the holy place returns again to the holy altar.'

'The blessed Godhead who rules over all, though in Its divine mercy It issues forth into fellowship with the holy ones who partake of It, yet It does not depart out of Its own proper and changeless position and state ; similarly It shines forth for the godly minded while truly remaining in Itself and without at all deserting Its own proper identity.'

Two other mystical interpretations of the same ceremony follow which are based upon the same general idea —the compatibility of unity with diversity ; one of them concerning the nature of the service, and the other concerning the pontiff who is a mystic and his con-

L

descension to the poorer conceptions of those who are not as enlightened as himself.

The example thus set and carried on was maintained in the East by a series of writers of whom Germanus has already been cited as an example.[12] For the present purpose it will be best not to follow out the development in the East, but to turn to the West, where the detailed application began rather earlier than in the East, so far as extant treatises are concerned. The exposition of the Gallican liturgy attributed to S. German of Paris belongs possibly to the latter part of the sixth century; and, if so, it is the earliest available systematic exposition of a Western liturgy on mystical lines in the detailed and developed style which grew out of the more general exposition of pseudo-Dionysius.[13] The interest of this document is all the greater because information with regard to the ancient Gallican rite is so rare, and because apart from the exposition it would be difficult to get any full and connected idea of the service which was superseded when the Roman rite spread throughout Gaul in the days of Pepin and Charlemagne.

Here every item of the service has its mystical interpretation. The opening antiphon represents the patriarchs because it comes before the reading of the Old Testament. The Trisagion is sung in Greek as an introduction to the Greek New Testament scriptures, and is sung in Latin too to signify the union of the two Testaments. The Amen at the end being a Hebrew word recalls with the Greek and Latin the title set over our Lord's cross in the three languages. The three boys who sing the *Kyrie* may similarly recall the three languages, or the three ages of the world—before the law, under the law, and under grace.

So the little tract goes on. Enough has been quoted to show the detailed character of the interpretation, and its application even to small features of the rite. There is less notice taken of the ceremonial, but where this is alluded to, its treatment is on the same scale. The procession that leads up to the Gospel is like the power of Christ triumphing over the grave; the seven lights are the seven gifts of the Holy Spirit; the ascent of the deacon into the ambo to read the Gospel is like the return of our Lord to His Father's throne. The mixed chalice has the two interpretations of S. Cyprian; the commixture signifies the union of the heavenly and the earthly —this is but another form of the symbolism already noted in this ceremony — and has no further mystical interpretation.

Moreover, the ornaments now begin to receive a mystical meaning. The vessel in the form of a tower, in which the oblation was brought at the solemn procession of the offertory, is said to have that shape because the rock-hewn sepulchre of our Lord was in that form. This explanation takes for granted the view that the vessel containing the host represents the grave; and this mystical view dictates a piece of symbolism, viz. that the shape should be made to suggest the current conceptions of the sepulchre. It is, in short, a case where the mystical generates the symbolical.

There is no chronological sequence in the interpretation such as may be found in some other more systematic explanations; for after this reference to the tomb the exposition harks back to the passion for its explanation of the paten, to the seamless robe as the counterpart of the *palla linostima* or veil of mixed material made of flax and wool used to cover the oblation; while the *palla corporalis*, made of linen, on which the oblation rests, suggests the linen clothes in which our Lord's body was wrapped for the burial. There is further mention of a decorated covering of silk or embroidery, with jewels or gold, whose richness represents the glories of the resurrection and our Lord's abode in heaven, or else is a following of the divine directions given in the Law for the levitical vestments.

A similar character pervades S. German's exposition of the ceremonies of Baptism. The symbolism of unction is explained, and the feeling which led to the covering of the Gospel-book with a red veil as an emblem of the blood of Christ. More strictly mystical in character is the explanation given of the cushions and soft towels provided at the baptism; these must in fact be utilitarian in origin, but S. German explains them as part of the plan of treating neophytes like children.

'The catechumen is tender and new in the faith as an infant is tender and new in body; therefore his limbs must, like a child's, rest upon cushions so as to be better cared for.'

The analogies which the baptismal rite draws from the Old Testament—the identification of Easter Even with the Exodus, Baptism with the passage of the Red Sea, and so forth—make it natural to find traces of similar references in the ceremonial. The Easter *pallium* is to have bells on it like those of the high priest; the memory of S. John Baptist is recalled by the girdle of the white vestment worn by the priest who baptizes; while the Easter note is preserved in the white colour of the vestments—a colour chosen to copy the angel who announced the resurrection, and also because white is the colour of joy.

The exposition of Baptism passes along this line of thought into an exposition of the vestments of the clergy. There is no need to describe it in detail, but it deserves special mention, because it is one of the earliest signs that the vestments have ceased to be the common dress of the people, and are now a survival that is becoming an official custom. With this change there goes also the tendency to explain the vestments by reference to the levitical garments. As long as the dress was familiar and in common use it needed no explanation. From the sixth century onward the explanations, levitical or mystical, show that it has become a ceremonial dress and needs to be justified by religious exposition of some sort. Thus:

'The chasuble, also called *amphibalum*,[14] which the priest wears, being all of one piece, was clearly first instituted by Moses the Lawgiver. The Lord prescribed the unusual garment in order that the priest might wear such a dress as the people would never venture to wear. It was without sleeves, because the priest has more to do with blessing than with serving. It was all of one piece, not slit nor open, because there are many hidden mysteries of Holy Scripture which the learned priest should hide, as it were under a seal, and because he should keep the unity of the faith and not fall away into heresies or schisms.'

It has been worth while to deal at some length with these two letters of S. German, not only because they give the earliest systematic exposition of the rites and ceremonies in the West, but also because they contain the germ of all future developments along these lines. They deal with ritual and ceremonial alike; they deal with the ornaments as well as with the ceremonies; they contain the rudiments of two of the most popular methods of mystical interpretation in the Middle Ages, viz. the referring of Christian rites, ceremonies, and ornaments, either to the levitical system or to the passion, death, and resurrection of our Lord. Since these all emerge here, there will be the less necessity to trace them out in later writers.

But while S. German was the pioneer of later developments, he was not their parent. His work dealt with a liturgy which disappeared into remote corners; and therefore the future of his mystical interpretation lay not with the direct line, but with collaterals. Moreover, he was not himself a person of so great reputation that his modest little work could exercise a widespread influence. The case stood otherwise with Isidore of Seville (†636), who must be pointed out as the lasting progenitor of the mediaeval mystical interpretation.[15]

It is surprising that he was able to take such a position, for he too expounded a disappearing liturgy, viz. the Spanish form of that group of liturgies which was called Gallican in France, and Mozarabic in Spain, or Ambrosian at Milan, but which can best be negatively defined as Western but non-Roman. But apart from this work

S. Isidore had a worldwide reputation. Moreover, the part of his exposition which refers purely and solely to the non-Roman rite is small, while by far the larger part of it is taken up with the exposition of things which were in the main common to it and to the Roman rite—the system of canonical hours, the kalendar with its Sundays, fasts, and festivals, the ministry, the faithful, the catechumenate, and so forth. It is in fact an exposition of the whole ecclesiastical system.

Isidore therefore stands at the head of the ranks of mediaeval expositors. His exposition is pre-eminently business-like; it rests upon the writers who had preceded him, and views the whole matter from the primitive standpoint rather than from the mediaeval. The amount of mystical interpretation, therefore, is not large, and only a small part of it has to do with ceremonial. He gives the symbolical meaning of the episcopal investiture with staff and ring, of the carrying of lights at the Gospel and the consecration. As to the salt given at the exorcism of the catechumens, he says its purpose is that they may taste the flavour of wisdom and not lose the savour of Christ, and this is probably the original symbolism, not a mystical afterthought; but he goes on to link it with the pillar of salt into which Lot's wife was turned, and to treat it as meant to warn the catechumens against a return to the old life from which they have been drawn. This is, then, a real instance of mystical interpretation, and must be taken as sufficient exemplification of his method.[16]

After Isidore there is an interval of over a century and a half in which there was little or nothing of importance written concerning liturgical matters. The only great writer of the time, the English Bede, is singularly devoid of liturgical interest, and his use of the system of mystical interpretation is almost wholly with reference to the Bible. With the end of the eighth century the Carolingian period begins; and at once we are in a new world. The liturgical interests arising out of the adoption of the Roman rites and use in the Frankish empire are prominent, and literature upon the subject for the first time becomes copious. For the present purpose it is best to turn to the writings of Amalarius. In them the mystical interpretation of rites and ceremonies which we have traced in its early growth, and which has evidently sunk deep into the minds of the worshippers during the century and a half of silence, breaks forth into fully developed vigour, and is worked out by the writer into such an orderly system that the later mediaeval commentators on the services had little to do but follow the lines of Amalarius.

He took the Roman *Ordines* of his day with the Roman Sacramentary and went systematically through them, giving a mystical exposition not only of the rite and of its ceremonies, but also of all incidental things— the church, its parts and its ornaments, the grades of the ministry, the vestments, the arrangement of the church-year, etc., with reference first and foremost to the mass, but also to other services.

Some brief instances may be put together to form a sketch of his treatment of the ceremonial at mass, which is the part more especially in question here. The entry of the pope recalls the coming of our Saviour into the world; the incense signifies the body of Christ, which is filled with a good savour; the tapers tell of the light disseminated by the preachers, *i.e.* the subdeacons who follow; the Gospel is among them, and the bishop follows the Gospel-book, because Christ called His people to take up their cross and follow Him. Whatever number of deacons are in attendance, whether seven, five, three, or only one, a mystical interpretation of the number is forthcoming. The bishop bowing before the altar represents the Son humbling Himself to be obedient unto death; and as he gives the kiss of peace, he resembles the Son Who is our peace, and said 'Peace I leave unto you.'

The going up of the deacons to kiss the altar is like

the mission of the disciples who were to salute each house with 'Peace be to this house'; but the altar specially signifies Jerusalem, and therefore, when last of all the bishop goes up to kiss it, this is like our Lord's last journey to Jerusalem. The kiss of peace is given to the ministers as our Lord loved first His disciples; to the altar, as He loved Jerusalem and His own people to the end; to the Gospel-book wherein both Jew and Gentile are united, to recall that He reconciled the heathen also.

Another specimen may be given, extracted from the commentary on a later point of the service. When the Canon is over, Amalarius has to deal with the placing of the host in the chalice, and he notes that two methods were in use in his day, one derived from the old Roman ceremony of the *Sancta*, the other at communion from the old *Commixtio*. The former he explains thus:[17]

> 'The book in question says: "When he has pronounced the *Pax domini sit semper vobiscum*, he places the Holy in the chalice"; and very suitably in my judgement. For bodily life consists of flesh and blood. When both at once are effective in man, His spirit is there. Now this service shows us Blood outpoured for our souls' sake, and Flesh that was dead for our bodies' sake, returning to their proper state, and by the life-giving power of the Spirit a new man is in being, never to die any more, namely He Who for our sake both died and rose. The cross made with a particle of the obley over the chalice exhibits before our eyes His very Body which was crucified for us; and the touching of the chalice on the four sides shows that through it mankind, in the four quarters of the world, has come to the unity of one body, and to the peace of the Catholic Church.'

Amalarius then goes on to describe the commixture proper as directed in the *Ordo* at the pope's communion. This was evidently strange to him. He associates the formula *Fiat commixtio*, etc., with the earlier ceremony of the *Sancta* and not with this ceremony; his only comment upon it is that if any one wishes to know why the host should twice be placed in the chalice, there no doubt is a reason, and the Roman doctors can tell him. This comment is of special value, for it shows that mystical exposition of ceremonial was not in Amalarius's day what it seems to be in ours—an irresponsible method of attaching wild interpretations to anything and everything —but a serious explanation of a known ceremonial, which was only given in so far as it was of practical value to worshippers.

The exposition of the Canon also deserves special mention for its method and sense. With the greater part of it, concerning the prayer itself, we have here nothing to do ; but even from the point of view of ceremonial it is interesting to note the following facts. The exposition is divided into several parts : all the first section extends from the Salutation to the *Sanctus*, and is explained in reference to the angelic worship ; the second, from *Te igitur* to *Quam oblationem*, in reference to Gethsemane ; the third, to the end of the words of institution, in reference to the upper chamber ; the fourth, from *Unde et memores* to *Nobis quoque peccatoribus*, in reference to the crucifixion ; the fifth, to the *per omnia saecula saeculorum, Amen*, with reference to the descent from the cross ; the sixth, the Lord's Prayer, etc., in reference to the sepulchre. Now in all of the sections except the last a special and varying mystical interpretation is given to the altar, the corporal, and the chalice-cloth or sudary. In the first case the altar is the altar of incense, the chalice-cloth typifies the labours of the angelic ministry, and the corporal of pure linen their pure intention. In the second, the two cloths have a double meaning : the corporal signifies the humility of Christ as shown first in His prayer, and secondly in His betrayal ; while the chalice-cloth signifies His labours and toil in these two respects. In the third section the altar represents the table in the upper room, the corporal the towel girded on by our Lord, and the chalice-cloth His toil and trouble either in the washing of the feet or the dealings with Judas. In the fourth section the altar signifies the cross, the corporal the humility of Christ, and the chalice-cloth the toil of His passion. In the fifth, the altar is still the cross, the altar of burnt offering, the corporal is Joseph's winding-sheet, the chalice-cloth is the napkin about our Lord's head; and it is added here that the archdeacon recalls the part of Joseph, when he takes the chalice from the altar and wraps it in the chalice-cloth; that the two crossings are made over the chalice because Christ was crucified on behalf of Jew and Gentile; and that the uplifting of chalice and paten by celebrant and deacon shows the taking down from the cross.

There is plenty of method visible here when the exposition is carefully studied. Moreover, the method of comparison of the Eucharist with the passion of Christ was worked out in far more elaborate detail by later masters of mystical interpretation. There is no need to follow out the matter further forward.[18] Enough has been said to exemplify in its main features the principle of mystical interpretation of rite and ceremony. To be seen in its fullest exuberance it must be studied in the later writers, and especially in that great text-book of the later Middle Ages, the *Rationale Divinorum Officiorum* of William Durand, bishop of Mende.[19]

CHAPTER XIII

AUTHORITY IN MATTERS OF CEREMONIAL

THE discussions and disputes of the last half century have not merely brought into question a number of details of ceremonial, but have raised more fundamental questions. What is the authority that prescribes in such points? What is its source? How is it exercised? What are its limitations? These, and similar important questions as to the nature and scope of the authority, seem to need some discussion. Closely allied to them is another group of questions which have to do with the form in which ceremonial directions are clothed. These also seem to need discussion, as a settlement of such fundamental points is essential to the settlement of the countless detailed points.

The ultimate ecclesiastical authority for ceremonial directions is not far to seek. Ceremonies, like the rites which they accompany, are regulated by the Church, and by episcopal authority; and the ceremonial laws and customs of the Church form part of the general system of ecclesiastical discipline, of which the bishop is the normal source and safeguard. The bishop is the ordinary of his diocese, not only as ordinary judge, but also as ordinary promulgator of rules and regulations for the conduct of divine worship. The same limitations, however, of episcopal authority are observable here as in other parts of the sphere of discipline. The individual bishop is bound to some extent by custom, to a large degree by the actions of his predecessors; he is bound by the best precedents to carry with him either synodically or more informally the general assent of his clergy and the concurrence of the laity. Again, he is restricted by the action of his comprovincials, or by the former action taken by the province; and restricted also to some extent by action that has been taken in other provinces.

Such obligations and restrictions vary in force, partly through their own nature, and partly according to the importance of the matter in question. There are points of ceremonial of such importance, *e.g.* the use of water at Holy Baptism, that no bishop would be justified in ordering his diocese to diverge from the practice common to all other dioceses of Christendom. Such points, however, are very few; the greater number of ceremonial rules are not thus immutable; and even when a custom has been laid down by high authority, it may yet be open to revision by a minor authority, provided the point concerned is of small importance. Thus a General Council—the Council of Nicaea in 325—forbade kneeling throughout Eastertide. In practice, however, at the present time kneeling is usual during that period, and is even ordered in many provinces of the West. The contradiction is not serious, because the matter itself is small. It is only in an extreme case, and by giving up ceremonial customs of great importance and common to the whole Church, such as the withdrawal of the cup from the laity, that any real outrage is done to the unity of Christian worship.

This seems the simplest justification for the contradiction between present custom and the Nicene canon. But there is also another alternative way in which it might be justified. It is worth while to bring it forward here, as it will serve to exemplify a noteworthy principle which is common to all disciplinary regulations and therefore to be taken into account in connexion with ceremonial. It might be said that the canon of Nicaea had ceased to be operative through desuetude, *i.e.* through the effect of contrary custom prevailing over positive enactment. And certainly it is a recognized principle that canonical legislation does lose its force through desuetude. Canon law is not repealed, necessarily, as is statute law, when it is no longer required to be in force. It lapses through the prevalence of contrary custom or the indirect action of subsequent legislation. The principle is clearly exercised, though its application is often a matter of great obscurity.[1]

Ceremonial rules are therefore liable to be confused by the existence of contrary or inconsistent prescriptions of varying antiquity, or by the prevalence of custom over law. In this respect also ceremonial does not stand alone, for such circumstances as these are common to all ecclesiastical discipline. The reason for this state of things lies in the ecumenical character of the Church, and in the diversity of ways by which disciplinary rules are made or carried out. A civil State has no concern with the laws of other countries. It is self-contained, and its legislation therefore can the more easily be independent, consistent, and unmoved by what goes on elsewhere. This is not so with the Church. A province is not an independent, self-contained unit; nor is a National Church. Each is profoundly affected by what other parts of the Church have enacted in the past, or have in use at the present. A highly centralized ecumenical system of discipline might secure a unanimity, which is impossible so long as independent sectional action is maintained. It is this centralized system which the Roman Church has attempted to secure, to the practical exclusion of the right of sectional action in provinces and nations; and in doing so it has split Christendom into sections, and destroyed the very unity which it sought to secure. The result is to show clearly that Church discipline must submit to these puzzling and hampering conditions. The Church must be prepared to find itself continually in the position of having to solve troublesome problems connected with such points as these—the conflict between rival authorities, the present lesser authority against the past of greater dignity, or the local peculiarity against the general agreement elsewhere, or the conflict between law and prevailing contrary custom.

Premising, then, that the discussion of authority in matters of ceremonial will bring in before long some difficulties of this sort, we may come now to consider its normal character.

The ceremonial law of the Church rests, as has been already implied, partly on custom, and partly on enactment made either by a single bishop for his diocese or by a body of bishops for a larger area, acting not arbitrarily but by canonical procedure. Some early instances have already been given of canons which were passed by synods or councils in order to regulate various items of ceremonial. Far more common in early days was the action of individual bishops. Down to the time of the Reformation a very large part of the liturgical discipline was diocesan rather than provincial in character, and rested upon the authority of the bishop acting as ordinary. The largest part of all, however, was due to the power of custom. This was so from the beginning; and a clear witness to the fact, so far as the Middle Ages are concerned, exists in the term 'Use.' A service is performed, or a book is drawn up, 'according to the Use' of such and such a church. Some parts of this use may come from conciliar enactment; a good part of it is the common property of the Church as a whole; other parts of it may be backed by the constitutions or injunctions of the bishop or his predecessors; but the significant part, and perhaps the largest, is use.

This leads to the consideration of the second part of the subject, viz. the forms in which ceremonial authority finds expression. Our preliminary survey of Stages in the Growth of Ceremonial has given us sufficient material for the present purpose. We gather from it that the conciliar enactment takes the form of canons; the bishop gives his directions less formally, the customs grow up silently, until the time arrives for codifying, and an *Ordo Romanus* or a Sarum Consuetudinary is drawn up.

It is only to a small extent that early Service-books incorporate any of these directions. The early Roman sacramentaries, for example, presuppose the *Ordo Romanus* (or at any rate the customs and ceremonial laws that it records), but they do not as a rule cite it, or cover the ground that it covers. The early books are almost entirely destitute of directions. It is quite unusual to find, on turning to the Ordination Services in the sacramentaries, that the Gallican canons on the subject are fully cited there. The explanation of this and of other such exceptional directions is not difficult to see. Their presence is due to the fact that the service is not of purely Roman origin, but represents a fusion of Roman and Gallican elements.

This is the starting-point of rubric. As time went on, and especially as the Roman ritual and ceremonial spread about the West through the Frankish empire, the custom grew up of incorporating the Roman *Ordines* into the Service-books in the form of rubric. This was especially the case with the Occasional Services, such as the Consecration of a Church or the Making of a Nun. From the tenth century onwards these commonly had fairly full rubrics drawn from such sources—the Roman, or the modified Roman, *Ordines*. But for the round of ordinary services, the Mass and the Divine Service, it was not so. It was far easier and more convenient to keep the directions separate in an ordinal or a consuetudinary, or even in treatises like that of John of Avranches.[2] A monastic body naturally made the ceremonial directions part of the code of rules which it followed, or of the constitutions with which it supplemented for its own purposes some general rule, such as the Rule of S. Benedict. Thus—to cite only English instances—when S. Ethelwold made a compromise at Winchester between the monks whom he sought to restore and the canons whom he sought to displace there, he laid down in the *Regularis Concordia* rules for ritual and ceremonial with the other matters needed. Again, when Lanfranc gave statutes to the English Benedictine Houses, there was the same combination of topics.[3] Thus in all churches, both secular and monastic, until late in the Middle Ages, the ceremonial directions were kept apart from the Service-books, and there was very little in the shape of rubric.

Even when the process of combination came about by which the individual books belonging to the mass—sacramentary, gradual, gospel-book, etc.—were united to form the Missal, and the individual books of the Divine Service—psalter, legend, collectar, antiphonal, etc.—to form the Breviary, the incorporation was not extended to include the ordinal or other books directing the ceremonial. It was only in the fifteenth century, for example, that at Sarum the New Ordinal then current was cut up and inserted piecemeal in the Breviary, Missal, Processional, etc., in the form of rubric. The Old Ordinal had to the end of its days remained apart; while correspondingly the actual Service-books of the earlier days remained devoid of much rubric. The pre-Reformation books after that date varied widely as to the extent to which they included rubric. If they contained but little, it was because the ceremonial was adequately regulated by tradition, or by customs, which might, or might not, have been codified in a formal book of ceremonial directions, distinct from the Service-books.

Even when there was much rubric, the directions were far from being complete, or even from aiming at completeness. The rubrics, as at Sarum, might contemplate High Mass, and leave the ordinary masses of priest and serving-clerk to go on apart from rubrical regulation; or, on the other hand, the rubric might, as in the case of some continental missals, prescribe fully for the everyday mass of priest and server, but leave the ceremonial of the High Mass with three sacred ministers entirely out of account. This does not imply that no such developed ceremonial was usual in these churches abroad, or that there was nothing but the High Mass at Sarum; it only shows that it was not considered worth while to incorporate all the necessary directions in the Service-book. If rubric failed to provide full directions in such large matters as this, it naturally did not aim at fullness of direction in smaller points. Therefore the conclusion is clear, that, before the Reformation, rubric was not meant to be a complete guide as to what was to be done or not done. Rather it was a set of reminders or directions, more or less full, which always presupposed that the persons concerned had other means available for their guidance, either in tradition or custom, or in separate directories of ceremonial.

We turn now to consider how far the changes made in the Reformation in the sixteenth century made any difference in these respects. It will be well to keep to the same division already adopted, and to consider first how far they affected the authority that regulates ceremonial, and then how far the form in which the directions are given.

A distinct and interesting feature of the whole of the Catholic reform was the search after a closer uniformity in all matters ritual and ceremonial. With Protestantism the case was directly contrary. In Germany the reform movement produced endless and chaotic diversity of rite and ceremony. Almost every centre of importance had its own *Kirchen-Ordnung*; in Richter's collection alone there are no less than a hundred and sixty-five reprinted.4 Among the Calvinists and Evangelicals the case was not very different. Even in England there were several different forms in use among the bodies of Protestant refugees who found a welcome here under Edward VI. On the other hand, in the English Church and among the Catholics abroad there was a great desire for a better uniformity.

This affected the source of authority; for clearly uniformity among different dioceses can only be secured by the co-operation of the bishops, or even by a development of that plan of synodical action in regard to rites and ceremonies, which we have already seen to be one of the modes of action. So far the existing diversity was due not to diversity of view, but only to diversity in the ordaining authority. The diocesan uses had gone on side by side, each in theory being the pattern for all the secular churches in that diocese. But in fact some uses were better than others, some more popular than others ; and, as may easily be seen in the case of England, by the beginning of the sixteenth century there had been at work for some time a tendency for the popular use to spread far beyond the natural limits of the diocese. Thus the Use of Sarum was fast becoming general throughout the whole of the south of England, while the Use of York had a similar but more restricted sway in the north, and the Use of Hereford a still more restricted range in the west.5

In the countries that remained subject to the Roman obedience this uniformity was attained by papal and by conciliar action. Here too the process of assimilation had been going on for some considerable period before the sixteenth century. The nucleus of assimilation in this case was Franciscan in character ; that is to say, it was a use that was in its origin ' regular,' not ' secular,' which became the popular one. In the early days of the Franciscan movement, the Minorites obtained authorization for special books of their own ; in view of the active life of the friars, these were to be on a more restricted scale than those of other religious orders. The abbreviated rites became attractive to others. In time the privilege was given to members of the Roman Court, as people who also led a busy life, though concerned with less worthy matters than those that were supposed to occupy the friars, to enjoy the same exemption from long services and to use the Franciscan Breviary. Having thus become the book of the Roman Court, it was not surprising that the shortened service should only increase the more in popularity. Thus it came to pass that the Breviary of the Roman Court, and with it also, in some degree, the Franciscan-Roman Missal, spread not only throughout Italy, but elsewhere also. Here was one element telling for uniformity.

Another was the attempt at a novel Breviary set out by Cardinal Quignonez under papal authority. This had a wide currency between the year 1535 when the first edition was published, and the year 1558 when it was superseded by a further change. Hitherto there had been no conciliar action in this movement towards uniformity ; but that followed upon the summoning of the Council of Trent (1545 to 1563). One of the results of that council was the issuing of a set of books for general use where the Latin rite was dominant. The question of ceremonial also was affected by the same process. The Tridentine Missal was provided with a set of rubrics, directing the ceremonial of mass, which was far more considerable in bulk and more minute in character than what had been usual previously. This body of rubrical direction was closely allied with the latest of the series of Roman *Ordines*, and with the *Ordo Missae* of John Burckhard, first published at the beginning of the sixteenth century. Through this action a high measure of ceremonial uniformity was attained in connexion with the Latin rite, not only in the case cited of the Missal, but also in regard to other Service-books.

In England also there was a strong desire manifested among the more Catholic-minded for a uniformity of worship ; and the steadfastness of this desire was one of the lines of demarcation that separated them from the revolutionary reformers and from the later Puritans. The ideal of the advanced reformers was one of variety in worship, and they continually fought in order to gain leave for the minister to conduct the service in whatever way he pleased. The first serious step towards a new uniformity was taken in the Convocation of Canterbury in 1542, when it was decided that the Use of Sarum should be adopted throughout the province for the Hour Services.[6] From that point forward uniformity in worship was one of several ideals that guided the course of liturgical reform ; and it could hardly be doubted that, whenever a revised form of the Service-books was carried through, it would be promulgated for use throughout the kingdom with a more than diocesan, and even more than provincial, authority behind it. In point of fact, as is well known, the State made a new departure by taking the matter up, and enforcing for its own ends the new ideal of uniformity. Indeed, the earlier English Prayer-Books owed more in the way of formal authority to parliament than to the direct action of ecclesiastical synods.

The issue of the First Prayer-Book of 1549 was accompanied by the first Act of Uniformity. It is doubtful whether or not the book had the direct authorization of Convocation. When this was superseded by the Second Book of 1552, it is clear that the new rites had no such authorization. This is equally clear in 1559 in the case of the Elizabethan revision, so far as the original promulgation of the book goes; but the book had ample approval from the Sacred Synod subsequently. It was only at the revision in 1661–62 that the procedure was fully orderly. The Prayer-Book received first the ecclesiastical authority essential to it from the Church. Then was added the incidental support given to it from the State, on the ground that it was thought well, from the politician's point of view, that the uniformity should be secured not merely by ecclesiastical canon and censure, but also by civil enactment and penalty.

As the result of this procedure the Prayer-Book of 1662 has had a far more established position than any mediaeval Service-book, or indeed any previous English Prayer-Book had.

In the recent revision the precedent of 1661 has been followed, and thus the New Prayer-Book enjoys the same authority.

Having seen by what authority the Prayer-Book holds its position, it remains to inquire by what authority it is enforced or not enforced, and in what degree its rules can be modified. The contents of the book rest on the double authority, conciliar and parliamentary. Now it

AUTHORITY IN MATTERS OF CEREMONIAL 165

may be said in general that, in order to effect a change of practice in such matters as these, there is required an authority equal to that which prescribed the original practice. One bishop of Sarum was (and is) as good as another; and any one of them could alter regulations that rested merely on the authority of one of his predecessors. Similarly, a council could alter the rules laid down by a council of equal or inferior dignity. All this is evident. But if a bishop on his own authority were to supersede the rules laid down by a synod of his province, or a small synod to override a large one, the action would require some special justification. It has been already pointed out that on the principles of ecclesiastical law such special justification may readily be forthcoming, and might justify bishop and synod in acting in the way stated. Such cases would not be breaches of the general rule, but exceptions to it. Thus a single bishop might well allow the ceremonial law of the province to be infringed in some respect, on the ground that it was a small or temporary matter. Or again, he might allow it, even in greater things, on the ground of desuetude. Instances of the first case will readily occur to the reader; while the non-use of the Long Exhortation at every Eucharist, or again, the omission of the invitation to communicate and previously, if need be, seek absolution, which is prescribed to be read before each communion, will serve as examples of the recognized force of desuetude in regard to the provisions of the Prayer-Book of 1662. Such special justifications are not however recognized (at least to the same extent) by the civil law, and proportionately the bishop's power to countenance such technical irregularities is restricted by the civil enactment. There have been cases where the State wished to intervene and enforce conformity, even though the bishop might have preferred to let well alone; and in such cases the bishop has no alternative but to enforce the provision laid down. The same would also hold good if it was the province that called for the enforcement of conformity where an individual bishop had not pressed for it. This power of forcing the hand of an unwilling bishop is the necessary result of the limitation of the simple episcopal power that has come about through the action of the synod on the one hand and of the parliament on the other. But there may well be also cases, and there were such before the recent revision, where all parties concerned were quite content not to press for conformity. In any such the bishop practically had a dispensing power, at any rate for the time being. But the toleration was liable to cease if either he or his successor on the one part, or on the other part either the synod or the parliament, entered upon the opposite policy to enforce conformity. It is still more clear that if a single bishop could be allowed in certain circumstances what is practically a dispensing power, *a fortiori* it would belong to the synod in similar circumstances where the State was quiescent, though it will always be more difficult to take synodical action than individual.

In the case of ancient directions which through circumstances had not had the opportunity of revision for a large number of years—as the rubrics of the Caroline Prayer-Book previous to the late revision—this was particularly likely to happen. Deviations such as these from the strictness of civil procedure were then the more easily to be justified, and the connivance at formal irregularities was the more readily to be tolerated on the civil side and to be adopted on the ecclesiastical side. But the authorization of the New Prayer-Book has altered that position.

Now, apart from special circumstances, the individual bishop is restricted in those spheres where the synod has stepped in and taken joint action. This is made more clear in the sixth General Rubric of the New Book. The bishop of the diocese may still settle doubts or diversity as to how to understand, do, and execute the things prescribed, but this power is subject to the rules made by the province.

In the earlier edition of this book it was thought necessary to argue on historical grounds that the bishop by his own inherent authority or *jus liturgicum* had power to issue or sanction forms of service supplementary to the Prayer-Book. That argument is omitted now. The power is now recognized formally in the new Prayer Book Measure to belong both to the province and to the diocesan bishop; and with it there must be held to go the power to determine the ceremonial suitable to any such rite.

We must now turn from the question of the authority itself to consider the form in which that authority expresses itself; and to examine the nature and extent of the ceremonial directions given in the rubrics of the Prayer-Book.

CHAPTER XIV

THE RUBRICS OF THE PRAYER-BOOK

IN approaching the rubrics of the Prayer-Book the past history of rubric will necessarily lead us to expect something incomplete rather than something finished, something that to a large extent presupposes a tradition, rather than something that is self-sufficient. Such expectations will be amply justified so far as the First Prayer-Book is concerned. In the first place, a mere comparison, bulk for bulk, with the Latin Service-books shows that the new ceremonial rules cannot even be as complete as the old ones were. In the Missal, for example, there is page after page which contains almost as much rubric as text ; but on turning to the Prayer-Book there is nothing at all comparable to this.

In order to realize how slight are the directions of the book, it will be worth while to put together in full all the directions, other than the merely formal ones which order the execution of the various parts of the service in turn.

'Upon the day and at the time appointed for the ministration of the Holy Communion, the priest that shall execute the holy ministry shall put upon him the vesture appointed for that ministration, that is to say, a white alb plain with a vestment or cope. And where there be many priests or deacons, there so many shall be ready to help the priest in the ministration as shall be requisite ; and shall have upon them likewise the vestures appointed for their ministry, that is to say, albs with tunicles.'

'Then the clerks shall sing in English for the Office (or Introit as they call it) a psalm appointed for that day.'

'The priest standing humbly afore the midst of the altar shall say the Lord's Prayer with this collect.'

'Then shall he say a psalm appointed for the Introit : which psalm ended, the priest shall say or else the clerks shall sing . . . " Lord have mercy . . ."'

'Then the priest standing at God's board shall begin "Glory be to God on high." The clerks, "And in earth . . ." Then the priest shall turn him to the people and say, "The Lord be with you . . ."'

'The collects ended, the priest or he that is appointed shall read the Epistle.'

'Immediately after the Epistle ended, the priest or one appointed to read the Gospel shall say, "The Holy Gospel . . ." The clerks and people shall answer, "Glory be to Thee, O Lord." The priest or deacon then shall read the Gospel: after the Gospel ended the priest shall begin, "I believe in one God." The clerks shall sing the rest.'

(Sermon, homily, or exhortation.)

'Then shall follow for the Offertory one or more of these sentences of Holy Scripture, to be sung whiles the people do offer, or else one of them to be read by the minister immediately afore the offering.'

'Where there be clerks they shall sing one or many . . . Whiles the clerks do sing the Offertory, so many as are disposed shall offer into the poor men's box . . .'

'Then so many as shall be partakers of the Holy Communion shall tarry still in the quire, etc.'

'Then shall the minister take so much bread and wine as shall suffice for the persons appointed to receive the Holy Communion, laying the bread on the corporas or else in the paten, or in some other comely thing prepared for that purpose. And putting the wine into the chalice or else in some fair or convenient cup prepared for that use (if the chalice will not serve), putting thereto a little pure and clean water: and setting both the bread and wine upon the altar. Then the priest shall say, "The Lord be with you . . ."' (Preface and *Sanctus*).

'Then shall the priest or deacon turn him to the people and say, "Let us pray for the whole state of Christ's Church." Then the priest turning him to the altar shall say or sing plainly and distinctly this prayer following, "Almighty and Everliving God . . ."'

(At the Consecration.)

'Here the priest must take the bread into his hands . . Here the priest shall take the cup into his hands . .'

'These words before rehearsed are to be said turning still to the altar, without any elevation or showing the Sacrament to the people . . .'

'Here the priest shall turn him towards those that come to the Holy Communion and shall say, "You that do truly and earnestly . . ."'

'Then shall this general confession be made . . . all kneeling humbly upon their knees. "Almighty God . . ."'

'Then shall the priest stand up, and, turning himself to the people, say thus, "Almighty God, our heavenly Father . . ."' (Comfortable words.)

'Then shall the priest, turning him to God's board, kneel down and say . . . "We do not presume . . ."'

'Then shall the priest first receive the Communion in both kinds himself, and next deliver it to other ministers . . . and after to the people . . .'

'And when he delivereth the Sacrament of the Body of Christ, he shall say to every one these words, "The Body . . ."'

'And the minister delivering the Sacrament of the Blood, and giving every one to drink once and no more, shall say, "The Blood . . ."'

'If there be a deacon or other priest, then shall he follow with the chalice . . .'

'In the communion time the clerks shall sing, "O Lamb . . . ," beginning so soon as the priest doth receive the Holy Communion . . .'

'Then the priest shall give thanks to God in the name of all them that have communicated, turning him first to the people, and saying, "The Lord . . ."'

'Then the priest, turning him to the people, shall let them depart with this blessing . . .'

'Where there are no clerks, there the priest shall say all things appointed here for them to sing.'

Such are the rubrics that regulate the ceremonial. There follows at the end of the service a number of other rubrics on other points, such as the Ante-Communion Service and the vesture appointed for it, the number of communicants required for a celebration, the method of their reception in their mouths, etc. These fall naturally outside the service itself, as do also the

'Certayne Notes,' or general rubrics at the end of the book. The incompleteness of these provisions is evident; they are insufficient ritually as well as ceremonially. They could only suffice on the ground that there was behind them a well-known traditional order which the priest would be expected to follow wherever he was not commanded otherwise. A careful examination will confirm this impression ; and it is to be noticed, first, that the rubrics themselves continually appeal to this tradition ; and secondly, that, of the rubrics that are given, almost all are intended to call attention to something unusual, either in the way of novelty or in contradiction of the familiar ways ; in other words, they exist in order to be either supplementary or corrective.

The following are some instances of the appeals to custom in the book. 'The accustomed blessing' is prescribed for the end of the Ante-Communion Service ; the banns of marriage are to be published 'after the accustomed manner,' and in fact the familiar form of publication was not inserted in the book until 1661 ; 'the English Litany shall be said after the accustomed manner' on Ash Wednesday ; and the *Miserere* is to be said 'where they are accustomed to say the Litany.'

Apart from these definite references to custom, it will be clear on studying the rubric that there is hardly a part of the services which the priest could carry through without falling back upon precedent for his guidance. How does he reach the altar ? Where does he vest ? In what position are the Epistle and Gospel read, the same or different ? Where has the deacon been up to this point ? and where will he be until he is next required, *i.e.* after the *Sanctus* ? Where is he until the distribution of Communion ? So there rises a series of questions which the rubrics do not answer ; and this for the obvious and natural reason that they are only rubrics and do not profess to be all-sufficient.

But when custom is altered and innovation is made,

the rubric suddenly becomes remarkably full. This is especially noticeable in two places—the offertory and the communion. At the former point there are at least two new features, the offering into the poor men's box, and the more elaborate provision of the holy elements on the ground that now the people are to communicate in considerable numbers at each mass, and to communicate in both kinds. These are fully and clearly provided for. Equally clear are the places where the rubric is prohibitive. There is to be no elevation or showing the Sacrament to the people ; there is to be no cutting short the psalm of the Introit ; no saying the Canon inaudibly. Thus it can hardly be doubted that every word of the rubric has a special significance, not as being an independent Order of ceremonial, but as correcting or amplifying an already familiar Order.

How far, then, was the old ceremonial to be continued ? This question came home to every priest under the new Order. The retention of some of it was inevitable, but how much ? The desire of the authorities, in issuing the new book, to cut down the old ceremonial was also indubitable ; but in fact, of ceremony proper, as distinct from rite, they had prohibited very little except the elevation. This, no doubt, was the main thing to be abolished ; other points had been already dealt with by episcopal authority outside the Prayer-Book, and others again would be similarly dealt with subsequently. Meanwhile there remained a large amount of liberty, of which the conservative-minded were not slow to avail themselves. Where the priest was so minded, the new English service to the outward eye looked almost identical with the old Latin service. So far as the rubrics were concerned, this was perfectly justified ; and if the bishops thought it undesirable, as they did, it was for them to take further action and supplement the deficiencies of the rubrics by directions of their own. This is exactly what in fact they did. Originally it seems to have been intended that these prohibitions of the old ceremonial should go out by royal authority; a Visitation was projected and articles were drafted for it. But it is not clear that this ever took place, and the prohibitions embodied in these draft-articles were actually issued by bishops, and not, as far as can be traced, by the Crown. Thus, for example, the king designed to order thus: 'Item, For an uniformity that no minister do counterfeit the popish mass, as to kiss the Lord's Table; washing his fingers at every time in the Communion; blessing his eyes with the paten or sudary, or crossing his head with the paten; shifting of the book from one place to another; laying down and licking of the chalice of the Communion; holding up his fingers, hands, or thumbs joined towards his temples; breathing upon the bread or chalice; showing the Sacrament openly before the distribution of the Communion; ringing of sacrying bells, or setting any light upon the Lord's board at any time; and finally, to use no other ceremonies than are appointed in the King's Book of Common Prayers, or kneeling otherwise than is in the said book.'[1]

This, with slight differences, was issued as one of Ridley's Injunctions at his visitation of his diocese of London in 1550; and again by Hooper of Gloucester in the year following.[3] Action such as this on the part of bishops was entirely defensible, even though it tended to restrict the liberty which the Prayer-Book allowed. Indeed, such action was entirely necessary, especially as regards the ornaments of the church, on which the Prayer-Book was almost silent; and it is only through such action that the burden of many unedifying ceremonies has been loosed off the back of the Church. But it must be noted that both Ridley and Hooper went somewhat further than was defensible in their treatment of the orders of the Prayer-Book. Ridley forbade the saying of the *Agnus* before the communion, though the book ordered it to be sung in the communion time at the priest's communion. He also added a new formula to the rite by laying down 'That the minister in time of the Communion immediately after the Offertory shall monish the communicants, saying these words or such like : " Now is the time, if it please you, to remember the poor men's chest with your charitable alms." ' Hooper went expressly contrary to the rubrics by adding the following novel direction : ' Further, that the minister in the use of the Communion and prayers thereof turn his face towards the people.' It was not, therefore, a tender solicitude on behalf of the integrity of the Prayer-Book that made them forbid all the ceremonies that were not expressly ordered there, but rather a wish to cut all ceremonial down to the simplest level that was permissible by the book.

As regards the First Book it is therefore clear that the rubrics were admittedly incomplete, and that it rested with the bishop, with or without the direction of the Crown, to take action about such things as were not regulated by them.

Turning now to the book of 1552 it is clear upon the face of it that no attempt was made on any considerable scale to make these a more absolute and all-sufficient directory. The bulk is much the same as it was before. On going into detail, and comparing the one book with the other, the same observation is much confirmed. The new additions do not, as a rule, fill up gaps in the old, but are chiefly concerned with fresh innovations. Thus a rubric at the opening of the book expressly contradicts the previous order about vestments.

'The minister . . . shall use neither albe, vestment, nor cope : but being archbishop or bishop, he shall have and wear a rochet ; and being a preest or deacon, he shall have and wear a surplice onely.'

The alteration as to the nature of the bread is equally clearly meant to introduce a change. Another rubric directs the saying of the Commandments, a new feature, and another the collection of the alms by the churchwardens, which also seems to be an innovation. More

The Rubrics of the Prayer-Book

interesting are the new provisions about the table. The altar has gone from its customary position, and it is necessary to say expressly that a table takes its place, to define the position in which it is to stand, and to provide that in spite of this change the fair linen cloth shall be retained. Similarly, circumstances have called for a clear direction as to communion. The people are now to receive in an unfamiliar though ancient manner, in their hands ; and, as there has recently been much rebellion rising against the old custom of kneeling to receive, it is necessary to say explicitly now, in a way that was not necessary three years before, that the old custom is to be retained. The only two rubrics that seem merely to provide for a gap in previous information are those about the giving of notices and the payment of dues on the offering days. Probably these two were really necessitated by some special circumstances of the moment not now in evidence.

We turn now to the omissions, in order to see how far there is a definite intention to be gathered from them. It is clear that in many cases a rubric has gone because the formula with which it dealt has been cut out; as, for example, in the case of the Introit, Postcommunion, etc. Apart from these, it is possible also that signs of a deliberate intention are discernible in the omission of most of the directions to the priest to turn to the people. He now stands in a new position at the table, and the turning may have been designedly omitted. Possibly the same is also the case with the omission of the Manual Acts in consecration and of the mixture of water with the wine in the chalice. But even so it can hardly be maintained that there is such intention in the case of every omission. The order to say the Prayer of Consecration aloud has gone : this can hardly imply that it is not to be so said. The direction to drink once only of the cup has gone, and omission can hardly mean prohibition here. All references to music have had the same fate, except the order to say or sing the *Gloria in excelsis* ;

but it can scarcely be supposed that the revisers meant to forbid the singing of the *Kyrie*, Creed, etc. Lastly, there is now no room left for any one but the celebrant to read the Epistle or Gospel ; but it would be ridiculous and unhistorical to say that the book of 1552 brought to an end the custom of having them read by others.

The only possible conclusion is that the rubrics remained in the same position in 1552 that they had occupied at all previous points in their history. Where they decided a point, they were decisive ; but where they left it undecided, it was for other ecclesiastical authority to settle.5 In fact, provision had been carefully made for this appeal to ordinary authority to settle undecided points from the very first. The preface of 1549 had contained the following passage :

'And forsomuche as nothyng can, almoste, be so plainly set furth but doubtes maie rise in the use and practisyng of the same ; to appease all suche diuersitie (if any arise), and for the resolucion of all doubtes concernyng the manner how to understande, do, and execute the thynges conteygned in this booke ; the parties that so doubt or diuersely take any thyng shall alwaye resorte to the Bishop of the Diocese, who by his discrecion shall take ordre for the quietyng and appeasyng of the same ; so that the same ordre be not contrary to any thyng conteigned in this boke.'

No clearer recognition could be needed of the insufficiency of the existing rubrics, and of the need that they should be supplemented by the decisions of bishops as occasion demanded.

In 1552 this policy was further emphasized by the provision of an appeal from the bishop of the diocese to the archbishop, over and above the previous provision. This still remains the guiding rule of present practice.[6]

Here again it is necessary to consider whether these plans are in fact nullified by the civil authority added to the Prayer-Books by the Acts of Uniformity. It has been sometimes argued, especially by civil lawyers, that rubric has altered its character by being annexed as a schedule to acts of parliament ; and that by reason of this association the rubric must be interpreted by the narrow and precise methods appropriate to a penal act of the legislature. It is contended, moreover, that in this case the value of the liturgical custom as supplementary to the rubric can be little if at all recognized—unless it be merely to elucidate what the rubrics expressly contain ; that it is valueless to supplement ; and that therefore whatever is not expressly provided for in the rubric is in fact excluded. It was very natural that such a contention should arise ; indeed, it arose very early in the day, and has arisen again at intervals. It will be well, therefore, to call attention to some of the decisions that have been made on the subject.

As early as 1559 the question was first raised. The Elizabethan Act of Uniformity had recently passed enforcing the use of the Prayer-Book, which, so far as rubrics were concerned, was almost identical with the book of 1552, except for the opening rubrics. In the summer the Royal Visitation took place, and in the course of it the Visitors came to Exeter, and there gave Injunctions to the cathedral. They ordered not only an early morning service quite different from any in the Prayer-Book, though made up of bits of three of them, but also a compulsory divinity lecture in the quire at nine o'clock, preceded by the singing of the *Veni Creator* in plainsong, and followed by the singing of ' The Lord's Prayer in English,' with a Collect. This involved the introduction of the metrical psalter, where the versified Lord's Prayer was to be found. Two months later some Londoners who had come down for S. Nicholas' fair, and some of the natives of the place, insisted on introducing ' certain rhyming songs which they called psalms ' at the early morning service, to the great scandal of the Chapter. They were warned to discontinue them, being without lawful authority and contrary to the express words of the statute. The innovators persisted, and appealed to the Visitors, who sent down a rebuke to the Chapter, and ordered the continuance of the psalms. The Chapter replied to the Visitors that the Act of Uniformity was 'so precisely made and under so great paynes' that it had felt bound to stop them. The answer came back, not from the Visitors, for their work and temporary authority had come to an end, but from the archbishop and other ecclesiastical commissioners. It was, however, to the same effect, that the Genevan psalms were to be admitted, the Act notwithstanding.7 There is no suggestion that this action was taken under the proviso of the Act for the publishing of further rites, or that the queen had any hand in the decision. It was simply settled by the Ecclesiastical Commission that the insertion of these psalms was not a contravention of the Act. The results of this decision have lasted ever since. From that time forward the metrical additions to the services were generally recognized, and they have been widely utilized at very various positions in the various services.

In this case it was ritual rather than ceremonial that strictly was in question; in the next case both were to some extent involved. In February 1574 Robert Johnson, a noted puritan divine, was charged before the Commissioners with having administered unconsecrated wine at the Communion, when the consecrated wine was all consumed, and also with having not 'repeated the words of institution or, as they commonly say, not having consecrated' the wine when he delivered it to the communicants. His rejoinder was that partly he held it unnecessary to repeat the words, the whole being one action; this was his theological argument. And that partly he so acted 'for that in the Book of Common Prayer there is no such order appointed'; this was his legal defence. It was not, however, accepted as satisfactory, though it was quite true that the book, as it then stood, ordered no additional consecration. There had been a provision for this in the *Order of Communion* of 1548, but it had been omitted ever since. This omission, definite though it was, was not held to prohibit; on the contrary, Johnson was told that he 'should have repeated the Institution.'

'There is no such caveat nor proviso appointed in the book,' he repeated; but the court replied that this was the intention of the book, and he should have adhered to it. As he was not forbidden in any place to use the repetition, he should have used it. This condemnation of Johnson throws valuable light on the interpretation of the rubrics and the Act, as it was then understood. It bears out the contention that when the rubric gives no direction the officiant, so far from being prohibited from taking unspecified action, is merely thrown back on to other things than the rubrics, in order to find the guidance that they fail to give.[8]

Over fifty years passed before there occurred the next instance to be cited, and in the interval a great deal had happened. At the beginning of the seventeenth century a great deal of ceremonial was revived. This revival had its starting-point in the practice of that great reformer and propagator of religious ideals, Andrewes, bishop of Winchester. It is, however, clear that the introduction of 'additional ceremonies,' other than those expressly ordered by the rubric, does not begin with him. Such additional ceremonies had been maintained from the first, as has already been shown, in general. The ordinary service of a cathedral contained many traditional details, such as the ceremonial of the assistants at the Eucharist, or the ceremonial of the vergers. The solemn funeral services, especially when they were managed by such a conservative body as the College of Heralds, contained others of a more striking and unfamiliar kind. In the middle of the church stood a great hearse on which the corpse rested under a canopy. The service began with a proclamation of the style of the deceased by the herald in charge of the funeral. Then came the Communion Service; the Creed seems to have been omitted according to old custom. At the offertory, while a metrical psalm was sung, there was a prolonged ceremony of offering. An usher laid down a carpet and cushion for the chief mourner, who offered a purse of gold ; then the coat-of-arms, the sword, target, and helm were offered also to the priest at the altar by the chief persons present ; others went up solemnly in their turns to offer money. Then came the sermon, followed by the funeral service, and at the end, when the body was placed in the vault, the attendants broke their wands and threw them upon the top of the coffin.9

The accounts that survive of Elizabethan services are very few, but they are enough to show that there were many ceremonies that survived, though not ordered by the rubrics. When the Jacobean period opened there began to appear features in the services more significant than mere survivals. Old ceremonies were revived, and new ones introduced, until there was formed a perfectly definite and characteristic ' Use,' which prevailed through the first half of the seventeenth century, and exercised a powerful influence on the revision of 1661. It will be worth while to attempt to put together from somewhat scattered and meagre sources a general description of this Jacobean or Caroline type of service.[10] It will be a valuable successor of the general descriptions already given for earlier epochs, and it will further throw much light on the true significance of the rubrics of that date.

The altar stands possibly in the old puritan position, that is to say, tablewise and lengthways with the church ; but more probably, as it did in Andrewes' own chapel, altarwise and against the east wall. The position of altars had long been ambiguous, and early in the century the movement, which was to set all of them altarwise, had already begun. In Durham Cathedral, for example, the change seems to have been made about 1617 ; elsewhere it was earlier made, and it went on steadily till Archbishop Laud gave a strong impulse to the movement for change, and it became one of the battle grounds with the Puritans. Perhaps in consequence of this history the altar is squarer than the pre-Reformation or the modern altars, so that it is not very obvious whether it is placed altarwise or tablewise, the difference between its side and its end being not very marked. It stands on a carpeted footpace with two steps below it. In the centre there is a cushion bearing the almsdish, and flanked by two candles on either side. At each of the ends there is a hassock, and at the north end a cushion on which the book is to rest.

At the south side of the sanctuary there is a side-table or credence. There stands here before the service a canister containing the wafers, a cruet or a small tun containing the wine, and another for the water. In Andrewes' chapel this last cruet was one with three spouts of a curious design, and called by the curious name of *Tricanale*. Besides these there is also a basin and ewer with a towel, for the Lavatory. Westward of the altar are the rails; behind it is a tapestry reredos, in front possibly a special upper frontal as well as the lower frontal or altar cloth. In some cases these were marked with a cross, which caused great dissatisfaction in certain quarters.

After Morning Prayer has been said from the reading-pew or lower pulpit, the Litany follows, which is said at the litany-desk at the eastern part of the nave. Very probably the sermon is preached at this point; for in spite of the rubric it became a common custom to put it here, not merely as a matter of convenience, but as a matter of principle—so Andrewes explains in giving the reasons for the change.[11] The sermon is probably preceded by a bidding prayer. The battle that once raged on this subject has now died down since the canon of 1604 which regulated the matter; but there had been in earlier days a great controversy as to the interpolation of a pulpit-prayer into the service. It is observable that the question whether this was allowable or not by the rubric seemed quite a minor matter; the legality or illegality of the pulpit-prayer was not argued on these grounds, but on the general consideration as to whether it was desirable or not to allow a liberty of prophesying to the preacher.

When the Litany or sermon is over, the clergy go up through the chancel screen into the chancel and ascend to the altar, making at least three adorations or reverences to the altar on their way. This custom is a survival of the old ceremonial reverences of the Sarum rite rather than an innovation; but it is only now that it is becoming again prevalent, and stirring up the wrath of the Puritans. In a cathedral or collegiate church the officiating clergy are vested in copes according to the canon. The same is the case with some episcopal chapels, but it is not necessarily so at episcopal functions. For example, Laud's chaplains officiating in the Communion Service at the Consecration of S. Catherine Cree wore their surplices with hoods and tippets. It is customary to have, as a rule, only two clergy occupied at the altar; any others who are present take their seats in the sanctuary. These two kneel at either end of the holy table upon the hassocks, or if one is a deacon he kneels at the door into the sanctuary. But in the later Caroline times there was restored the custom that the celebrant should stand on the west side of the altar; and with this apparently there returned the custom of his having two assistants. The position at the north end was a survival of the puritan position when the altar was tablewise. It was the natural logical outcome of the change of position of the altar from tablewise to altarwise that the clergy should change their position also, and with their position their number; so that gradually a return was made to the pre-puritan custom.[12] Those who are to communicate come forward from the church and are kneeling at the altar-rail; very possibly this is done at the beginning of the service, but if not, then they advance at a later period, invited by the Short Exhortation.

The celebrant says the Lord's Prayer and introductory Collect at the north end. He then goes down to the door of the sanctuary to say the Commandments, returning to his former position for the Collect of the day. At all these movements there are continual reverences made to the altar. The Epistle is read by the assistant standing close to the door of the sanctuary. The Gospel is read also by him, or else, according to another custom, by the celebrant. The familiar response to the giving out of the Gospel is in use, though it was among the things omitted from the existing Prayer-Book. It was probably at this point that, in Andrewes' chapel at any rate, incense was burnt. The censer in use was seemingly a stationary one : in the bishop's chapel it stood upon the music table, where the singers were placed, together with the ship from which the clerk put the incense into the censer ' at the second lesson.' Elsewhere when the censer was in use it seems to have stood upon the altar.[13]

There follows after the Creed, which is said eastward and for which all stand, the elaborate ceremony of the offertory. First the alms-bason is set to the front of the altar. The celebrant with three low bows kneels before it, and makes a solemn offering of the oblations which are given to him by the assistants from the credence. The whole of this is an additional ceremony not ordered in the Prayer-Book of that time, though familiar now. After this he offers his own alms into the bason. The communicants then follow suit ; in some cases apparently a clerk gives an invitation to them to offer. It was becoming usual for them to come up singly and make their offering as the celebrant had done ; or else the chaplain stood holding an alms-bason, with a footstool before him, on which they knelt to offer their alms. This, again, was a ceremony much objected to by the Puritans. The rubrics definitely ordered the collection to be made by churchwardens, but Andrewes equally definitely set it on one side as favouring too much of Genevan customs. When there was no separate offering such as has been described, the chaplain collected the alms. Meanwhile the Offertory Sentences were read, and Andrewes seems to have authorized for use a number of supplementary ones.

After the Offertory and the Exhortations came the Confession, which was led by one of the clergy kneeling at the door with the people. He remained there with them during the Absolution and the Comfortable Words; but after they had been pronounced, he went back again to kneel by the altar at the *Sursum corda*.

Immediately before the Consecration-prayer came the lavatory, another additional ceremony. The celebrant washed his fingers, wiped them with the napkin, and then went on to select the wafers for consecration, and to prepare the chalice, mixing the wine and water. When a bishop celebrated, he very possibly did not execute any of the earlier part of the service, but merely came in at the Consecration-prayer. Sometimes, however, he intervened at an earlier stage of the service, as, for example, at the shorter Exhortation. In the Jacobean days the consecrator still stood at the north end, but in the Caroline days it became increasingly common for him to stand on the west side of the altar facing eastwards. No directions for Manual Acts were in force at this time ; in fact they had been expressly taken out from the rubrics of the Prayer-Book of 1552, and their continued omission had given great offence to the conservatives in 1559. But it had now become common to use them again. Andrewes was again, it may be, the leader in this restoration ; at any rate the practice spread quickly among his followers and disciples, such as Wren and Laud, until it came to be described as 'the custom of the Church of England' when the question arose in connexion with the Scottish Liturgy of 1637. There was no genuflexion at the consecration, but the old custom of deep reverences was either retained or restored. The Puritans ran riot in their wild descriptions of the gestures used at this point by the clergy whom they attacked. They even charged them with elevating the host. This, no doubt, was one of the things in which their party spirit led them to misrepresentation. But when all deductions have been made, there can be little

The Rubrics of the Prayer-Book 185

doubt that there was a great deal of prostration and a multitude of reverences customary at the consecration.

It is interesting to note, as bearing upon Johnson's case, that Andrewes himself on one occasion when consecrating a new church performed an additional eucharistic consecration when there were more communicants than had been prepared for.

The assistant minister followed the celebrant, administering the chalice. When all had communicated, chalice and paten were placed upon the altar and covered with a corporal. Some of these fair linen cloths, it was complained, bore upon them five crosses. The use of them at all was non-rubrical. For the closing of the service the celebrant stood at the north end and the congregation remained at the rails until it was time for the Blessing. They then went back to their seats, and on their way contributed to the poor men's box, according to the somewhat unexpected arrangement which Andrewes recounts, and which was perhaps peculiar to him. This was a sort of second almsgiving, and was accompanied by the reading of further Offertory Sentences. When the people had reached their seats the service was closed with the Blessing.

A description such as is here attempted may be taken to represent the type of an advanced service in the first half of the seventeenth century. It does not represent the use of any one place or any particular moment, for places varied ; the whole time was one of great liturgical expansion, and changes were being continually made.

It is not surprising to find that all these developments provoked immense hostility, and from the midst of an electrical atmosphere at Durham there came in 1628 a notable explosion which again bought the interpretation of the Act of Uniformity into question. The development there began after the death of Bishop James in 1617. In 1624 John Cosin was appointed prebendary, a disciple of the new school, though not the first in Durham to attempt to recover more of decency and order in the cathedral and its services than had prevailed at the end of the previous century. He was, however, young and vigorous, and had considerable influence with the bishop and chapter; consequently, a senior prebendary, by name Peter Smart, fastened upon him as responsible for the novelties which he disliked, and made a violent attack upon him in a sermon preached in the cathedral on July 27, 1628. The virulent and untrue abuse with which the sermon was crammed was so scandalous that proceedings were at once taken against him by the chapter in the High Commission Court at Durham. The affair became notorious; the proceedings were removed to London, and ended ultimately in a crushing condemnation of Smart and a sentence of degradation. But before this had come about, Smart took proceedings against Cosin in the civil court on his own account. The assizes were at hand, and in August 1628 Smart prosecuted Cosin under the Act of Uniformity. The chief charges were the position of the communion table, the singing of the Creed standing up, the use of candles, Cosin's own attitude at the communion table, and apparently some others less easy to define. The result was reported by Cosin to Laud in the following terms: 'The Grand Jury found nothing, and the judge, Sir James Whitlock, with whom they consulted (as the use is) rejected the indictments in open court, letting the country know that he knew no law whereupon they should be grounded; and adding that the man deserved no small punishment, who in this unwonted sort, hath gone about to disgrace the Church and to dishonour the solemnity of God's service there, where himself had been both an ear- and an eye-witness that all things were done in decency and in order.'

He further charged 'the Jury to admit of no such presentments, but if any doubts were about the manner of celebrating any church service, to refer the parties that doubted to the Bishop,' as directed in the Preface of the Prayer-Book.

The Rubrics of the Prayer-Book 187

Not satisfied with this interpretation of the Act of Uniformity, Smart returned to the charge a year later at the assizes of July 1629. He was probably induced to do this by the fact that he had now to deal with Chief-Justice Yelverton, a strong Puritan. The judge showed his own partiality in an interview which he had with the prebendaries on the Sunday before the assizes. He denied the right of the bishop as Ordinary to order standing at the Nicene Creed, and said that this attitude was only allowable at the Apostles' Creed. In charging the jury on the day of trial, he laid down, ' That as it was against the law to do less than was commanded (as not to wear the surplice, etc.), so it was against it also to do anything more than is thereby expressly appointed to be done. And that such that did more than was therein specified might be indicted at the assizes, as well as they that did less.'

If this interpretation had held, Cosin ought to have been condemned, for there was no order in the Prayer-Book for candles, unless they were covered by the Ornaments Rubric, none certainly for the standing up at the Creed, a ceremonial innovation which was then much contested ; and the book definitely ordered the Creed to be said, not, as other books had it, to be said or sung. On further thoughts, however, though the jury in court thought this doctrine decisive against Cosin, the judge seems to have receded from his position. He did his best privately to make up the quarrel, told Smart that he ought to stand for the Creed as the bishop ordered, and finally confessed that he saw no direct law whereon the indictments could be grounded after taking the matter into fuller consideration. Cosin's account of the earlier stage of the matter is as follows : ' But it should seem the law is fallen out to be otherwise this year than it was the last, and it is false doctrine to say now as Judge Whitlock did : for we are taught, and the Jury stood by, That as some men have been punished and deprived for refusing to use some ceremonies commanded in the

Church by law, so other some are as punishable, if they shall dare to use any other rite, ceremony, ornament, or order whatsoever, which is not expressly appointed in the Book of Common Prayer, and if any such were indicted, that they should then be punished at the Assizes. Whereupon we are like (they say) to be indicted the next time for our organs and our cornets, together with the candlesticks and tapers upon the Communion Table, there being no such things expressed in the book. . . . In the mean while the Judge hath stayed the indictments from any further public view or prosecution, until he hath consulted with your Lordship, my Lords of Durham and Winchester, for reasons best known to himself.' Thus the case ended; Yelverton retired from the position that he took up, finding it untenable.[14]

This was not, however, the end of the troubles at Durham, nor of the persecution of Cosin, nor of the discreditable proceedings of Smart. In 1641 Cosin was among the prelates who were attacked by the House of Commons, and Smart was again his prosecutor. But at this stage of the attack upon the worship of the Church other expedients than the narrow interpretation of the Act of Uniformity were adopted; and it is significant that a good lawyer like Prynne in preferring similar charges against Laud did not rely upon the Uniformity Act to secure his condemnation.

When the Restoration came, Bishop Wren emerged from prison, and with Cosin became one of the leaders in the revision of 1661. In considering the rubrical changes then introduced, it is interesting to note that there are considerable ceremonial additions made to them, and the bulk of ceremonial rubric is distinctly larger than it was before. On examining these additions it soon becomes clear that they are little else than a definite prescribing of some of the most widespread of the 'additional ceremonies' that we have seen in vogue without rubrical authority in the preceding era. They represent a triumphant vindication of the men who were attacked by the Puritans. Wren himself is seen to be the direct inspirer of some of these additions, and Cosin of others. Their policy now takes its place not merely as a plan permissible in the absence of direction, but as a plan henceforth to be enjoined. Thus the Creed is now to be said or sung, and the attitude is to be standing. The same attitude is required for the Gospel. At the Offertory the alms-bason is now required; and, while the collection by the churchwardens is to be maintained, there is henceforth to be added a solemn presentation of the alms by the celebrant. Here too it is to be noted that the offering of the elements is henceforward compulsory. Again, at the consecration the Caroline customs are to be observed. The celebrant will stand before the table: he will order the bread and wine in view of the Manual Acts that now are restored to universal use. Provision is definitely made for a second consecration when required, for the placing on the altar and covering with a fair linen cloth whatever is over, and for its reverent consumption at the end of the service. In some of these respects the precedent of the Scottish Book of 1637 is followed, for this liturgy had already stereotyped some of the Caroline customs so far as it could.

By this process, undoubtedly, the rubric attained a greater measure of fullness than it had previously had. This was not merely an accident; it seems to have been part of the deliberate plan of the revisers to bring this about; and in many small ways, as well as in the greater ones quoted, they amplified the rubrical directions. This is, however, a very different thing from making them complete and all-sufficient. They took away some points of doubt, but they left more than they removed. In some instances they seem to have acted thus by design. There are a good many signs of compromise in the book. This is noticeable in more important things than the ceremonial. Even upon some doctrinal points it was desirable to leave a margin of ambiguity wherein men of divergent views could lie down together in peace. The same was the case with the ceremonial. The position of the celebrant is a conspicuous instance of a point that was left designedly ambiguous. The same may probably be said of the Ornaments Rubric. And in other points of ceremony, great and small, where there was much divergence of custom, no attempt was made to secure a rigid uniformity. Other points are left unsettled, but probably without any such reason. Thus there is no direction for communicants to come to the altar-rails, nor for the officiant to return the infant whom he is baptizing. Such things are certainly done, but there is no direction for them.

Thus even when a new Act of Uniformity had added civil sanctions to the new book and civil penalties to nonconformity, the directions of the book retained their old character. Where they were precise they were to be precisely followed—except in so far as authority allowed deviations; but there were many points undecided, with which it was left to episcopal authority to deal, according to the provision of the preface.

That this view of the law was the one present to the minds of those who in the ecclesiastical and civil spheres made the law, may be shown by the events of the time and the conduct of those in authority. The old additions to rite and ceremony went on unchecked. For example, the Gospel was still read by another than the celebrant, and the people still answered 'Glory be to Thee, O Lord!' as had been ordered in 1549, but not since. The turning eastward for the Creed, a Jacobean innovation, went on unhindered. The metrical psalms and hymns, far from being put down through any change of policy, multiplied and grew. The funeral ceremonies still on occasion were performed. The vergers continued. The interpolation of additional functions into the normal services still was allowed. Thus not only were prayers from the Visitation of the Sick [15] combined with Divine Service, or prayers, other than the bidding prayer according to the canon, added at the sermon 'at the discretion of the ordinary,' but it was usual to hold at the close of the Second Lesson a long and elaborate penitential exercise when any one had been condemned in the courts to do open penance in his or her parish church. Some ordinaries went to great lengths in acting independently of the rubrics even where their rule was explicit; as, for example, Bishop Overall had done, when he habitually said the Prayer of Oblation in the Communion Service before communicating the people instead of afterwards. But it was noted of him with apparent approval, so the example was not disavowed in his own or the next generation, even if it were not followed.

At the beginning of the eighteenth century the troubles that fell upon the Church, and later the paralysis that overtook it, caused a gradual and steady disappearance of the ideals of worship. More survived of decency and order than is usually supposed, but slovenliness and disorder became painfully common. It was not until the days of the Oxford movement that interest in services revived with the revival of the fuller use of the services themselves. Since then there has been another period of remarkable liturgical expansion, similar to that of the seventeenth century, and history has strangely repeated itself. The circumstances were, however, in some ways very different. The disastrous and unintentional substitution of the Court of the Privy Council for a final court of ecclesiastical appeal had thrown all the Church's courts into utter confusion, as it soon proved; and when 'ritual' suits began, the lawyers were found to take up the old narrow line of interpretation of the rubrics that Yelverton had tried and abandoned. The inability of the courts to deal satisfactorily with the situation was patent to all after the Liddell suits of 1855, the Mackonochie suits of 1868 and 1874, and the Purchas suits of 1871. The judgements were contradictory as well as unparalleled; the sentences were impotent. Consequently the Public Worship Regulation Act was passed in 1874, with the avowed object of putting down ritualism. Though it mainly dealt with procedure against offending clerks, it incidentally incorporated the view current among the narrow school of interpreters by enumerating among the offences unlawful addition to, alteration of, or omission from the rites and ceremonies of the Prayer-Book. The phrase is, of course, in itself unexceptionable ; it is a mere truism ; but it tells a tale.

After the passing of that Act, the confusion only became worse so long as prosecutions went on. It could hardly be otherwise while such novel and indefensible interpretations of the rubrics were in vogue. The tangle was a far greater one than can be undone by any single expedient.

One expedient has now come into operation through the approval given by the Church Assembly in the Convocations to the Revised Prayer-Book. But it is clear, that, apart from the new General Rubric interpreting the Ornaments Rubric, so far as it bears on the vesture of the celebrant, it adds little to the Caroline book so far as directions for ceremonial are concerned. All the chief alterations of rubrics concern the rite : the ceremonial remains mostly untouched. The actual changes are as follows :

The second General Rubric of the book gives direction about collections of alms at other times than that at Communion.

At Morning and Evening Prayer in the Introduction the minister is directed to turn to the people when saying the Exhortation. At the opening versicles he is given the option of singing. At the collects the direction to kneel is confined to the people.

At the Holy Communion the fifth General Rubric directs that the service shall be said throughout in a distinct and audible voice. The thirteenth expressly authorizes the use of wafer-bread. In the Alternative Order the priest is directed to stand '*at God's board*,' not '*at the North-side of the Table*.' Provision is made

The Rubrics of the Prayer-Book

that another, not the celebrant, may read the Epistle, and another, being deacon or priest, the Gospel. The reader in each case is directed so to '*stand and turn himself as he may best be heard of the people.*' It is no longer implied that the celebrant preaches. The option is given of singing the Offertory Sentences. Permission is implied for the Mixed Chalice. The Short Exhortation is allotted to the minister, not the priest. Either priest or minister is to lead the Confession.

In the Alternative Baptismal Service some change is made in favour of standing at certain points instead of kneeling. The priest is directed to take the child '*into his arms or by the hand.*' New directions as to posture are given in the Order of Private Baptism and Baptism of Adults; and again in the Alternative Marriage Service. The mention of clerks as forming part of the procession to the altar in the Marriage Service is omitted, but the bride and bridegroom are directed to go up then. At the Churching the woman is no longer directed to come '*decently apparelled.*'

It is clear that in 1928 as in 1662 the changes of ceremonial which appear in the rubric are, almost without exception, intended to give explicit sanction to already existing custom. No attempt is made to make the rubric a complete directory of ceremonial. A deacon about to be ordained priest has still to learn from outside sources how he is to perform the detailed acts implied in celebrating. He might ask, When are chalice and paten brought in and where are they set? He finds a corporal in use, perhaps two; probably also a silk burse and veil; what is he to do with them? Where is the Epistle read, or the Gospel? Where is he to stand for the Creed, for the notices, for the Offertory? Whence does he get the bread and wine? How does he stand for the Intercession? All these questions arise before the consecration: and if there are others associated with him in the sanctuary, further questions will have arisen as to them, and as to his relation to them.

The consecration itself raises a number of further questions. It will not be necessary to recite them, or to do more now than call attention to the fact that the new Consecration-prayer implies some difference in ceremonial from what has been customary with the old prayer.[16]

In the Caroline book the consecration is complete when the Institution has been recited: for thereupon the prayer is ended. There is therefore no doubt at what point actions or gestures intended to mark the consecration should take place. With the new prayer it is different. It does not end till the *Anamnesis* and Invocation have been said and the sacrifice explicitly offered: and it is followed at once by the Lord's Prayer. If it is desired to emphasize the completion of the whole action, that can be still done by action and gesture at the close of the prayer. If it is desired to single out a moment or moments in the course of the prayer for hailing the consecration—a much more dubious and controversial proceeding—it is not legitimate to regard the Invocation as having no part in the 'consecration,' using the term in this narrow sense. If genuflexions and bells follow at the Institution they should also follow at the Invocation: otherwise the ceremonial would distort the prayer.

It still remains true then that the rubrics are in themselves incomplete. The Use of the Church of England is not set out in them. Recourse must be had to other liturgical authority as described in chapter xi. Omission is not prohibition: and regard must be paid to matters unexpressed but ancillary to the rite.

A new generation has yet to find a way out of the tangle inherited from the nineteenth century. But in the altered circumstances, with a new Prayer-Book, a reform of the Church Courts, the recovery of synods, and a return to the ancient principles of interpretation, it may be trusted to recover order, reasonable liberty, and peace.

CHAPTER XV

THE APPLICATION OF PRINCIPLES

THE ceremonial of the Church of to-day is the result of the experience of many centuries; and we are thus led to give great value to any traditions which can show the character of permanence. Similarly, we note that a considerable part of the ceremonial of the Catholic Church is in essentials common to all the divergent rites at present in use in different places; and where customs agree in spite of difference of surroundings, we are again led to give to them special consideration and reverence. It is therefore one of the first principles to be applied throughout all the discussion and settlement of ceremonial, that there is a presumption in favour of that which is old and that which is widespread in the Church.

It follows from this that particularism is to be avoided, both in the local Church and in the individual, unless there are special circumstances that justify it. For one branch of catholic Christendom to be unlike another in matters of ceremonial is not in itself a thing to be desired; on the contrary, wherever similarity can suitably be obtained or preserved, it is important that it should be done. This principle has an important application to such a point as the use of a distinctive dress for the Holy Communion Service. The divergences in fabric, shape, and colour which are actually found in the vestments which are in use in different branches of Christendom, are small and unimportant. What is great and eminently valuable, is that upon which all historic Churches are agreed, viz. the use of a distinctive and traditional dress.

On the other hand, while laying all due stress on

catholicity, it is right also to recognize the privilege of local Churches to have their own ways in such matters of ceremonial wherever diversity seems justifiable and desirable. It is right also to recognize concurrently the obligation of loyalty in the individual to the local and national Church, in whose rites he takes a part, and to whose ordinances he is bound. The adjustment of these two claims—the universal and the local—when there is any discrepancy between them, must necessarily be a matter of some delicacy. It will depend to a large extent, so far as ceremonial is concerned, on a sane examination and a sympathetic but searching criticism of the ceremonial issues that are involved, based upon considerations both historical and theological.

We pass on from discussing the application of broad principles such as these, to discuss the application of the more special principles of ceremonial which have been brought out in the previous chapters. Ceremonial which is in dispute must be considered with a discriminating judgement. A distinction must be drawn between the right adherence to tradition and the wrong adherence which is mere traditionalism. Again, a distinction must be drawn between the right deference to practices and customs which are in widespread use in other parts of the world, and the wrong deference which may merely be mimicry.

As an instance of the first of these take the question of utilitarian ceremonial. Again and again it must be asked, Is such and such a ceremony still utilitarian, as it was when it first justified its claim to a position in church worship? The wearing of a head-covering by the clergy, for example, was utilitarian in the days when everybody else equally wore a head-covering at services, and churches were not warmed. But what is to be said of the wearing either of a priest's cap of the old English shape or of the Italian biretta in church at the present time? Is it good adherence to tradition, or is it mere traditionalism? In old days the subdeacon lifted the priest's chasuble when he turned, because it was full and heavy. Shall he do so still, with a chasuble which is much less full, and perhaps from the following of evil traditions has been pared down till it is hardly an adequate garment at all ?

The same discrimination is needed with regard to the interpretative ceremonial. It must be inquired whether it still interprets something or not ; for therein lies the true distinction between ceremonial that is edifying and ceremonial that is ' dark or dumb.'

With equal care ceremonial must be scrutinized for fear of that mimicry, which has always been a potent degenerating influence in the development of ceremonial, and especially for fear of the mimicry which copies abuses. Take, for example, the question of overlapping the different parts of the service in the Eucharist. It has already been shown that there are certain parts of this rite which are designed to accompany some action, or even to go on simultaneously with some other devotion. The singing of the *Agnus Dei*, for example, is meant to go on during the priest's communion, just as the Communion-psalm is meant to go on during the people's communion. There is no wrong overlapping in this. The opposite is the case with regard to the Creed or *Gloria in excelsis*. These are substantive parts of the rite ; and every one, from the celebrant to the humblest worshipper, is expected to take his part in them in common. It is therefore merely an abuse, superadded as a rule to another abuse, viz. inordinate music, that the clergy should say their Creed or *Gloria in excelsis* independently of the public performance of it, and then occupy themselves with something else. In individual cases, no doubt, exceptional circumstances may justify it ; but it is an instance of mimicry at its worst, when both the inordinate music and the slovenly habits of the clergy are introduced into our churches as a general practice, or as being the correct thing.

A more serious instance may be taken from the questionable uses of the Sacrament. These have been many and various in the history of the Church. The Holy Sacrament has been used as a charm; it has been used as a complimentary present; it has been used as a substitute for relics, to be placed in an altar or carried about in a procession; it has been used to add solemnity to a service of benediction. But the fact that such uses have been made, in some quarters or at some periods, is no argument that they should be copied at other times and in other places. Here again great discrimination is required to decide what is legitimate and what is not.

A valuable method of exercising discrimination will be to test ceremonial by analogy. Is it in a right analogy with doctrine, or with the rite to which it is annexed? Ceremonial has constantly been the expression of the less educated or more superstitious mind, rather than the better educated or more reverent conscience of the Church. Ceremonial acts must therefore be continually tested, to see how far they are according to the analogy of the faith. To genuflect in honour of our Lord present in the Blessed Sacrament is an act which accords duly with the reverent belief in the real presence; but such a belief does not necessitate the precision with which some on returning from communion ostentatiously direct their genuflexion towards the exact point where one or other priest happens to be administering.[1]

Still more fruitful in mistakes is the tendency to let ceremonial grow in false analogy with the rite itself. When it is supposed that because great festivals as a rule have a first Evensong, therefore Easter must have one, the whole liturgical arrangement is thrown into chaos; for the Prayer-Book rightly recognizes that the evening of Saturday in Holy Week forms no part of Easter Day, but only of Holy Saturday. It is again false analogy that in restoring the midnight Mass makes it the close of Christmas Eve instead of the first function of Christmas Day. It may, or may not, be desirable that Christians should begin their Christmas Day at midnight with a Eucharist. It was natural at any rate to do so in former days, though it may be questioned whether it is equally natural now. But it is only by false analogy that it can become something for which the faithful sit up specially late on Christmas Eve, instead of something for which they get up specially early on Christmas morning. It is only the growing habit of going to bed late at night and getting up late in the morning that has made such an idea seem possible.

False analogy again is responsible for the introduction into the usual service of a number of details which are not really fitted to it. For example, at the offertory our English rite makes provision for the offering of the alms and oblations, and gives the definite words for that purpose in the Prayer for the Church Militant. Such words are wanting in the old Latin rite, except so far as the 'Secret' performed that function, and they were only supplied in mediaeval times by the semi-official private prayers of the celebrant. It is therefore false analogy which leads the celebrant in the English rite to make a ceremonious offering of the alms and oblations, with private prayers borrowed from late Latin sources, before he begins the Prayer for the Church Militant, instead of doing it as the rite provides. It is more mistaken still to have the alms removed from the altar before that prayer.[2]

One more instance may perhaps be allowed, owing to the importance of this branch of the subject. The introduction of processions and processional hymns, which has become common of late, in many ways violates the analogy. A procession, properly speaking, has always a definite objective, and is not merely a perambulation round the church. It was designed as a method of approaching the altar before the Holy Communion Service, or else at other services as a visit to some other altar, to the font, to the rood, and so forth. Popular feeling for a spectacle has introduced processions among us which have none of this justification. As has already been remarked, the use of a processional hymn on going into church for Morning or Evening Prayer is particularly out of analogy with the rite. The same is, of course, not the case with the procession before the Holy Eucharist, which is a definite approach to the altar. But perversely enough, the former has become much more common than the latter. Similarly, the processions held after Evensong are, as now conducted, generally meaningless ; for they have no real objective, and very constantly are not even given such point as might be attached to them, if a special collect was said as their climax. They neither belong to Evensong nor have a separate existence of their own.

These instances must suffice to show the way in which it is suggested that the principles which govern ceremonial must be applied to the practices in current use, and a testing process carried through. In the circumstances of to-day such a discrimination seems specially necessary. If we look towards the past history, we see the way in which divergent traditions have grown up, and acquired a venerable status. More recently fresh divisions of opinion have manifested themselves on the subject of ceremonial. At the present moment we are in the midst of a period of experiment and expansion. The result of all this is a great diversity in matters of ceremonial. There are signs, however, that the limits of this diversity have been reached ; and there are hopes that the moment has come for the attainment of a far greater measure of unity than has been possible at least during the last fifty years. If this is to be the case, the unity can only be secured through a testing of the customs in use by the standard of ceremonial principles. The net result of this will be, not so much an increase of ceremonial as a regulation of it, not a mechanical uniformity but a reasonable unity in diversity. As the testing process goes on, a good many customs now in common use, of high ceremonial or of unworthy slovenliness, will be shown to be unworthy to survive, because, it may be, they are inconsistent with doctrine or with the character of the English rite, or because they are in themselves unsuitable, perhaps on the one side through being too fussy, and on the other side by being too squalid. But *pari passu* others that are worthy and congruous will stand out tested and commended, and will secure adhesion and general approval. So there may be evolved, in God's good pleasure, a new beauty and a new unity in our worship.

NOTES

ABBREVIATIONS USED IN THE NOTES

A C. C	Alcuin Club Collections	H B. S.	Henry Bradshaw Society.
A C L	Anglo-Catholic Library	L E W.	Brightman, *Liturgies Eastern and Western*, vol 1 (Oxford, 1896).
A C. T	Alcuin Club Tracts		
B. C P	Book of Common Prayer		
C H S.	Church Historical Society	P G.	*Patrologia Graeca* of Migne
C S	Camden Society		
D. A C. L	*Dictionnaire d'Archéologie Chrétienne et de Liturgie* (in progress)	P. L.	*Patrologia Latina* of Migne.
		P. S.	Parker Society.
E. E T S	Early English Text Society.	S. P. C. K.	Society for Promoting Christian Knowledge

CHAPTER III

¹ For the development of Divine Service, see Batiffol, *History of the Breviary*; Duchesne, *Christian Worship*, 446 and ff.; or a brief summary in my *New History of the Book of C. P.*, 348 and ff. The clearest description of the transitional stage from private devotion to public is in the *Peregrinatio Etheriae (Silviae)*. The whole is printed in the Vienna Corpus, vol. xxxix (*Itinera Hierosolymitana*); Engl. Transl. in the publications of the Palestine Pilgrims Text Society, vol. 1. Another Trs. by McClure (*S.P.C.K.*). The passages bearing on this subject are printed at the end of Duchesne, *Christian Worship*, 490 and ff.

² *Peregr. Etheriae*, 57. Duchesne, *Christian Worship*, 495.

³ To prove this it is sufficient to look at the directions for a festival Mattins, *e.g.* of Christmas Day, in a mediaeval Consuetudinary or Ordinal. See, for example, *Use of Sarum*, i. 118 and ff., where the following figures emerge. There are required, first the hebdomadary who says the service; then to sing the *Venite* the four Rulers of the choir; nine singers to start the Antiphons of the Nocturns, two boys for the Versicles there; nine readers for the Lessons; seven singers for each of the three groups of Responds; a total of nearly fifty persons.

⁴ See the account given in chapter v.

⁵ See further descriptions at pp. 67 and ff. The elaborate apportionment of the music is described in Wagner, *Einfuhrung in die Greg. Mel.*, I. capp. iv–vi, or (E. T.) *History of Plainchant* (Plainsong Soc.); and also the process by which the choir in early days absorbed the parts that had at first belonged to the clergy or congregation.

⁶ Daily celebration was in use in Africa in Tertullian's time, and

thenceforward it was customary there to refer the 'daily bread' of the Lord's Prayer to the Eucharist. It is more difficult to discover the state of affairs in early days at Rome. Most of the evidence available there concerns the solemn papal services, which retained the old ideal of primitive days, when in each city there was but one Eucharist, and that celebrated by the bishop. But side by side with these papal services there were evidently the local and particular services. The clergy celebrated apart from any connexion with a central papal Eucharist in the various churches on ordinary days, even while the old ideas were still surviving in some modified form for solemn days. But it is difficult to discover details. Some evidence is collected in Stone, *Holy Communion*, 233–235, and Stone, *Conditions of Church Life* (*C. H. S.*, Tract xcii), 11, 12.

[7] The Liturgy is celebrated in the Eastern Orthodox Church, normally speaking, only on Sundays, Festivals, and other special days; and though in special places there is greater frequency, there is no general ideal of daily Eucharist.

[8] See the account of the *fermentum* at pp. 42, 59. It is not clear when it was given up in Rome, but it is significant that as early as 416 Pope Innocent did not advise that the custom should be in use elsewhere. See his letter to Decentius, *Ep.* xxv (*P. L*, xx. 551).

[9] See Imbart de la Tour, *Les Paroisses Rurales* (Paris, 1900), for an interesting account of the development of parishes in France.

[10] See *Italian Relation* (Camden Soc.), 23. 'They all go to hear Mass every day and say many paternosters in public, the women carrying long rosaries in their hands; and if any one can read he takes his Office of our Lady with him, and says it *sotto voce* in church with some others, verse and verse about, as the Religious orders do. They always hear Mass on Sunday in the parish church, and give good alms.'

[11] This is repeatedly shown in the instruments establishing chantries. See, for example, those in the *Exeter Registers*, edited by Hingeston-Randolph; *e.g.* in *Grandisson*, 620, 1155; *Brantyngham*, 241.

[12] See further on this subject at pp. 120 and ff.
[13] Some scattered indications are collected in *A. C. C.*, No. II.
[14] See Jessopp, *Before the Great Pillage*, 61.
[15] See further on this subject in chapter xiv.
[16] See Atchley, *The Parish Clerk* (*A. C. T.*, No. 4).

CHAPTER IV

[1] For a discussion of the interpretation of the events of Maundy Thursday, see Batiffol, *L'Eucharistie*, 5, 26–33, 40–46 (*Études d'Histoire*, 11).

[2] 1 Cor. xi, xii, xiv.
[3] Rev. iv, v.
[4] For a specimen of the early basilica of the catacombs see Marucchi,

Eléments d'Archéologie Chrétienne, ii. 276, from the Ostrian catacomb. On the development of the Christian church from the Roman dwelling-house, see *ibid.*, iii. 16-19. A valuable link between the early church of the catacombs and the later basilicas of the days of peace is to be seen in the catacomb of Domitilla (*ibid.*, ii. 105-112). A notable instance of the transformation of the house into a church is that by which the house of Pammachius became the church of SS. John and Paul. See Marucchi, *ibid.*, iii. 203 and ff., but it is probable that the dedication really refers to the apostles, and that the brothers John and Paul like their *Acta* are fictitious. See Delehaye, *Légendes Hagiographiques*, 254.

5 See Διδάχη, 10. 'But permit the prophets to offer thanksgiving as much as they desire' (εὐχαριστεῖν ὅσα θέλουσιν).

6 On the early history of the diaconate see Hastings, *Dict. Bib.*, *s.v.* Deacon: and *D. A. C. L.*

7 The office of the presbyter was rather to reduplicate and reinforce the part of the celebrant than to minister to him. In the bishop's absence he simply stepped into his place; and his change of position left no gap in the ceremonial, as would have been the case if the deacon had been despatched to some other function.

8 See the evidence collected in Wordsworth, *Ministry of Grace*, 152.

9 See the letter of Pope Cornelius to Fabius of Antioch (251) cited by Eusebius, *Hist. Eccl.*, vi. 43. The subdeacons and acolytes arose out of the extension of the diaconate, so that each deacon had seven men under him, a subdeacon and six acolytes.

10 S. Ambrose speaks thus of S. Lawrence, the deacon of Pope Sixtus; for as the pope was being torn away from his deacon, and haled to martyrdom, the following expostulation is put into the mouth of S. Lawrence:

'Whither goest thou, a father without his son? Whither hastest thou, a holy priest without his deacon? Thou wast never wont to offer the sacrifice without a minister. Hast thou found him unworthy? Nay, try whether the minister thou hast chosen is unfit. Thou hast committed to him the consecration of the blood of the Lord, and a share in the celebration of the sacraments, and wilt thou deny him partnership in thine own blood-shedding?' (*De Off.*, i. 41).

11 See a fuller description of this below, p. 60. Damasus, Carmen xviii (*P. L.*, xiii. 392), tells of Tarsicius (*levita fidelis*) killed on the Appian Way while carrying the sacrament in Pope Stephen's time. Some have supposed that he was an acolyte taking the *fermentum*. But clear testimony as to the acolyte's part in the *fermentum* is first found in the Epistle of Pope Innocent to Decentius (*P. L.*, xx. 556), dating from 416 or 417; and the institution of the *fermentum* is ascribed to Pope Miltiades (311-314), *Lib. Pont.*, i. 168.

12 See Brightman's essay in Swete, *Early History of the Church and Ministry*.

13 See the *Liber Pontificalis* (*s.v.* Silvester), i. 170-187 (ed. Duchesne).

This celebrated book contains a series of biographies of the popes; the earlier lives were written in the first half of the sixth century, but later revisions brought a good deal of modification of the already existing notices, as well as the addition of fresh ones.

14 For a survey of these and other kindred documents see Maclean, *Ancient Church Orders* (1910). The *Hippolytean Church Order* is a document of the first quarter of the third century. It is not now extant in its original form, but it is recoverable from later documents which were founded on it. These are principally the Ethiopic and Egyptian Church Orders, see Horner, *Statutes of the Apostles*; the Latin Fragments, *Didascaliae Fragmenta*, published by Hauler; the *Canons of Hippolytus*, as edited by Achelis in *Texte und Untersuchungen* vi (1891), and the above-mentioned *Testament*.

15 The sources from which this description is taken are the following: *The Apostolic Constitutions* (Brightman, *L. E. W.*, 3 and ff.), ii. 57 and viii. 5–14; *The Ethiopic Church Order* (ibid., 189 and ff.); *The Arabic Didascalia* (ibid., 510, 511); *The Testament of the Lord*, 19, 23 (edd. Maclean and Cooper); *The Syriac Didascalia*, xii (ed. Gibson); and the *Canons of Athanasius*, 5, 7, 13, 25, 39, 96, 106 (edd. Riedel and Crum, for the Text and Translation Society).

16 For the development of the Roman rite see further at p. 59; and see Duchesne, *Christian Worship*, or a more brief description, with some difference of detail, in *New Hist. B. C. P.*, 436 and ff.

17 See the passages collected in Warren, *Lit. Ante-Nicene Church*, 98 and ff. Tertullian goes so far as to say (*De Corona*, iii): 'Whatever occupation we are engaged upon, we mark our forehead with the sign of the cross.' ('Quaecunque nos conversatio exercet, frontem crucis signaculo terimus.')

18 S. Augustine says in this respect (*Tract. in Joh.*, cxviii): 'Unless this sign is set upon the foreheads of converts, on the water in which they are regenerated, on the oil wherewith they receive their unction, on the sacrifice whereupon they feed, none of these rites is duly administered.' ('Quod signum nisi adhibeatur sive frontibus credentium, sive ipsi aquae ex qua regenerantur, sive oleo quo chrismate unguntur, sive sacrificio quo aluntur, nihil eorum rite perficiuntur.')

19 See the mentions of it by S. Augustine collected in *D. A. C. L.*, i. 653, and cp. chapter ix, note 22.

20 This is to be inferred from the charge made by Optatus against the Donatists of having made a perverted use of it (*De Schismate*, vi. 6).

21 See the description in *D. A. C. L.*, i. 630 and ff.

22 Canons 28, 34, 35, in Bruns, *Canones*, ii. 6.

23 Canons 15, 21–26, 56, 57, in Bruns, i. 75–79.

24 See canons 6 and 24 of the third Council of Carthage in Bruns, i. 123, 126. The canons of the so-called Fourth Council are not cited, as they are really a later Gallican document.

CHAPTER V

¹ See in Cambridge Texts and Studies, *The Liturgical Homilies of Narsai*, ed. Dom. R. H. Connolly (Cambridge, 1909), and compare Brightman, *L. E. W.*, 247–305.

² The Eastern Liturgies are, for the most part, easiest found in Brightman, *L. E. W.* But for the text of S. James's Liturgy with full rubrics recourse must be had to Mai, *Nova Bibliotheca Patrum* (Rome, 1905), X. ii. 31–116, edited by F. Cozza-Luzi. Convenient modern forms of the current Liturgies in English have been published by Brightman (Faith Press, 1922), by A. Riley (Mowbrays,1922), and Pullan (S.P.C.K.). For a useful commentary see de Meester in Χρυσοστομικὰ (Rome, 1908), 245–357; Nikolsky, *Ustar Bogosluzhenia* (Petrograd, 1907), 355–454.

³ See the Greek Text reconstructed by Brightman in *Journal of Theol. Studies* (1908), ix. 248–267 and 387–397.

CHAPTER VI

¹ This change is more fully described in *New Hist. B. C. P.*, 436–448. See *D. A. C. L.* Canon.

² The letter is No. xxv of the collection of Innocent's Epistles (*P. L.*, xx. 551). See Kidd, *Documents*, ii, no. 128.

³ The custom has already been alluded to in another connexion; see above, p. 29 and note.

⁴ Epistle ix (*P. L.*, lix. 47).

⁵ The letter is among the collected letters of Vigilius (*P. L.*, lxix. 15), but wrongly addressed to Eutherius.

⁶ See for examples the Canons of Agde (506), 4, 18, 31, 44, 47, 63–66, in Bruns, ii. 145 and ff.

⁷ The masterly edition of Duchesne (2 vols., Paris, 1886) has already been referred to, and will be cited in future notes.

⁸ Johannes Diaconus, *Vita Greg.*, ii. 6, 17 (*P. L.*, lxxv. 90 and ff.), and Wagner, *l.c.*, 194 and ff. (*E. T.*, 168 and ff.).

⁹ This has been printed in four texts: Cassander's text originally published as *Ordo Romanus de Officio Missae* (Cologne, 1558 and 1561), and reproduced by Hittorp in *De Divinis Catholicae Ecclesiae Officiis*; Mabillon's text in his *Museum Italicum*, ii, reproduced in *P. L.*, lxxviii; Bianchini's text in his *Anastasius*, iii. xxxviii; and Grisar's text in his *Analecta Romana*. A proper edition of the *Ordo* is much needed, based upon the MSS., and giving a critical result not only of the study of the different texts of the First *Ordo*, but of the bearing of the subsequent *Ordines* (of Mabillon) on the first; for the second and third of the series are recensions of the first, and have readings more correct than the actual texts of the first. The document also needs further analysis and criticism of the higher sort to lay bare its composition and history. This task has not been attempted in Atchley's *Ordo Romanus Primus*, but the book is

valuable in many respects as a commentary. A critical edition is being prepared by Père Andrieu. Compare with these the *Ordo* of S. Amand printed in Duchesne, *Christian Worship*, 460, and the very different *Ordines* edited, with a rather wild commentary, by Silva-Tarouca in *Miscellanea de Rossi* (1923), i. 159 and ff.

¹⁰ For the 'Stations' at which the papal mass was celebrated see Probst, *Sacramentarien und Ordines*, 324 and ff., and Kirsch, *Die Stationskirche*.

¹¹ The basilica-form in church building is probably derived by a special line of Christian evolution from the Roman house. It was in such houses first of all that Christian worship took place, so the evolution was a natural one; and the form arrived at differs in so many respects from the form of the civil Roman basilica or public hall, that there is little likelihood that any direct connexion existed between the two. See above, p. 40 and note. See also Marucchi, *Élements d'Archéologie : III. Basiliques et Églises de Rome*, 13 and ff.; Lowrie, *Christian Art*, 89 and ff.; and for a general description of a Christian basilica, Grisar, *Geschichte Roms*, i. 342 and ff. Plans are given in Dehio and von Bezold, *Die Kirchliche Baukunst*, as well as, and more largely than, in the above-mentioned books.

¹² The directions, however, do not in all cases tally with this basilica; for example, the position *ad orientem* is contrasted with the position *ad populum*, which implies that the church was orientated. It was always the theory that a church was orientated (see above, p. 44), but at Jerusalem and Tyre Constantine's basilicas faced west, and in Rome exceptions to the rule were frequent for practical reasons. The Liberian basilican (S. Mary Major), in fact, is turned north-west, the Vatican and the Lateran west. Elsewhere the same custom was copied, e g. at S. Apollinare in Ravenna, which faces west; but at least from the fifth century onward this was noted as unusual, not only in Eastern Christendom (Socrates, *Hist. Eccl.*, v. 22), but also in Western parts (Paulinus, *Epist.*, xxxii. 13). See further, p. 77 and note, on the bearing that this has upon the ceremonial.

¹³ These curtains veiling the altar have left their mark behind them in the sockets for the rods, which still are to be seen in some ancient churches. They are the direct progenitors of the mediaeval curtains surrounding the altar on the north, east, and south sides. See some of the evidence in Braun, *Der Christliche Altar*, ii. 133.

¹⁴ Anciently the name *presbyterium* belonged to the apse as containing the seats of the presbytery; but it seems to have changed its meaning with the change of custom. The use of it in the *Ordo* (esp. §§ 5, 7, 8, 21) clearly indicates the space before the altar, not behind it. The change of position cannot be easily traced. The First *Ordo* clearly implies that the bishops and priests do not sit in the apse at the Liturgy; but seats for them are found in the apses at a much later date in the old traditional position.

¹⁵ For the *tabula* see §§ 4, 7, 9 of the *Ordo* of S. Amand: cp. Bishop, *Lit. Historica*, 151 and ff.

¹⁶ The use of the terms left and right is sometimes misleading, because it is not clearly stated whose hand is referred to—that of a person looking up the church or of one looking down. The former is the case here implied. The use of the terms north and south is similarly ambiguous, because of the uncertainty as regards the orientation of the church. A still further ambiguity is caused by the difference in the position of the celebrant, which might be either before or behind the altar from the point of view of the congregation; see below. Hence directions seemingly, and perhaps really, contradictory are not uncommon; for example, Amalarius (*Eclog.* and *De Off. Eccl.*, iii. 2) differs from the *Ordo* as to the position of the sexes, and differs from Pseudo-Alcuin (Hittorp, col. 280) as to the direction in which the Gospel is to be read.

¹⁷ This represents a change from the custom, noted above, in the East in the fourth century.

¹⁸ For an English exposition of this Stational Mass, and especially for an account of the *personnel*, see Atchley, *Ordo Romanus Primus*.

¹⁹ For a full description of the vesting see the *Ordo* itself, or Grisar's description of the rite, *La più antica descrizione della messa pontificia solenne*, in the number of *Civiltà Cattolica* for May, 1905.

²⁰ The water is the offering of the choir. It is made through the precentor, and not by the singers individually, as are the offerings of other groups, because the choir is busy with the singing.

²¹ This is not mentioned in the main *Ordo Romanus Primus*; but provision is made for it in the *Ordo* of S. Amand.

²² It is probable that the prefixing of the word *tacite* ('silently') by the Second *Ordo* to the phrase (§ 16) *intrat in Canonem* ('he begins the Canon') of the First *Ordo* marks more or less accurately the change of custom from saying the Canon audibly to saying it inaudibly. The unmodified text seems elsewhere to imply that the words were audible to those close at hand. The subdeacons (not *deacons*, as most of the texts have) are directed to stand upright when the pope says *Nobis quoque peccatoribus*, and the archdeacon to move when other words are said. He was placed at the time almost touching the pope, but the subdeacons were some distance off, and must have relied on their ears for their cue, as their heads were all the while bowed until the words were said. The custom of saying the Canon distinctly but inaudibly was general from the eighth century onwards. This Second *Ordo* is the earliest testimony for it available, in Roman documents; but Germanus of Paris seems to imply it in the Gallican Rite of the sixth century. The *Ordo* of S. Amand, in speaking of concelebration by the priests with the bishop, prescribes *dicit pontifex canon ut audiatur ab eis* ('the pontiff says the Canon so that they can hear'). This shows that the old custom of reciting the Canon audibly was retained on such occasions, and suggests that on other occasions it was

not (Duchesne, *Christian Worship*, 460). This evidence also points to the change having been effected between the seventh and eighth centuries. The monastic *Ordo*, printed by Martene in *Thes. Nov. Anecd.*, v. 103 and ff., says of the Secret, *dicat orationem secrete nullo alio audiente* (' he says the prayer secretly so that no one else hears '), but speaks otherwise of the Canon : ' When they have, with great reverence and fear, proclaimed the *Sanctus*, the priest begins the Canon in a different voice gently ' (' incipit sacerdos canonem dissimili voce leniter ').

Even when the custom of silent recitation came in, it did not at first apply throughout the Canon ; for the Second *Ordo* having inserted *tacite* ('silently') at the beginning, inserts another phrase corrective of it later on : ' And when in a loud voice (*aperta clamans voce*) he has said the *Nobis quoque peccatoribus* the subdeacons arise.' The ceremonial requirements still demanded that this part should be said aloud.

CHAPTER VII

1 For Amalarius see *Dict. Théol. Cath.* and *D. A. C. L.* His *Eclogae de Officio Missae* and his *De Ecclesiasticis Officiis* are in *P. L.*, cv. The convenient collection of Hittorp, *De Divinis Catholicae Ecclesiae Officiis*, contains not only the former of these, but a collection of liturgical writings, some *Ordines Romani*, and works of Isidore, Pseudo-Alcuin, Rhabanus, Walafrid, Berno, Ralph of Tongres, the *Micrologus*, the *Gemma Animae*, etc.

2 Amalarius, in describing the first salutation, *i.e.* before the Collect says (*De Eccl. Offic.*, iii. 9) that at the salutation the celebrant always turns to the people except at this point, and then he is too much engrossed with his high task to turn. ' Quando dicimus *Pax vobiscum* sive *Dominus vobiscum*, quod est salutatio, ad populum sumus versi. Quos salutamus eis faciem presentamus, excepto in uno quod est in preparatione hymni ante *Te igitur*. Ibi iam occupati sumus circa altare ita ut congruentius sit uno modo versos nos esse quam retro aspicere.'

3 The question has no great significance, but is mainly of archaeological interest. The fact that the celebrant faced the people was of little import, as there was a curtain, and perhaps a considerable screen as well, between him and them. Attempts to give great significance to the attitude from a puritan point of view, or any other point of view, are therefore vain.

In the East the veiling of the mysteries by the iconostasis, or by some screen or curtains, was ultimately more complete than in the West; but this came about there not earlier than the sixth or seventh century. No evidence is so far forthcoming to show that the westward position was ever in use there. The passage in Gregory Naz. (*Or.*, xlviii. 52) which is sometimes quoted seems quite ambiguous.

4 See Braun, *Der Christliche Altar*. Section IV.

5 Some further evidence that this was done thus on principle may be deduced from the basilicas with two apses, one at either end. Some of these may bear witness to a change of position of the celebrant, and show the device by which he was able to continue facing in the actual eastward direction, when he shifted from one side of the altar to the other. In the earlier days when he followed Roman custom and faced the people, the altar needed to stand in the western apse; in the later days when he stood between the people and the altar, it needed to be transferred to the eastern end of the church. Such basilicas seem to have been specially common in England and on the Rhine. At Canterbury, the classic English instance, the apses disappeared at Lanfranc's restoration; but they survive at Mainz, Bamberg, and elsewhere on the Rhine. There are instances in France of churches that had the two apses, *e.g.* that of Clermont (see Greg. of Tours, *Hist. Franc.*, ii. 14), but orientation with one eastern apse was the rule there. At Nevers the western apse survived as De Moleon notes (*Voyages*, 145). Now England was the place which reproduced most closely the customs of Rome of the seventh century, having been early imbued with the ceremonial of that century rather than (as France) with that of the eighth; and it might be natural to find the earlier Roman custom survive in England, but not introduced into France. For the old cathedral at Canterbury see Willis, *Architect. Hist. of Cant. Cath.*, 10 and ff. The Rhineland churches were in close connexion with England and also in very direct connexion with Rome in the seventh century. See Scott, *Hist. Engl. Gothic Arch.*, 14 and ff.

6 See the Bayeux Ordinal (ed. Chevalier), 26, and Le Brun, *Explication de la Messe*, i. 160.

7 Amalarius, *De Eccl. Off.*, iii. 36.

8 He also implies the same thing in the passage where he speaks of the *Sursum corda*. See above, note 2.

9 It is difficult to get clear evidence as to the drawing of the curtains as well as to their subsequent abolition. But see Atchley, *l.c.* 20.

10 See Haddan and Stubbs, *Councils*, iii. 367.

11 The earliest express mention of the importation into England of the well-known *Ordines* seems to be in Alcuin, *Epp.* 114 (72), 226 (167). For the books brought by S. Augustine and those sent to him by Pope Gregory in 601 see Bede, *H. E.*, i. 29. Silva-Tarouca's theory (see ch. vi, note 9) of an *Ordo* of John the Archicantor is not tenable. See *Jahrbuch fur Liturgiewissenschaft*, iv. 178; v. 153.

12 The Pontifical of Egbert is printed in Surtees Soc., vol. xxvii. The service in question is analysed, with the results quoted in the text, in *Pontifical Services* (*A. C. C.*, III), 11 and ff. See there also the description of a number of early English Pontificals which are in close dependence upon Roman *Ordines*, and in some cases (Nos. xi and xii) are simply collections of Roman *Ordines* of the later type. See also *D. A. C. L.* under 'Egbert.'

¹³ For this section see in general *Use of Sarum*, vol. 1, and especially pp. xix and ff.

¹⁴ *Ibid.*, 58 and ff. In some respects the later *Customary* is drawn upon for this description as well as the *Consuetudinary*. Both are included in the above-cited volume.

¹⁵ See for example the Second *Ordo* of Mabillon's series ; and other passages bearing on the development are collected in *The Case for Incense*, 65 and ff. On the whole subject of incense see Atchley in *A. C. C.*, XIII.

¹⁶ Some details of the procession are taken from the Sarum Processional, and are not in the Consuetudinary.

¹⁷ The latest developments of all may be seen in Maydeston's tract, *Crede Michi*, § 31. (*H. B. S.*)

¹⁸ The only English mediaeval authority that can be discovered for such a censing is of late date and for one place only, though it was probably not uncommon. It existed however at Chichester as the result of a special benefaction for the purpose from 1304 onwards. See *Archaeologia*, xlv. 212.

¹⁹ There is a certain amount of discrepancy here between the Consuetudinary and the Customary.

CHAPTER VIII

¹ This has already been noted. See pp. 66 and ff.

² It has been shown that in the Roman Stational Mass there was no cross set upon the altar. Pictures of early altars bring similar evidence. See *A. C. C.*, I, pl. i, No. 1, for an example. The companion illustration, No. 2, shows the presentation of a cross to the church as a reliquary. This belongs to the eleventh century, and shows one of the ways by which the altar cross came into existence as a regular institution. A later picture, pl. ii, No. 2, seems to show an altar with the processional cross actually set up behind it. From this use of the cross it was a natural development to have a cross head, which could be fixed either into a staff for processional use, or into a socket to stand upon the altar. It was only one step further to distinguish the processional cross finally from the altar cross.

³ See above, p. 89.

⁴ For the paten cp. pp. 71, 87.

⁵ See the direction as to this in the Sarum rite, *Use of Sarum*, 1. 67.

⁶ This description is that of the later mediaeval Mass. For the earlier method see above, p. 87.

⁷ See above, p. 42.

⁸ *Use of Sarum*, i. xxxix. (66), 81 : ' teneat (hostiam) inter manus suas non disjungendo pollicem ab indice, nisi dum facit benedictiones tantum.'

⁹ *Ibid.* : ' Fricet digitos suos ultra calicem propter micas.'

NOTES 213

¹⁰ *Ibid.*, 87. See the history of the ablutions in Lockton, *The Remains at the Eucharist*, chaps. viii and ix. Bishop Wordsworth of Salisbury (*Considerations on Public Worship*, 1898, p 72) questioned the utility of an ablution of wine, on the ground that formerly the pouring of fresh wine into the chalice was held to consecrate it by contact with that already consecrated in the chalice. But both procedure and intention so widely separate the two acts, that they can hardly be said to concern one another. In the one case wine is poured into a chalice which is not empty, and for the purpose of consecrating more; in the other it is poured into a chalice which has been emptied as far as possible, and for a totally different purpose. For the custom in question see Andrieu, *Immixtio et Consecratio* (Paris, 1924).

¹¹ *Ibid.*, 88, and see *Boexken van der Missen* (*A. C. C.*, V), plate xxxii.

¹² In fact an ablution of the paten if it had been used was ordered by Abp. Edmund (*c.* 1240). See Lyndwood, *Provinciale*, III 23.

¹³ See Batiffol's essay on the history of vestments, in his *Etudes de Liturgie*, no. 11; Braun, *Die liturgische Gewandung*; Macalister, *Ecclesiastical Vestments*. The value of eucharistic vestments at the present day rests on their universal and distinctive character. Like the eastward position of the celebrant, they are part of the uniformity that for centuries has prevailed in broad outline through catholic Christendom. They therefore do not represent the eucharistic doctrine of a party, but the fundamental agreement of the whole Church on the main facts (apart from theories) of the Eucharist, just as the slight divergences between the shapes of the vestments may be taken to represent the more superficial divergences, the special views and theories of the Eucharist. It may seem paradoxical and strange, but in fact on a wide-minded survey it cannot but be clear, that the use of the surplice for the Eucharist was a peculiarity of a particular party in its origin. It won its way in defiance of the rubric under strong puritan influence early in Elizabeth's reign, and has been allowed to dominate the English Church, till recent years brought in obedience to the rubric in its obvious meaning and the recovery of the dress which stands for catholic unity and not party views.

CHAPTER IX

¹ For the contest about the psalms see the proceedings of the Subcommittee of the House of Lords in 1641. Among the innovations there noted was the standing up at the hymns in church and always at the *Gloria Patri*. Cardwell, *Conf.*, 243. Cp. *Hierurg. Angl.*, ii. 52 and ff. for this and the eastward attitude. See also the Orders of Wren for his diocese of Norwich in 1636 (Cardwell, *Doc. Ann.*, cxliii).

² The turning eastward at the *Gloria Patri* is ordered in mediaeval rites; *e.g.* see *Use of Sarum*, 1. 19.

3 *The Lay Folks' Mass Book* says at this point (l. 303, ed. *E. E. T. S.*, p. 26):

> To he come til the altar middis
> Stande up thou als men thee biddis,
> Heart and body and ilk a dele
> Take good keep, and hear him wele.
> Then he begynnes *Per omnia*,
> And sithen *Sursum corda*;
> At the ende he says *Sanctus* thrice,
> *In excelsis* he nevens twice.
> As fast as ever that he has done
> Look that thou be ready sone,
> And say these words with stille steven
> Privily to God of heaven.
> . . . . .
> When this is said, kneel thou down
> And that with good devocioun.

4 See the account in *New Hist. B. C. P.*, 422, and cp. Edwardine Injunctions, 23, in *A. C. C.*, XV. 124, and Cranmer's article 35, *ibid.*, 181, for the change to a kneeling position.

5 *E.g.* in the procession of the Knights of the Garter on S. George's Day at Windsor. See Machyn's *Diary* (*C. S.*) in 1561, 257-8, etc. It was apparently not till 1673 that a hymn was substituted for the Litany at this procession (*Hierurg. Angl.*, ii. 18). This was clearly not held to be forbidden by the eighteenth canon of 1604.

6 Standing for the Gospel is ordered as early as the *Apostolic Constitutions* (ii. 57), which date at latest from the latter part of the fourth century. See Brightman, *L. E. W.*, i. 29.

7 See *New Hist. B. C. P.*, 83 and ff.

8 Genuflexion was adopted for other purposes though not for this. There was a genuflexion, for example, prescribed in the Sarum rite at the beginning of each of the Hours of the days in Lent, at the *Veni Creator* on Maundy Thursday, at the *Gloria in excelsis* of the Mass of Easter Even. (See *Use of Sarum*, i. 23, 204, 24, 151.) A genuflexion also preceded the censing of the altar, and this apparently at other altars than the High Altar where the pyx hung (*ibid.*, 44, 114, 183). There was no genuflexion customary then before the reserved Sacrament. It must be remembered too that genuflexion was not the most profound posture of worship; prostration was commonly used at penitential prayers and other occasions of humiliation; but the two postures were on some occasions interchangeable.

9 See *Ordinale Exon.*, c. xix (*H. B. S.*, i. 10). 'They should bow to the altar or rather genuflect as the Roman Church does at the clause *Et incarnatus est.*' ('Ad altare se inclinent vel potius genuflectent more

ecclesiae Romanae cum dicitur haec clausa, " Et incarnatus est." ") It will be observed that even this does not involve genuflexion at the Canon. The chapter is mainly taken from the *Sarum Consuetudinary*, but this passage is an alteration.

[10] The direction of the rubric at Morning Prayer *all kneeling* is not repeated at Evensong; it refers to the congregation, as it does also in the Baptismal Services (which also are not uniform in the matter) and still more clearly in the Order of Confirmation. The rubric in the New Prayer-Book clears away any ambiguity.

[11] To confirm the force of this questionable canon there is also a strong tradition. The canon itself appeals to the custom as a practice of the Church of England for many years of the reign of Queen Elizabeth, and commends its revival. (Canon vii in Cardwell, *Synodalia*, i. 406.) See further evidence from 1560–1857 in *Hierurg. Angl.*, ii. 75 and ff.

[12] *Sarum Consuet.*, xiii (2), in *Use of Sarum*, i 14. A similar bow was prescribed to the clergy as they passed before the altar (*ibid.*, xv (3), in *Use of Sarum*, i. 16). The canon touches only the congregation and their entry to or departure from church.

[13] Indulgences of 100 days were granted to those who adopted the custom by Urban IV (1261–1265) and John XXII (1410–1417); and this fact is noted in the Exeter Ordinal, cap. xix (p. 10).

[14] See *Hierurg. Angl.*, ii. 75 and ff. The canon gives an interpretation of the gesture.

[15] *Sarum Consuet.*, xvii (13), in *Use of Sarum*, i. 19.

[16] These are the directions of the *Sarum Customary*, 66, § 21 (*Use of Sarum*, i. 74), but the directions can be traced back as far as the Second *Ordo Romanus*, § 8. There the deacon is directed to cross only his forehead and breast; the bishop and people are to do the like.

[17] English directions for the crossing by the people are found, *e.g.*, in the *Lay Folks' Mass Book*, 175, and a further cross is ordered when the Gospel is done in this form, 195:

Somewhere beside when it is done
Thou make a cross and kiss it sone.

This custom of the people can also be traced back as far as the Second *Ordo*. See further the notes in *E. E. T. S.* edition of the *Lay Folks' Mass Book*.

[18] For other instances of the same tendency in words to suggest gestures even when not specially suitable see De Vert, *Explication*, i. 177; and for *benedicere* see pp. 119 and ff. But for an alternative explanation see next note.

[19] *Sarum Consuet.*, xvii (13). (See *Use of Sarum*, i. 21, 22.) It was noted by Durandus (*Rationale*, v. 2, 15) here as at the end of all the chief hymns of the Eucharist, and even at the Gospel canticles. Cp. similar orders in the Lincoln Customary of 1236 (Bradshaw and Wordsworth, *Linc. Cath. Stat.*, ii. 153).

216 THE PRINCIPLES OF RELIGIOUS CEREMONIAL

²⁰ At Exeter the Roman custom of kneeling for two clauses was adopted (see above, note 9), and it was explained that there was to be no kneeling at *crucifixus*, 'because the Jews then bowed the knee in mockery.' There was also customary there a further genuflexion instead of the bow at the last clause of the Creed. This seems to discount in some degree De Vert's explanation of the kneeling in the Creed, deriving it from the influence of the word *descendit* (see his *Explication*, 1. 164); but probably the reverence in the middle of the Creed is both older and more significant than that at the end. The former stands alone in expressing humiliation at the thought of our Lord's condescension; the latter is a mere closing gesture.

²¹ The analogy which suggested the practice is in one sense false, but in another not. The Creed in the English Divine Service is publicly recited as it is in the Eucharist: in the Latin services the use is different, as the Apostles' Creed is said privately. There is therefore much to be said for the sign of the cross as a public gesture of faith at the end of the public recitation of the Creed.

²² Nahum ii. 7; Luke xv. 13, xxiii. 48; S. Augustine, *Enarr. in ps. xxxi.* 11; *in ps. clxvi.* 7; *Sermo xix.* 2; *Sermo xxii.* 8; *Sermo xxix.* 2; *Sermo lxvii.* 1; *Sermo cccxxxii.* 4. It is a curious recurrence to a practice noted as in use in his time by Rufinus (†410), *Com. in Symb. Ap.*, 43. The cross then accompanied the words ' the resurrection of *this* flesh,' and defined the word *hujus*, this.

²³ *Exposition de la Messe* (*A. C. C.*, III), plates 7, 8, 9. *The Lay Folks' Mass Book* says at the offertory, l 282 :

> It will thy prayer mykel amende
> If thou wilt hold up both thy hende
> To God with good devocioun
> When thou sayes this orisoun.

And see a similar passage (l. 405) directing it at the elevation.

²⁴ Lupton, *Life of Colet*, 291. ' Lyfte up your lytel whyte handes for me, which prayeth for you to God.'

CHAPTER X

¹ Mommsen, *Romisches Staatrecht* (1871), i. 347. Cp. Ammianus Marcellinus, xxi. 10, 11. Similar honour to the pope is directed in the First *Ordo Romanus*, § 4, so far as the incense is concerned.

² This practice was cited in the Seventh General Council on the subject of the use of images. (Actio 1.) Labbe, *Concilia*, viii. 705 c. (Venice, 1759.) Εἰ γὰρ βασιλέων λουράτοις καὶ εἰκόσιν ἀποστελλομένοις ἐν πόλεσι καὶ χώραις ἀπαντῶσι λαοὶ μετὰ κηρῶν καὶ θυμιαμάτων, κ.τ.λ.

NOTES

³ See above, pp. 70, 90. The censing at the Gospel is mentioned by Etheria at the end of the fourth century. See chapter iii, note 1.

⁴ See above, chapter vi, p. 70; vii, p. 85.

⁵ Compare with the *Ordo* the Sarum directions in *Use of Sarum*, i. xxxix (66), pp. 61–105.

⁶ *Use of Sarum*, i. 82.

⁷ Justin Martyr, *Apol.*, i. 65; Kidd, *Documents*, no. 42. See further passages in Warren, *Lit. Ante-Nicene Church*, 131 and ff.

⁸ See Rock, *Church of our Fathers* (ed. Hart and Frere), iv. 187 and ff. for illustrations.

⁹ See *Tracts on the Mass* (H. B. S.), 259.

¹⁰ See above, chapter iv, note 18.

¹¹ This was introduced as a protest against the views of Berengarius. It proved only too powerful in its effect, for it became the central point of the service; and the ill-instructed or conventional worshipper went to church in order to 'see his Maker,' rather than to worship or communicate. Its abolition in the Order of Communion of 1548 and the First Prayer-Book was the result of this abuse.

¹² See *Gelasian Sacramentary* (ed. Wilson, 288, 289).

¹³ See for an early example Origen, *In Exod.*, iii. 3, and for the later use Rock, *Church of our Fathers*, iv. 114 and ff.

¹⁴ Text C, line 240; and notes, p. 228.

¹⁵ *Tracts on the Mass*, 25.

¹⁶ So Langforde, *Ghostly Meditations* (*ibid.*).

¹⁷ Cyprian, *De Oratione*, 31, also *A. C. T*, *Primitive Consecration Prayer*, and Kidd, *Documents*, no. 121.

¹⁸ S. John xx. 22.

¹⁹ Acts ix. 17, xiii. 3.

²⁰ Acts vi. 6.

²¹ 1 Tim. iv. 14, v. 22; 2 Tim. i. 6.

²² Cyprian, *Epp.* lxxi and lxxiv. Cp. *Epist.* ix.

²³ Exorcism was also extended to inanimate objects, for experience showed that evil spirits might be latent there. Thus the salt, water, etc., employed in Christian rites were first exorcized and then blessed. This may be seen most easily in the case of Holy Water, which is hallowed by the following steps: first, the exorcizing of the salt and then a blessing pronounced over it; then a similar exorcizing and blessing of the water; then the casting of salt into the water in the form of the cross; and lastly, the blessing of the mixture. This involves, it will be noted, no imposition of hands. See *e.g. Missale Sarum* (ed. Dickinson), 29**.

²⁴ Tertullian, *Apol.*, 23. The point came up in the contest as to the rebaptism of heretics in the middle of the third century, and it was expressly mentioned by one African bishop, Vincent of Thibari, that exorcism with imposition of hands was a preliminary to baptism. See No. 37 of the *Sententiae Episcoporum* among Cyprian's works.

When we reach a rite of ordination to the office of exorcist, it clearly assigns to him the imposition of hands. He was given a book containing the formulas of exorcism, and the bishop accompanied the action with the words, 'Take and commit to memory; and have thou authority to lay hands on the possessed, the baptized, or the catechumen' ('Accipe et commenda memoriae; et habeto potestatem imponendi manus super energumenum, sive baptizatum, sive catechumınum '), *Statuta Ecclesiae Antiqua*, c. vii (Bruns, *Canones*, i. 142). It is a Gallican rite of the beginning of the sixth century in origin, and became the nucleus of the service adopted throughout the West.

²⁵ The First Prayer-Book of 1549 directed thus : ' *Then the priest casting earth upon the corpse shall say*, I commend, etc.' In 1559 this was altered to the following : ' *Then, while the earth shall be cast upon the body by some standing by, the priest shall say*, Forasmuch, etc.' The object of the change, no doubt, was to save the priest the trouble of casting the earth, but it does not preclude his doing so. The same ambiguity existed in the old rubrics. The York Manual ordered thus : ' *Hic aspergatur corpus et incensetur; postea proiciatur terra super corpus in modum crucis, sacerdote dicente*, De terra, etc.') (p. 99). The Sarum Manual on the contrary has ' *Finitis orationibus executor officii terram super corpus ad modum crucis ponat*, etc.' (p. 83*). See for both the Surtees Society edition of the York Manual.

²⁶ The use of oil for the sick was in its origin probably utilitarian, being regarded as medicinal. But it was more than this ; it gave a very necessary definiteness to the prayers for recovery, and acted as a strong method of ' suggestion.' Elsewhere it had of course no medicinal connotation, and simply served as object-lesson.

²⁷ The bearing of palms and the veneration of the cross were both in use as early as the fourth century. It was the misuse of such things, and not their own character, which really made it necessary that they should be laid aside in the sixteenth century.

²⁸ See p. 102.

²⁹ It is due to a misunderstanding of the history and rationale of incense when ' censings of persons and things ' are classed together without discrimination. The earliest use of incense, other than the prophylactic use, which is utilitarian in a sense, but not a part of religious ceremonial, is probably honorific; and the censing of persons is mainly so to be interpreted. But incense has a meaning like that of Holy Water. When the person censed drew to himself some of the smoke, he regarded the incense as representative of a hallowing influence. (See the Second *Ordo Romanus*, § 9.) This then is a second signification. There is also a third, the one discussed in the text here, viz. the signification of prayer. In censing the altar and sanctuary, a practice which is at least as old as the fifth century, this is the one intended, but in censing an object that is being blessed it is

the second meaning; while in censing images the action is honorific, *i.e.* it has the first meaning. There can be no use of incense that does not cense some thing.

CHAPTER XI

1 Gen. xxv. 15; xxxv. 18.

2 The earliest allusion seems to be that of the *Epistle of Barnabas*, vi. 17. 'First of all the child is nourished with honey and then with milk.' (πρῶτον τὸ παιδίον μέλιτι εἶτα γάλακτι ζωοποιεῖται.)
Tert., *De Corona*, iii: 'When we are going to enter the water, but a little previously, in the church and under the hand of the bishop, we profess that we renounce the devil and his pomp and his angels. Then we are thrice immersed, making a somewhat fuller profession than our Lord laid down in the Gospel. On being received from thence we taste a mixture of milk and honey.' ('Aquam adituri ibidem sed et aliquanto prius in Ecclesia sub antistitis manu contestamur nos renuntiare diabolo et pompae et angelis eius: dehinc ter mergitamur, amplius aliquid respondentes quam Dominus in Evangelio determinavit. Inde suscepti lactis et mellis concordiam praegustamus.') Tertullian speaks again elsewhere (*Adv. Marcionem*, i. 14) of this mixture of honey and milk wherewith God nourishes His children (' mellis et lactis societatem qua suos infantat ').

3 Jerome, *Adv. Lucif.*, c. 8, speaks of 'the practice of dipping the head three times in the laver, and then, after leaving the water, of tasting mingled milk and honey as a representation of infancy.'

4 The two passages in the *Hippolytean Church Order* are as follows (*Canons*, ed. Achelis, xix. §§ 144, 148): § 144, 'The presbyters bring other cups of milk and honey in order to teach those who receive them that they are born like little children, because little children receive milk and honey.' § 148, 'Thereupon they are to receive milk and honey as a reminder of the world to come, and of the sweet delights on which is set the heart of a man who does not return to bitterness.' For Baptism in the Church Orders see Thompson, *Baptism and Confirmation*, chap. iii.

5 Clement of Alexandria speaks thus (*Paed.*, I, vi. § 45): 'As soon as we are regenerated, we are ennobled by the news of the hope of rest, even the Jerusalem above, where, it is written, honey and milk fall in showers.' (εὐθὺς δὲ ἀναγεννηθέντες τετιμήμεθα τῆς ἀναπαύσεως τὴν ἐλπίδα, τὴν ἄνω Ἰερουσαλήμ, εὐαγγελιζόμενοι, ἐν ᾗ μέλι καὶ γάλα ὀμβρεῖν ἀναγέγραπται); and cp. *ibid.*, §§ 50, 51.

6 The Leonine Sacramentary speaks of God nourishing the baptized with milk and honey according to His promise given to the patriarchs that He would bring them to the Promised Land. The following formula is given at Pentecost (p. 318): 'Benedic, domine, et has tuas creaturas fontis mellis et lactis, et pota famulos tuos ex hoc fonte aquae vitae perennis qui est Spiritus veritatis: et enutri eos de hoc lacte et melle

quemadmodum patribus nostris Abraham, Isaac, et Jacob [promisisti] introducere te eos in terram promissionis, terram fluentem melle et lacte,' etc.

The formula and the ceremony alike disappear after the date of this book, and are not found in the succeeding Roman sacramentaries ; they disappeared also from the Alexandrian Church, but survived in the Coptic and Ethiopic rites. (Duchesne, *Christian Worship*, 330.)

[7] See above, note 2.

[8] The directions of the *Hippolytean Church Order* are as follows (*Canons*, ed. Achelis, xix. 108 and ff.) : § 108, ' Die autem Sabbati Episcopus convocet eos qui baptizandi sunt et moneat eos ut genua flectant, capitibus ad orientem conversis, et manibus super eos expandat orans ut malignum spiritum ab omnibus membris eorum expellat . . .' § 119, ' Qui autem baptizatur facie ad occidentem versa dicat " Renuntio tibi, O Satana, cum omni pompa tua . . ." ' § 122, ' Antequam in aquam descendat facie ad orientem conversa stans super aquas ita dicit postquam oleum exorcismi nactus est " Ego credo et me inclino coram te et coram tota pompa tua, O Pater, et Fili, et Spiritus Sancte " '

Cp. Stone, *Holy Baptism*, 166.

[9] Ps. cxxxviii. 2 ; Dan. vi. 10.

[10] Tertullian defends the custom of praying eastward (*Apol*. xvi) in spite of the misapprehension : ' Others . . believe the sun to be our god . . . I suppose because they have discovered that we pray towards the East.' (' Alii . . . solem credunt deum nostrum . . . Denique inde suspicio quod innotuerit nos ad orientem regionem precari.')

Clement of Alexandria explains it with reference to the sunrise (*Strom* , vii. 7). Origen reckons it among the ecclesiastical ceremonies which are in common use even among people who could not give a reason for them (*Hom. in Num*., v. 1). See p. 142.

[11] This is shown by the *Apostolic Constitutions*, ii. 57, which here represents earlier custom. For indeed a reference to a similar habit in Africa may be found in Tertullian ; where, speaking of the Christians as dovelike in contradistinction to the Valentinians, who were like serpents and crouched in holes, he says (*Adv. Valent*., iii) : ' The house of our dove is simple, always in a high and open position and turned to the light.' (' Nostrae columbae domus simplex, in editis semper et apertis, et ad lucem.')

[12] This matter, as regards the earlier stages of its history, has been discussed above, see pp. 76, 77 and notes. For the later stages see the Lambeth Judgement in Read *v*. Bishop of Lincoln.

[13] Cyril, *Cat. Myst*., iv. 8. Cp. Ambrose, *De Myst*., vii.

[14] Clem. Alex , *Paed* , ii. 10 (*alias* 11) ; iii 11.

[15] *Canons of Hippolytus* (ed. Achelis, c. xxxvii. 201), p. 118. *Apostolic Constitutions*, viii. 62 : ὧν γενομένων (*i e*. after the dismissals and the preparation for the service of the faithful) οἱ διάκονοι προσαγέτωσαν τὰ δῶρα

τῷ ἐπισκόπῳ πρὸς τὸ θυσιαστήριον, καὶ οἱ πρεσβύτεροι ἐκ δεξιῶν αὐτοῦ καὶ ἐξ εὐωνύμων στηκέτωσαν . . . εὐξάμενος οὖν καθ' ἑαυτὸν ὁ ἀρχιερεὺς ἅμα τοῖς ἱερεῦσι, καὶ λαμπρὰν ἐσθῆτα μετενδὺς, καὶ στάς πρὸς τῷ θυσιαστηρίῳ, τὸ τρόπαιον τοῦ σταυροῦ κατὰ τοῦ μετώπου τῇ χειρὶ ποιησάμενος, εἰπάτω 'Η χάρις τοῦ παντοκράτορος Θεοῦ καὶ ἡ ἀγάπη τοῦ Κυρίου ἡμῶν, κ.τ.λ. Cp. Warren, *Lit. Ante-Nicene Church*, 290.

[16] See, for the transition, Duchesne, *Christian Worship*, 379 and ff. The clerical dress was not different in shape from that of the laity as late as the fifth century (see *Ep.* iv of Pope Celestine to the Bishops of Narbonne and Vienne in 428; Kidd, *Documents*, ii, no. 192); but the reservation of special clothes for use in church began at least as early as the middle of the third century (see life of Pope Stephen, *Lib. Pont.*, 1. 154). Cp. below, chapter xii, p. 148.

[17] For the mediaeval development of the symbolism of colours see Innocent III, *De Mysterio Missae*, i. 65, and Durandus, *Rationale*, iii. 18. Earlier ritualists did not deal with the question fully. And for details as to colour sequences see Hope and Atchley, *English Liturgical Colours* (1918).

[18] Heb. x. 32; vi. 4.

[19] De Vert, *Explication*, ii. 436; and Le Brun, *Explication*, i, pref. xxviii.

The ceremony was subsequently adopted elsewhere, and the following passage may mark one transition.

S. Ambrose thus addresses a consecrated virgin who, after being professed one Easter day as a nun, had proved untrue (*De Lapsu Virg.*, v) : 'Did you not call to mind the holy day of the Lord's resurrection when you presented yourself to be veiled at the holy altar of God ? For in such a solemn assembly of the Church of God thou hadst taken thy place, shining out in the lights of the newly baptized, conspicuous among the white-robed procession as one who was to be wedded to the King.'

At a later date candles were regularly carried, and white robes worn by nuns to be professed. See *Pontifical Services* (*A. C. C.*, III), 78.

S. Gregory Nazianzen interprets the lights in a further sense by reference to the lights of the Wise Virgins (*Oratio*, xl, c. 46): αἱ λαμπάδες, ἅσπερ ἀνάψεις, τῆς ἐκεῖθεν φωταγωγίας μυστήριον, μεθ' ἧς ἀπαντήσομεν τῷ νυμφίῳ, φαιδραὶ καὶ παρθένοι ψυχαί, φαιδραῖς ταῖς λαμπάσι τῆς πίστεως.

For later instances, and later forms of the ceremony, see Martene, *De Ant. Eccl. Rit.*, I, cap. 1, Art. xv, 9, 10; or Duranti, *De Ritibus*, I, xix, No. 41. Cp. Muhlbauer, *Geschichte und Bedeutung der Wachslichter* (Augsburg, 1874), 67–77. And for an exposition of the Latin Baptismal Services belonging to the epoch of the Reformation see the *Rationale* of *c*. 1541 (*A. C. C.*, XVIII, pp. 6 and ff.).

[20] Justin, *Apol.*, 1. 65 (Kidd, *Documents*, i. 42); cp. 66 and 67. Irenaeus, *Adv. Haer.*, v. 11. 3 (*ibid.*, 1, no. 79).

[21] Cyprian, *Ep.* lxiii.

§ 5. Vinum mixtum declarat, id est calicem Domini aqua et vino mixtum prophetica voce praenuntiat, ut appareat in passione dominica id esse gestum quod fuerat ante praedictum.

§ 13. Nam quia nos omnes portabat Christus, qui et peccata nostra portabat, videmus in aqua populum intelligi, in vino vero ostendi sanguinem Christi. Quando autem in calice vino aqua miscetur, Christo populus adunatur, et credentium plebs ei in quem credidit copulatur et iungitur. Quae copulatio et coniunctio aquae et vini sic miscetur in calice Domini ut commixtio illa non possit ab invicem separari.

[22] Most explicitly in the Pseudo-Ambrosian treatise, *De Sacramentis*, v. 1 (*P. L.*, xvi. 475), which is probably North Italian, and of the fifth century.

[23] *Test. Dom.*, ii. 10.

[24] For Germanus see *P. L.*, lxxii. 93 and below, p. 169; and for Isidore the *De Eccl. Off.*, i. 18 (*P. L.*, lxxxiii. 755). For the *Rationale* see above, note 19. It is doubtful whether the two letters attributed to Germanus are really his.

[25] In the Syrian rite the commixture is denoted by the word Ἕνωσις, and the formula is Ἕνωσις τοῦ παναγίου σώματος καὶ τοῦ τιμίου αἵματος τοῦ Κυρίου κ.τ.λ. In the Byzantine rite it is πλήρωμα, with some corresponding formula (Brightman, *L. E. W.*, 62, 341, 393). There is also a form of commixture in the Nestorian rite (*ibid.*, 291). In the West the name 'commixture' comes from the Roman formula *Fiat commixtio et consecratio corporis et sanguinis D. N. J. C. accipientibus nobis in vitam eternam. Amen.* (See *Ordo* I, § 19.) In the Gallican rite the formulas were different, but the ceremony was identical. The eighteenth canon of the fourth Council of Toledo (671) shows its antiquity better than any existing Service-book: 'Post orationem dominicam et conjunctionem panis et calicis benedictio in populum sequatur' (Bruns, i. 228). Germanus of Paris, a century earlier, also bears witness to it in France (*P. L.*, lxxii. 94).

No primitive mention is made of the ceremony, so the chief sign of its high antiquity lies in the fact that it is common to the Syrian, Byzantine, Roman, and Gallican rites. See the careful study of Andrieu, *Immixtio et Consecratio*.

[26] See Martene, *De Ant. Eccl. Rit.*, I. 4. viii. 11, or Mabillon's *Commentary on the Ordines*, § 12 (*P. L.*, lxxviii. 893, or *Mus. Ital.*, II, lxxvi).

[27] See above, pp. 60, 72, 84.

[28] The symbolism is not explained by Amalarius in the ninth century (*De Eccl. Off.*, iii. 31). He was puzzled by it, and by the confusion which subsisted in his day in France between the commixture and the *sancta*. (See p. 177.) A century later Pseudo-Alcuin (*De Off. Divinis*) (Hittorp, 294) states the object to be 'that the chalice may contain the fullness of the sacrament' ('ut calix Domini totam plenitudinem contineat

sacramenti '). Micrologus, a century later, is clearer (§ xvii, *ibid.*, 741) The commixture is ' to show the union of body and soul in the resurrection of Christ' (' ad designandum corporis et animae coniunctionem in resurrectione Christi '). Cp. the English *Rationale*, p. 27.

²⁹ Brightman, *L. E. W.*, 393.

³⁰ See Binius, *Tractatus de Liturgia Antiqua Hispanica*, c. ix, in *Liturgia Antiqua Hispanica*, I, xc (Rome, 1746), or the Mozarabic Missal in Migne, *P. L.*, lxxxv. 557. Cp. Duchesne, *Chr. Worship*, 218 and ff.

³¹ Canon III in Bruns, ii. 226. ' Ut corpus domini in altari non in imaginario ordine sed sub crucis titulo componatur.'

³² See for example in the Stowe Missal (*H. B. S.*, vol. xxxii), pp. 41, 42.

³³ Jerome, *Adv. Vigilantium*, 7 :

'As to the questions of tapers, however, we do not, as you falsely represent, light them in the daytime, but by their solace we would enliven the darkness of the night. And if some persons . . . adopt the practice in honour of the martyrs, what harm is thereby done to you ? . . . Throughout the whole Eastern Church, even when there are no relics of the martyrs, whenever the Gospel is to be read, the candles are lighted, although the dawn may be reddening the sky, not, of course, in order to scatter the darkness, but to testify our joy.'

CHAPTER XII

¹ 1 Cor. x. 4.

² Origen, *De Princ.*, iv. 11.

³ Origen, *Hom. in Num.*, v. 1.

⁴ See above, p. 136, and Pseudo-Ambrose, *De Sacr.*, v. 1. Amalarius (*De Off. Eccl.*, iii. 19) copies S. Cyprian, but with some enlargement; and then follow Pseudo-Alcuin (Hittorp, col. 281), Micrologus (cap. x), and others, adding in more or less degree other touches, and reproducing the original reference to the passion.

⁵ See his *Catech.*, xxiii=*Mystag.*, v.

⁶ For the general bearing of the Church Orders on the subject of ceremonial see p. 44 and notes.

⁷ *Apost. Const.*, ii. 26 :

'Ὁ δὲ διάκονος τούτῳ (ἐπισκόπῳ) παριστάσθω ὡς ὁ Χριστὸς τῷ πατρὶ, καὶ λειτουργείτω αὐτῷ ἐν πᾶσιν ἀμέμπτως, ὡς ὁ Χριστός, ἀφ' ἑαυτοῦ ποιῶν οὐδέν, τὰ ἀρεστὰ ποιεῖ τῷ πατρὶ πάντοτε. Ἡ δὲ διάκονος εἰς τύπον τοῦ ἁγίου πνεύματος τετιμήσθω ὑμῖν, μηδὲν ἄνευ τοῦ διακόνου πράττουσα ἢ φθεγγομένη, ὡς οὐδὲ ὁ παράκλητος ἀφ' ἑαυτοῦ τι λαλεῖ ἢ ποιεῖ, ἀλλὰ δοξάζων τὸν Χριστὸν περιμένει τὸ ἐκείνου θέλημα.

The roots of such interpretation are to be found in the Ignatian letters; but here the conception is liturgical and ceremonial.

⁸ *Testam. Domini*, xix. Other instances of the same tendency are

to be found scattered elsewhere : *e.g.* on the subject of incense in *Athan. Canons*, 7, and on vestments in Celestine's letter mentioned above, chapter xi, note 16.

9 For the Dionysian Writings see Westcott, *Essays on Religious Thought in the West*, 142 and ff.; Rolt, *Dionysius the Areopagite* (*S.P.C.K.*, 1920). They are printed in *P. G.*, iii and iv.

10 The outline of the service itself is disentangled from the commentary in Brightman, *L. E. W.*, 487.

11 Dionysius, *De Ecclesiastica Hierarchia*, III. iii. 3.

12 See above, p. 53.

13 There are two letters of S. Germanus containing the exposition; the first deals with the Liturgy, the second with Baptism. See *P. L.*, lxxii. 89–98, and the account of them given in Batiffol, *Études de Liturgie*.

14 This seems to be the earliest use of the terms *casula* and *amphibalum*; they are Gallican names corresponding to the Roman term *planeta*.

15 The works of S. Isidore comprise writings on many different subjects—commentaries on the Scripture, polemical and historical treatises, educational manuals, etc. For the ecclesiastical system his two books *De Ecclesiasticis Officiis* are of chief importance; but references to the subject may be found scattered elsewhere in his writings. For example in the twenty books of his *Etymologies*, which form a sort of encyclopaedic dictionary, there is much of ecclesiastical interest, especially in books vi–viii. His works are to be found in *P. L.*, lxxxi–lxxxiv.

16 See Isid., *De Eccl. Off.*, II. v. 12 : xiv.

17 Amalarius, *De Eccl. Off.*, iii. 21. See chapter vi, note 1.

18 For later expositions of the Latin service see Franz, *Die Messe im Deutschen Mittelalter*.

19 The latest development of English origin is in an early document of the Reformation, the Rationale of the reformed Latin services composed *c.* 1541. See *A. C. C.*, XVIII.

CHAPTER XIII

1 See Lacey, *Handbook of Church Law*, 8 and ff.

2 See John of Avranches, *De Officiis Eccles.*, in *P. L.*, cxlvii, or new edition by Delamare (1923).

3 The *Regularis Concordia* is in *P. L.*, cxxxvii, and the Statutes of Lanfranc are to be found in *P. L.*, cl. The first is also printed in Reyner, *Apostolatus Benedictinorum* and in the *Monasticon Anglicanum* (London, 1846).

4 Richter, *Die Evangelischen Kirchenordnungen* (Weimar, 1846). The collection of Sehling (1904–1913) is more comprehensive still.

5 For the extension of these Uses see *Use of Sarum* (Introd.).

6 See Wilkins's *Concilia*, iii. 861, and for the general outline of the development and for references to authorities see *New Hist. B. C. P.*, 30.

NOTES

CHAPTER XIV

1 See the Draft Articles c. 1549, in *A. C. C.*, XV. 191 and ff.

3 Ridley's Visitation Articles and Injunctions are printed, *ibid.*, ff., 230 and ff. See especially p. 241, and for Hooper, p. 276.

5 Accordingly there is not only a series of judgements in ecclesiastical courts enforcing the rubrics, but also a series of episcopal injunctions regulating the ceremonies. These sometimes forbid special things, *e.g.* Parkhurst's Injunction 4 of 1561 forbidding ' the gestures of the popishe mass . . . as shifting of the boke, washing, breathing, crossing or such like ' (*A. C. C.*, XVI. 98); sometimes they are more restrictive, and forbid any ceremonies not appointed by the Prayer-Book (Grindal's Art. 7 of 1571, *ibid.*, 255). Additional ceremonies were, however, continuously in use, such as were held to be unobjectionable.

6 The Lambeth Opinions of 1899 were an outcome of this principle; but the actual Opinions then given rested on a method of interpretation very different from that which is here maintained as alone being historically justifiable.

7 See Reynolds, *Chapter Acts of Exeter Cathedral*, p. 53.

8 Johnson's case was fully reported by the Puritans in their collectanea called *Parte of a Register* (c. 1590 : see Brit. Mus., 697, f. 14). It has been partly reprinted in Brook's *Lives of the Puritans*, i. 176, and in Fuller Russell, *The Form and Order of the Consecration of the Parish Church of Abbey Dore* (London, 1874).

9 For such funeral services see *Hierurg. Angl.*, ii. 187 and ff.

10 The sources of this description are chiefly the following: Andrewes, *Minor Works* (*A. C. L.*), 150 and ff.; Fuller Russell, *l.c.*; and *Hierurg. Angl.*, ii. 82, 83, 90, 96, 98, 100 and ff.

11 See his *Notes on the Book of Common Prayer* in *Minor Works* (*A.C L.*).

12 For a full discussion of the eastward position see the Lambeth Judgement (Read *v.* the Bishop of Lincoln) in the Archbishop's Court (1890).

13 Passages with regard to the incense are collected in *The Case for Incense*, 162 and ff.

14 See for this two volumes of the Surtees Soc., *Acts of the High Commission Court at Durham*, App. A., and Cosin's *Correspondence*, i. 145, 155 and ff.

15 See Cardwell, *Doc. Ann.*, cxliii. 10.

16 The following directions for the saying of the latter part of the New Canon are offered by way of illustration and suggestion.

Then shall the priest continue thus, standing in the middle of the altar with uplifted hands, All glory be to Thee. *At* Who in the same night *he lowers his hands to carry out the manual acts, and first to uncover the paten. At* took Bread *he holds the paten in both hands. At* given thanks *he holds the paten in his left hand and signs it with his right. He breaks with thumb and forefinger of each hand, holding the paten with the other fingers. The words* Take, eat, etc., *he says over the paten, laying on his right hand. He keeps the thumb and forefinger of each hand joined thenceforward until the ablutions, except when handling the Holy Sacrament. At* Do this, etc., *he holds the paten again by the fingers of both hands, lifts it up, and then replaces and covers it. He then makes his reverence.*

Similarly with the chalice at Likewise after supper *he uncovers the chalice with his right hand ; at* He took the Cup *he holds it firmly with the fingers of the left hand at the base or round the stem, while the right hand rests on the bowl, is free to sign at the words* given thanks, *and then is replaced. The words* Drink ye all, etc., *he says over the chalice, laying on his right hand as directed. At* Do this *he holds the chalice again in both hands, lifts it up, and then replaces and covers it. He then makes his reverence.*

Then with arms outstretched he says Wherefore, O Lord ; *at* These Thy holy gifts *he signs paten and chalice together. In the Invocation he makes not more than seven crosses,* i e. at the words, bless, sanctify, us, *at* Bread *and* Wine, *at* Body *and at* Blood. *At the end of the Invocation he makes his reverence after the words* body and soul.

At the offering And we entirely *he stands with uplifted hands, and crosses at* this our sacrifice. *Note that all these crossings are made with the right hand, and the left hand simultaneously is dropped to correspond. At* although we be unworthy *he beats his breast once with his right hand.*

At the doxology he uncovers paten and chalice and makes crosses over them both, first at by Whom and with Whom ; *secondly at* Holy Ghost. *At* all honour and glory *he lifts paten and chalice, and he replaces them on the altar and makes his reverence. Then he covers both paten and chalice, and joins his hands, raising them again at* Our Father, *until they are joined for the doxology.* The peace of God, etc., *is said without turning round, but disjoining hands and reuniting them : the blessing is said after a half-turn to the right, with the right hand uplifted, and the left resting on the altar.*

CHAPTER XV

[1] See the profound statement of Cardinal Newman, *Via Media,* ii. 220 *n.* :

' Our Lord is *in loco* in heaven, not (in the same sense) in the Sacrament. He is present in the Sacrament only in substance, *substantive,* and substance does not require or imply the occupation of place. But if place is excluded from the idea of the Sacramental Presence, therefore division or distance from heaven is excluded also, for distance implies a measurable interval, and such there cannot be except between places. Moreover, if the idea of distance is excluded, therefore is the idea of motion. Our Lord then neither descends from heaven upon our altars, nor moves when carried in procession. The visible species change their position, but He does not move. He is in the Holy Eucharist after the manner of a spirit. We do not know how; we have no parallel to the "how" in our experience. We can only say that He is present, not according to the natural manner of bodies, but *sacramentally*. His presence is substantial, spirit-wise, sacramental; an absolute mystery, not against reason, however, but against imagination, and must be received by faith.'

INDEX

ABLUTIONS, 86, 91, 98, 99
Absolution, 109, 184.
Acolyte, 42, 65–74, 83
Additional ceremonies, 94, 115, 179–185.
Africa, liturgy and ceremonial of, 46, 203
Agape, the, 47
Agnus Dei, 26, 27, 73, 91, 121, 134, 173, 197
Alb *See* Vestments
Alcuin, 75
Alleluia, 26, 54, 57.
Almoner, 65, 66
Alms, 94, 174, 183, 185, 189, 192.
Alms-dish, 181, 183, 189.
Altar, 40, 47–58, 153, 168–170, 186, position of, 44, 63, 82, 175, 180; veil in front of, 44, 52, 77, 80
Altar-rail, 181, 182, 190
Amalarius, 75, 79–81, 150–154, 210, 222, 224.
Ambo, or pulpit for Epistle and Gospel, 64, 69, 83, 147; in Eastern Church, 56
Ambrose, Saint, 133, 144, 205, 220, 221.
Ambrosian rite, 149
Anamnesis, 194.
Anaphora. *See* Canon
Andrewes, Bishop, 179–185
Antiphons, 57
Apocalypse See *Revelation*
Apostolic Constitutions, 43, 144, 206, 220, 223
Apse, 40, 44, 63–74, 78
Aquileia, 61
Archdeacon, 66–74, 87
Ashes, 124
Athanasian Canons, 206
Atrium, 65.
Augustine, Saint, 114, 118, 206, 216
Avranches, John of, 159, 224

BALDACHIN-CANOPY, 64
Banns, 171
Baptism, ceremonies of, 47, 61, 93, 107, 109, 147, 193,

Baptism cross, 46,
giving of honey and milk, 129;
turning east and west, 130,
chrysom, 132,
giving lighted taper, 133,
unction, 46, 147,
cushion and towel, 148
Baptistery, 44.
Barnabas, 219
Basilica, 40, 44, 62, 63–65, 82, 208.
Bason, 183
Beating on the breast, 8, 46, 114.
Beatitudes, 57.
Bede, The Venerable, 150
Bell, 120, 173, 194
Bema or *tribunal*, 63
Benedict Biscop, 81.
Benedict, Saint, Rule of, 159
Benediction, 46, 51, 171
Benedictus qui venit, 112, 113
Berengarius, 85, 217.
Bidding of the bedes, 88
Bidding-prayer, 50, 88, 181, 190
Biretta, 196
Bishop, the, as celebrant, 29, 42, 44, 83, 152,
ordaining, 110,
confirming, 110,
the throne of, 40, 63–74, 78–80,
authority of, 155–158, 165–167.
Black Rubric, 108
Blessing, 170, 171, 185.
Boniface, Saint, 119
Bowing, 53, 111, 112, 116,
to the altar, 111,
at the Holy Name, 112,
in the Creed, 112
Breviary, the, 160
Burckhard, J, 163
Burial *See* Funeral
Burse, 193
Byzantine *See* Liturgy of S Chrysostom

Cancelli, 64, 83
Candles, 54, 63, 65, 83, 96, 134, 139, 151, 181, 186–188.

INDEX

Canon, the 45, 50, 59, 61, 75, 78, 85, 97, 119, 120, 144, 153, 172, 175, 184
Canons at Salisbury, 89
Canon law, 156
Canons of 1604, 112, 181, 182, 190, of 1640, 111
Canopy, 83
Canterbury Convocation, 163
Cap, 6
Caroline Use, 180–191
Carolingian period, ceremonial of, 4, 75, 150
Catechumens, dismissal of, 45, 49, 55, 118
Celebrant, 25–28, 42, 49–58, 76–80, 83–91, 98–101, 109, 131, 168–185, 189 ;
gestures of, 95, 117–120,
See Communion
Celestine, Pope, 221
Celtic customs, 81
Centralized worship, 17–21
Ceremonial, religious, a cause of contention, 1, attitudes of mind towards, 2, cycles recurring in its history, 4, in relation to Erastianism, 5, to ' No popery,' 6, to legal misconceptions, 6, to panic, 7, viewed as external, 8, in relation to general ceremonial, 11–43 ; analogous with habit, 12, with manners, 13, how far natural, 15, is centralized, 16, 21, in relation to individualism, 19, feature of corporate worship, 20–37, in parish churches before the Reformation, 31, affected by the Reformation, 32, traditions subsequently surviving, 32–45 ; in the primitive era, 38–48, grows along with rite, 40 ; regulated by councils, 47, in the East, 49–58, the West in the earlier mediaeval period, 59–74, and in the later, 75–91, utilitarian in character, 92–103, or interpretative, 104–126, or symbolical, 127–139, mystical interpretation of, 140–154 ; authority for, 155–167, principles to be applied, 195–201
Chalice, 42, 51, 54, 84, 89, 90, 96–99, 118, 152, 169, 185, 193,
mixed, 135–137, 147, 169, 175, 184, 193
Chantries, 30
Chasuble *See* Vestments

Cherubic Hymn, 55–57.
Choir, 64, 91. And *see* Music and *Schola cantorum*
Chrism, 66, 67
Chrysom *See* Baptism.
Chrysostom, Saint, liturgy of *See* Liturgy
Church Militant prayer, 106, 199
Church of S Mary Major, Rome, 62, 208,
of S Lawrence, Rome, 63,
of S. Peter, Rome, 64, 208,
of Sarum, 82, 87–91,
of S Catherine Cree, 182
Church Orders, 43–46, 144, 206, 223
Churches, form of *See* Basilica
orientation of, 44, 76–80, 208, 209, 211
Ciborium, 63, 99
Clement of Alexandria, Saint, 130, 132, 219, 220
Clergy of the Roman Church, 65
Clerk, 30, 31, 32, 35, 168–170, 183, 193
Colet, Dean, 114
Collect, 69, 74, 76, 78, 88, 89, 110, 168, 182.
Collection *See* Alms
Colours, liturgical, 133.
Comfortable Words, 170, 184
Commixture, 51, 72, 73, 91, 137, 147, 152
Common sense, 8
Commonwealth, 6
Communion of the celebrant, 73, 79, 91, 170,
of the laity, 51, 55, 73, 84, 170, 172, 175, 182, 190,
of the sick, 93,
to the dead, 47,
in one kind, 84, 156
Communion-psalm, 26, 27, 36, 73, 74, 197
Concelebration, 71.
Confessio, 63, 70, 77, 82.
Confession, the, 34, 106, 170, 184
Confirmation *See* Bishop.
Congregation, ceremonial of, 21,111, 113.
Consecration of a church, 46, 61, 81, 159, 182,
of the eucharist, 45, 46, 50, 51, 76–78, 97, 194,
a second, 178, 179, 185, 189,
of the font, 46
Consecration-prayer, the *See* Canon
Constantine, the Emperor, 43

INDEX

Consuetudinary of Sarum, 82, 90, 158
Convocation, 163
Cope, 88, 168, 174, 182
Cornelius, Pope, 205
Corporal, 54, 56, 74, 87, 89–91, 96–98, 102, 118, 153, 169, 185
Cosin, Bishop, 185–188
Councils,
  Elvira, 47,
  Nicaea, 47, 156,
  Laodicea, 47,
  African, 47,
  Braga, 61;
  Cloveshoo, 81,
  Tours, 138,
  Trent, 163,
  Carthage, 206,
  Agde, 207,
  Toledo, 222
Court ceremonial, 2, 11, 14, 16, 18, 20, 115
Credence table, 181
Creed, the, 26, 27, 36, 50, 70, 85, 90, 113, 114, 121, 175, 179, 183, 186, 187, 189, 190, 197
Creeping to the cross, 124
Cross on altar, 50, 96, 212,
  carried, 55, 63, 88, 96, 212,
  held, 56,
  on ornaments, 181, 185
Cross, sign of the, 46, 74, 86, 89, 98, 112–114,
  in consecrating, 50–53, 87
  See also Baptism
Crucifer, 88, 90
Crucifix, 9
Cruet, 71, 89, 96, 181
Curtains, 64, 71, 80, 82 *See* Veil
Cushion, 181
Custom, the power of, 93–95, 158, 171–173
Customary of Sarum, 86, 90
Cyprian, Saint, 120, 122, 135–137, 143, 147, 217, 222, 223
Cyril of Jerusalem, Saint, 52, 132, 143, 220

DAILY CELEBRATION, 28–30
Dalmatic *See* Vestments
Damasus, Pope, 205
Deacon, 25, 26, 42, 44, 45, 49–58, 65–74, 83–91, 96–99, 152, 168–172, 182
Deaconess, 44.
Decentius, 48, 59, 60, 204, 205
Defensores, 65
Desuetude, 156, 157, 165

De Vert, Dom Claude, 133, 134
Didache, The, 43, 205
Dionysius the Areopagite, 144–146, 224
Dismissal of Catechumens, 45, 49, 55
Diptychs, 50
Dispensing power, 166
Divine Service, 22 and ff,
  origin, 23, 24
Doorkeeper, 43
Doors, 51–58
Drama, 13, 36, 37, 51, 100
Durand, Bishop of Mende, 154
Durham Cathedral, 180, 185–188

EARLY CHURCH CEREMONIAL, 4, 38–41, 140–143
East and West contrasted, 25, 26, 28, 45, 48, 59, 106, 139
East, turning to, 1, 89, 90, 105, 130
Easter Even, 147, 198
Eastward position, 1, 74, 76, 131, 132, 182, 184
Edward VI, 5, 161
Egbert, Pontifical of, 81, 211
Eikon, 116
Ektenia, 50–58
Elevation, the,
  in East, 56,
  in West, 80, 85, 86, 91, 118, 169, 172
Elizabeth, Queen, 4, 5, 107
Elizabethan Act of Uniformity, 177–179
Elizabethan Injunctions, 112, 177
England, 81
Episcopal authority *See* Bishop.
Epistle, 26, 33, 54, 66, 98, 107, 108, 169, 183, 192
Epistoler, 33, 96 *See also* Subdeacon
Erastianism, 5–7
Ethelwold, Saint, 159
Eucharist, Holy, 25, and *passim*,
  daily celebration of, 28, 30;
  multiplication of eucharists, 28–30
Eugubium, 60
Exeter Cathedral, the Royal Visitation of, in 1559, 177, 178
Exeter Use, 109, 214–216
Exhortation, 192
Exit of ministers, 101
Exorcism, 123, 218
Exorcist, 42, 123
Externals, relation to internal ideas, 8–10

INDEX

FAIR LINEN CLOTH, 175, 189.
Fans, 49, 50, 52.
Fermentum, 29, 42, 60, 84, 137.
Finger and thumb closed, 98
Font, 46, 88.
Formulas accompanying ceremonies, 86.
Fraction of the host, 51, 72, 85, 118, 134.
Fragments of the host, symbolical arrangement of, 138.
Franciscan Use, 162.
Funeral services, ceremonies of, 48, 95, 123, 179, 190

GALLICAN, 81, 138, 146, 158, 222.
Garter, service of Order of, 214.
Gaul, 46, 61, 76, 77, 146, 149.
Gelasius, Pope, 60
Genuflexion, 50, 53, 108, 184, 194, 198, 214
German, Saint, of Paris, 137, 146-149, 209, 222, 224.
Germanus, Patriarch of Constantinople, 53, 146.
Girdle, 148.
Gloria in excelsis, 26, 27, 69, 76, 89, 105, 112, 121, 169, 175, 197.
Gloria patri, 105.
Gloria tibi, 89, 90, 112, 183, 190.
Gospel, 33, 44, 66-70, 88-90, 100, 107, 112, 147, 152, 169, 176, 183, 189, 193
Gospel-book, 44, 50, 53, 66-70, 85, 87-90, 115, 147, 152.
Gospel procession, 54, 83, 85
Gospel, Last, 91
Gospeller, 33. *See* Deacon.
Gothic architecture, 78, 82.
Gradual, 26, 57, 67, 69, 89, 121.
Great Entrance, 52, 54.
Gregory the Great, Saint, 62, 81
Gregory Nazianzen, Saint, 133, 221

HANDS, position of, 101, 120, 122-124
Heralds, 115, 179.
Hereford, Use of, 162
High Mass, 31, 87-91, 160.
Hippolytean Church Order, 43-45, 120, 130, 206, 219, 220.
Holy Water, 46, 88, 124, 217.
Homily, the, 45.
Honey and milk, 129.
Hoods, 182.
Hooper, Bishop, 173.
Host *See* Loaf, Obley.

ICONOSTASIS, 25, 51, 54, 210.
Ignatius, 223
Imposition of hands, 122.
Incense, 45, 48, 50-58, 67, 85, 86, 90, 91, 97, 115, 116, 124, 125, 141, 145, 152, 183, 218
Injunctions, 173, 174, 225
Innocent I, 48, 59, 60, 204, 205, 207.
Intercession, 50, 60
Introit-psalm, 26, 36, 68, 74, 85, 88, 90, 168, 172, 175.
Investiture of bishops, 150
Invitation to dine, 72
Invitatory, 57.
Invocation, 50, 53, 194
Irenaeus, 135, 221.
Isidore of Seville, 137, 149, 222, 224
Ite missa est, 74, 91

JACOBEAN 'USE,' 180-185.
James, Bishop, 185
Jerome, 129, 139, 219, 223
John of Avranches, 159, 224.
John, Saint, 18, 40.
Johnson, Robert, the case of (1574), 178, 179, 185, 225
Jus liturgicum, 158, 167.
Justin Martyr, 117, 135, 217, 221

Kirchen-Ordnung, 161
Kiss of peace, 45, 46, 50, 59, 68, 72, 87, 91, 116, 117, 144, 145, 152
Kissing the altar, ceremony of, 88, 152, 173;
  of the Gospel-book, 90;
  celebrant, 116.
Kneeling, 47, 92, 104-109, 156, 173, 175, 192
Kyrie, 26, 27, 36, 69, 88, 121, 146, 169, 175.

LAMBETH JUDGEMENT, 118, 220
Lamps, 50, 64, 83.
Lance, 55
Lanfranc, Archbishop, 159
Langford, J., 120, 217
Lateran, 66, 208.
Laud, Archbishop, 5, 180, 182, 184.
Lavatory, 45, 70, 86, 89, 90, 96, 97, 145, 173, 181, 184.
Lay Folks' Mass Book, 120, 214-215
Lay officials of the Roman Church, 65-73.
Le Brun, 134.
Lent veil, 83,
  collects, 89.
Leonine Sacramentary, 219.

INDEX

Lessons, 35, 44, 45, 55, 98, 191
Levitical ceremonial, 17, 38, 47
Liber Pontificalis, 43, 61, 205
Liddell lawsuits, 191
Lights *See* Candles
Linen bags, 66, 72, 84
Litany, 35, 44, 107, 171, 181,
 deacon's, 44–46, 50–58.
Litany-desk, 6, 181
Little Entrance, 52
Liturgy of the Faithful, 45, 52,
 the Roman, 46, 59–74,
 the Western non-Roman, 46, 59–61, 76, 149,
 the African Latin, 46,
 of S James, 53, 207,
 of S Mark, 53,
 of S Chrysostom, 53–58, 138, 207
Loaf, 66–74, 84, 138, 139, 174.
Long Exhortation, 106, 165
Lord's Prayer, 51, 56, 57, 97, 168, 182, 194.
Low Mass, 27, 28, 30, 31, 33, 95, 96
Lucania, 61.

MACKONOCHIE lawsuits, 191
Manual Acts, 117–120, 169, 175, 178, 184, 189.
Marriage, 123, 193
Mass *See* High, Low
 midnight, 198, 199;
 papal, 62–74.
 See also Eucharist
Mattins, 24
Maundy, 38, 39
Maundy Thursday, 38
Memorials, 110
Mensa, 63
Metrical psalms, 177–179, 190.
Milanese rite, 61, 149
Miserere, 171
Missal, formation of, 31, 160
Mixed chalice *See* Chalice
Mozarabic rite, 138, 149
Music, 22, 23, 25–27, 35, 36, 56–58, 121, 175, 183, 192
Mystical interpretation, 140–154

NARSAI, 49–53, 144, 207.
Nave, 50, 51, 64, 83
Nestorians, 49
Nicaea. *See* Councils
Nisibis, 49, 52
Nomenclator, 65

Oblationarius, 66.
Oblation, Prayer, 191

Oblations, 189, 199
Obley, 66–74, 96, 152. *See* Loaf
Offertory-psalm, 26, 27, 70, 90, 169
Offertory ceremony, 27, 44, 45, 70, 71, 75, 76, 84, 90, 147, 169, 172, 179, 183, 199.
Offertory Sentences, 106, 183, 185
Officers of the papal palace, 65–73
Oil, 124, 218.
Optatus, 206
Order of Communion (1548), 178
Ordinale, 160
Ordinary, the, 187, 191
Ordination services, 33, 107, 110, 158
Ordo Missae of John Burckhard, 163.
Ordo Romanus, 62–87, 116, 151, 158, 207.
Organs, 6, 83, 188.
Orientation of churches. *See* Churches
Origen, 142, 143, 217, 223
Ornaments Rubric, 5, 187, 190, 192.
Osculatorium, 117
Overall, Bishop, 191

PALL, 68
Palla, 147
Pallium, 148
Palms, 124, 218.
Papal Curia, 65–74
Paraphonista, 65
Parker, Archbishop, 4
Parliament, 5, 164
Paten, 54, 56, 71, 84, 87, 90, 91, 96, 97, 99, 102, 169, 173, 193
Patrick, Saint, 127
Paul, Saint, 4, 39, 116, 122, 138.
Pax, 87
Pax-brede, 117
Penitents, 44, 191
Peregrinatio Etheriae, 203, 217.
Pergula, 64
Planet, 67, 68, 70
Pontifical of Egbert, 81
Poore, Bishop, 82.
Postcommunion, 74, 79, 80, 91, 175.
Prayer-Book, authority of, 161–164;
 First (1549), 21, 32, 94, 108, 132, 139, 164, 168–172, 176, 190, 218,
 Second (1552), 108, 117, 132, 164, 174–176, 184,
 of 1559, 164, 184,
 of 1662, 33, 117, 164–166, 180,
 Scottish, of 1637, 184, 189.

Prayer-Book (1928), 95, 164, 166, 192–194
Precentor, 67.
Preface, 56
Presbyter, 29, 44, 45, 66, 79, 88
Presbytery, 44, 64–74, 88, 208
Private devotions in the Service-books, 86
Privy Council, 191
Procession, 93, 107, 199, 200 *See also* Gospel procession, Cross
Profuturus, Bishop of Braga, 61
Prokeimenon, 54.
Prothesis, 52
Psalms, 35, 36, 45, 105, 213.
Pseudo-Ambrose, 144, 222, 223
Public Worship Regulation Act, 191
Pulpitum, 83, 89, 90
Pulpit-prayer, 181.
Purchas lawsuits, 191
Puritan, 6, 105, 112, 163, 178, 180, 182, 183, 189
Pyx, 63, 83.

QUAKER, 3, 19
Quignonez, Cardinal, 163
Quire, 83, 88–91.

Rationale (1541), 137, 221, 224
Rationale divinorum officiorum, 154, 215
Reader, 43, 47
Recessional, 94.
Reed, 73
Reformation, 4–6, 32–35, 139, 161
Regularis Concordia, 159, 224
Relics, 63, 77, 90, 198
Renunciation in baptism, 130
Reredos, 181.
Reserved Sacrament, 64, 68, 72, 83, 84.
Respond, 88
Responsorial psalmody, 45, 47
Revelation of S John, 18, 39, 40, 68, 124, 132, 141.
Reverences, 182, 183, 185
Ridley, Bishop, 173.
Rochet, 174
Roman Church, clergy of, 65, lay officials of, 65–73
Roman emperor, 115
Rome, primitive rite, 45, 46, later evolution, 59–74, contrast with non-Roman, 46
Rood, 83, 88
Rubrics, the origin of, 32, 159–161, interpretation of, 168–194

Rubrical directions, incompleteness of, 92–96, 167
Rulers, 91.

Sacellarius, 65.
Sacerdotalism, 33–35.
Sacrarium or *Secretarium*, 67–74, 88.
Sacring bell, 120, 173
Sacristy, 44, 65
Salisbury Cathedral, 82, 87–91
Salt, 150.
Salutation, 69–71, 74, 76, 78, 89, 91, 153
Sancta, 68, 72, 84, 137, 152
Sanctuary, 45, 49–58, 88–91, 182.
Sanctus, 26, 57, 91, 106, 121, 153
Sarum, *see* Consuetudinary
Sarum, Use of, 31, 32, 87–91, 116, 118, 158, 160, 162, 163
Sarum Ordinal, 160
Schola cantorum, 26, 27, 62, 65
Secondary prayers, 125, 126
Secret, 71, 91, 199.
Screens, 64
Sedilia, 88
Senatorium, 64, 70
Sequens, 66
Sermon, 56, 70, 169, 180, 181, 193
Server, 27, 30
Sexes divided in church, 44, 64
Short exhortation, 106, 182, 193
Sign of the cross *See* Cross *and* Baptism
Singers, 47 *See* Choir
Sitting, 105–110
Smart, Peter, the case of, 186–188.
Spain, 46, 61, 149
Standing, 92, 105–110
State, authority of the, 6, 164–166.
Station, 62, 88, 208
Stationarius, 66, 67
Stoles, 47
Subdeacon, 26, 42, 44, 65–74, 83–91, 96–99, 196.
Subpulmentarius, 65
Sudary, 153, 173.
Suffrages, 110
Surplice, 6, 88, 174, 187
Sursum corda, 45, 76, 92, 106, 120, 144, 184.
Symbolism, 8, 52–54
Symmetry, 101

Tabula, 64, 209
Taper, lighted, giving of *See* Baptism.

INDEX

Taperers, 26, 66–74, 83, 88, 90, 152.
Tarsicius, 205.
Tertullian, 129, 130, 203, 206, 217, 219, 220
Testament of the Lord, 43–45, 136, 144, 222, 223.
Theodore, Archbp., 81.
Theotokia, 57.
Throne, episcopal. *See* Bishop
Thurifer, 26, 85, 88, 90, 111.
Tippet, 182.
Tower, 147.
Tract, 69
Trent, Council of. *See* Councils
Tribunal, 63, 73
Tricanale, 181.
Trisagion, 54, 57, 146.
Troparia, 57.
Tunicle *See* Vestment.

Umbraculum, 83.
Unction in Baptism *See* Baptism
Uniformity, Acts of, 164, 179, 185–188, 190 *See also* Elizabethan Act of Uniformity ;
of rite, growth of, 161–173.
Use, 158, 160–162, 180, 194

VEIL OF ALTAR *See* Altar, Curtain ,
of elements, 49, 54, 193 ,
of the sanctuary, 52, 83 ,
of the paten, 54, 83 ;
of the chalice, 71, 72, 89, 96, 153 ,

Veni creator, 177.
Verger, 88, 115, 175, 190.
Vestments, eucharistic, 45, 67, 87, 102, 133, 148, 149, 174, 192, 195, 213 ;
chasuble or planet, 1, 67–70, 87, 168, 196 ;
alb, 89, 168, 174 ;
dalmatic, 87 ;
tunicle, 87, 89, 168.
Vestry *See* Sacristy.
Vestry-prayer, 97.
Vicar, 89.
Vice-dominus, 66.
Vigilius, Pope, 61, 207
Virgins, 23, 44, 45.
Visitation, Royal, 173, 177
Visitation of the sick, 190.

WAFER-BREAD, 84, 98, 138, 181, 184, 192
West, turning to, 76–81, 90, 95, 130
White colour used, 132, 133, 148.
Whitgift, Archbishop, 4
Whitlock, Sir James, 186, 187
Widows, Order of, 44, 45
Worship, centralization of, 17–21.
Wren, Bishop, 184, 188, 213

YELVERTON, Justice, 187, 188, 191.
York, Use of, 162

ZACHARIAS, Pope, 119.

www.ingramcontent.com/pod-product-compliance
Lightning Source LLC
Chambersburg PA
CBHW070733160426
43192CB00009B/1427